Spanish politics today

John Gibbons

Manchester University Press
Manchester and New York

distributed exclusively in the USA by St. Martin's Press

Published by Manchester University Press
Oxford Road, Manchester M13 9NR, UK
and Room 400, 175 Fifth Avenue, New York, NY 10010, USA
http://www.man.ac.uk/mup

Distributed exclusively in the USA by
St. Martin's Press, Inc., 175 Fifth Avenue, New York,
NY 10010, USA

Distributed exclusively in Canada by
UBC Press, University of British Columbia, 6344 Memorial Road,
Vancouver, BC, Canada V6T 1Z2

British Library Cataloguing-in-Publication Data
A catalogue record for this book is available from the British Library

Library of Congress Cataloging-in-Publication Data applied for

ISBN 0 7190 4945 8 *hardback*
      0 7190 4946 6 *paperback*

First published 1999

06 05 04 03 02 01 00 99   10 9 8 7 6 5 4 3 2 1

Typeset in Photina
by Servis Filmsetting Ltd, Manchester
Printed in Great Britain
by Biddles Ltd, Guildford and King's Lynn

For Amanda, Joseph and Florence

Contents

Acknowledgements

To compose a list (such as is the custom) of the many colleagues and friends who, in one way or another, have helped me to write this book would, almost certainly, require an application for a further deadline extension from Manchester University Press. In gratitude for the patience of their staff I will refrain from such a course of action. However, some expressions of thanks are essential: to the anonymous Manchester University Press reader for the very useful and detailed observations, clarifications and corrections of an earlier draft; to my colleagues at the Department of Politics and Philosophy at Manchester Metropolitan University for their help and encouragement; to Kirstin for her patience and good humour in typing my many 'final' drafts; to the Miguelez Val family of Santiago de Compostela for their hospitality; to my parents for their support, when I needed it most; to Amanda for her serenity, especially in time of chaos; and to Joseph and Florence for arriving in our lives and entertaining us during the writing of this book.

Glossary

administración periférica	central government delegated administration in the provinces
administración única	proposal for organising centre – region relations using a 'single administration'. Suggested by Manuel Fraga, President of Galicia
alcalde	local mayor
asesores	advisers
ayuntamientos	municipal council/town hall
'barons'	term used to describe party or regional political élites
Boletín Oficial de las Cortes	official parliamentary journal of Spain
cacique	local political boss engaged in clientelist politics, an activity referred to as 'caciquismo'
Carlism	a monarchist cause, particularly strong in Navarre
Caudillo	leader/warlord; the title assumed by Franco
Comisión de Asuntos Económicos	(Cabinet) Committee for Economic Affairs
comisiones delegados del gobierno	cabinet committees
Comunidades Autónomas	regional governments called 'autonomous communities' in the 1978 Constitution
concejales	town councillors
conciertos económicos	traditional Basque and Navarrese economic privileges

ix

conferencias sectoriales	sectoral committees with regional representatives which discuss centre-region policy matters
Congreso de los Diputados	lower house of Cortes (parliament)
Consejo de Ministros	the Cabinet
Consejo General del Poder Judicial	General Council of the Judiciary
Cortes (Generales)	Spanish Parliament comprising *Senado* and *Congreso*
continuistas	advocates of continuity of the regime after Franco's death
cuerpos	(civil service) corps
Defensor del Pueblo	(parliamentary) Ombudsman
delegado del gobierno	government representative (in the regions)
diputación provinciale	provincial council containing *diputados* (councillors)
enchufe	a 'plug'. In political terms, putting a 'word in for' a client in clientelist politics, hence *enchufismo*
Ertzaintza	Basque police force
felipismo	political ideas and policies associated with Felipo González the PSOE leader, 1974–98
fueros	traditional rights of the Basque Country and Navarro
Generalitat	government of the autonomous community of Catalonia
gobernador civil	civil governor (central government representative in the provinces)
Grupo Mixto	Mixed Group (of independent and small party MPs in the Cortes)
Grupo Patrimonio	the National Assets Company (a state holding company)
Guardia Civil	civil guards – long-established Spanish police force
hechos differenciales	distinctive traits of the *nationalidades históricos*
Junta de Portavoces	(parliamentary) Board of Spokespersons (each member represents a parliamentary party

latifundio	large landed estates concentrated especially in Andalucia and Extremadura
ley orgánica	organic law (highest parliamentary law e.g. used for changes to the constitution)
ley ordinaria	ordinary act of parliament
Lhendakari	Basque president
ministro	minister
Mossos d'Esquadra	Catalan police force
nationalidades históricos	historic nationalities of the Basque Country, Catalonia and Galicia
Nuevo Estado	Franco's 'New State'
pluriempleo	'moonlighting'; working at more than one job at a time
poderes fácticos	*de facto* power of élites in Army, Church and the Falange, especially during the Franco era
presidente	prime minister of Spain
projecto de ley	parliamentary bill
proposición de ley	private member's bill
reformistas	advocates of evolutionary reform of the regime after Franco's death
rupturistas	advocates of a complete change of regime after Franco's death
secretario de estado	secretary of state (junior minister)
secretario general	secretary general (of the government)
Senado	Senate (upper house of *Cortes*)
soberanía compartido	shared sovereignty, an idea for further autonomy advocated by Catalan nationalists
transfuguismo	parliamentary defection to another party
Tribunal Constitucional	Constitutional Court
tribunal superior	high court
Tribunal Supremo	Supreme Court
Xunta de Galicia	autonomous community (regional) government of Galicia

List of abbreviations

AEB   *Asociación de Banca Privada* (Spanish Banking Association)

AECA   *Asociación Española de Co-operativas Agrarias* (Association of Spanish Farms Co-operatives)

AEI   *Agencia Industrial Español* (Spanish State Industrial Agency)

AES   *Acuerdo Económico y Social* (Economic and Social Agreement)

AMI   *Acuerdo Marco Interconfederal* (National Agreement on Employment)

ANNP   *Asociación Nacional de Productores de Pollo* (National Association of Broiler Producers)

AP   *Alianza Popular* (People's Alliance)

AP–CP   *Alianza Popular–Coalición Popular* (People's Alliance–People's Coalition)

ASAJA   *Asociación Agraria de Jóvenes Agricultores* (Agricultural Association of Young Farmers)

BNG   *Bloque Nacionalista Galego* (Galician Nationalist Bloc)

CAP   Common Agricultural Policy

CC   *Coalición Canaria* (Canary Islands Coalition)

CCOO   *Comisiones Obreras* (Workers' Commissions)

CD   *Coalición Democrática* (Democratic Coalition)

CDC   *Convergència Democrática de Catalunya* (Democratic Convergence of Catalonia)

CDS   *Centro Democrática y Social* (Social and Democratic Centre party)

CEOE   *Confederación Española de Organizaciones Empresariales* (Confederation of Spanish Employers Organisations)

CEPYME   *Confederación Española de Pequeñas y Medianas Empresas* (Spanish Confederation of Small and Medium-Sized Firms)

CES	*Consejo Económica y Social* (Economic and Social Council)
CESID	*Centro Superior de Información de la Defensa* (Spanish Secret Service)
CGPJ	*Consejo General del Poder Judicial* (General Council of the Judiciary)
CGT	*Confederación General del Trabajo* (General Labour Confederation)
CIAC	*Conferencia Interministerial para Asuntos Comunitarios* (Interministerial Committee for Community Affairs)
CIG	*Converxencia Intersindical Gallega* (Galician Trade Union)
CiU	*Convergència i Unió* (Convergence and Union)
CNAG	*Confederación Nacional de Agricultores y Ganadores* (National Agricultural and Livestock Farmers Federation)
CNJA	*Centro Nacional de Jóvenes Agricultores* (National Centre of Young Farmers)
CNT	*Confederación Nacional de Trabajadores* (National Workers Confederation)
COAG	*La Co-ordinadora de Organizaciones de Agricultores y Ganaderos del Estado Español* (The Co-ordinating Body for Spanish Agricultural and Livestock Producers)
COREPER	Committee of Permanent Representatives
DG	director/ate general
EA	*Eusko Alkartasuna* (Basque Solidarity)
EBRD	European Bank for Reconstruction and Development
EC	European Community
ECOFIN	Economics and Finance Council of Ministers
ecu	European currency unit
EEC	European Economic Community
EH	*Euskal Herritarrok* (Basque Nation)
EJC	European Court of Justice
ELA–STV	*Eusko Langileen Alkartasuna – Solidaridad de Trabajadores Vascos* (Basque Workers Solidarity)
EMU	Economic and Monetary Union
EP	European Parliament
EPP	European People's Party
ERC	*Esquerra Republicana de Catalunya* (Republican Left of Catalonia)
ERM	Exchange Rate Mechanism

ESC	Economic and Social Committee
ETA	*Euskadi Ta Askatasuna* (Basque Homeland and Liberty)
EU	European Union
FCI	*Fondo de Compensación Interterritorial* (Interterritorial Compensation Fund)
FET	*Falange Española Tradicionalista* (Spanish Fascist Party)
FIAB	*Federación Española de Industrias de Alimentación y Bebida* (Food and Drinks Federation)
FRAP	*Frente Revolutionario Antifascista y Patríota* (Revolutionary Anti-fascist and Patriotic Front)
GAL	*Grupos Antiterroristas de Liberación* (Anti-terrorist Liberation Groups)
GATT	General Agreement on Tariffs and Trade
GDP	gross domestic product
HASI	*Herriko Alderdi Sozialista Iraultzailea* (People's Revolutionary Socialist Party)
HB	*Herri Batasuna* (Basque Homeland and Freedom party)
IGC	Inter-Governmental Conference
IMF	International Monetary Fund
INEM	*Instituto Nacional de Empleo* (National Employment Forum)
INH	*Instituto Nacional de Hidrocárburos* (National Oil Company)
INI	*Instituto Nacional de Industria* (National Industrial Company)
INSALUD	*Instituto Nacional de Salud* (National Health Service)
INSS	*Instituto Nacional de Seguridad Social* (National Social Security Service)
IRI	*Istitutio per la Ricostruzione Industriale* (Industrial Reconstruction Institute)
IRYDA	*Instituto Nacional de Reforma y Desarrollo Agrario* (National Agricultural Reform Body)
IS	*Izquierda Socialista* (Socialist Left)
IU	*Izquierda Unida* (United Left)
IVA	*Impuesto sobre el Valor Añadido* (value added tax)
LEADER	*Liasons Entre Actions de Développement de l'Economie Rurale* (Integrated Rural Development Programme)
LGS	*Ley General de Sanidad* (General Health Law)
LOAPA	*Ley Orgánica de Armonización del Proceso Autonómico* (Organic Law on the Harmonisation of the Autonomy Process)

LODE   *Ley Orgánica del Derecho a la Educación* (Organic Law on the Right to Education)

LOFCA   *Ley Orgánica de Financiación de las Comunidades Autónomas* (Organic Law on the Financing of the Autonomous Communities)

LOGSE   *Ley Orgánica de Ordenación General de Sistema Educativo* (Organic Law on the General Organisation of the Education System)

MAPA   *Ministerio de Agricultura, Pesca y Alimentación* (Ministry of Agriculture, Fisheries and Food)

MEP   Member of European Parliament

MP   Member of Parliament

NATO   North Atlantic Treaty Organisation

OECD   Organisation for Economic Co-operation and Development

OPEC   Organisation for Petroleum Exporting Countries

OSE   *Organización Sindical Española* (Spanish Syndical Organisation)

OSI   operational service inspection

PA   *Partido Andalucista* (Andalusian Party)

PAD   *Partido de Acción Democrática* (Christian Democratic Party)

PAR   *Partido Aragonés Regionalista* (Arragonese Regional Party)

PASOC   *Partido de Acción Socialista* (Party of Socialist Action)

PCE   *Partido Comunista de España* (Spanish Communist Party)

PER   *Plan de Empleo Rural* (Rural Employment Plan)

PNV   *Partido Nacionalista Vasco* (Basque Nationalist Party)

PP   *Partido Popular* (People's Party)

PSBR   Public Sector Borrowing Requirements

PSC–PSOE   *Partit del Socialistes de Catalunya–Partido Socialista Obrero Español* (Socialist Party of Catalonia–Socialist Workers Party of Spain)

PSE   Party of European Socialists

PSE–PSOE   *Partido Socialista de Euskadi–Partido Socialista Obrero Español* (Basque branch of the PSOE–Socialist Workers Party of Spain)

PSOE   *Partido Socialista Obrero Español* (Socialist Workers Party of Spain)

PSP   *Partido Socialista Popular* (People's Socialist Party)

PTA   peseta

PTE   *sociedades mercantiles* (public trading companies)

REA   *Régimen Especial Agrario* (Special Agricultural Regime)

RTVE   *Radio-Televisión Española* (Spanish state-owned radio and television network)

SCA   Special Committee on Agriculture

SEA   Single European Act

SEM   Single European Market

SEPI   *Sociedad Estatal de Participaciones Industriales* (State Holding
           Company)

SPD   *Socialdemokratische Partei Deutschlands* (Social Democratic Party
           of Germany)

UCAE   *Unión de Co-operativas Agrarias de España* (Spanish Farms Co-
           operatives Union)

UCD   *Unión de Centro Democrático* (Union of the Democratic Centre)

UDC   *Unió Democràtica de Catalunya* (Democratic Union of Catalonia)

UGT   *Unión General de Trabajadores* (General Workers' Union)

UM   *Unió Mallorquina* (Mallorcan Union)

UN   United Nations

UPA   *Unión de Pequeños Agricultores* (Small Farmers Union)

UPN   *Unión del Pueblo Navarro* (Navarrese People's Union)

USO   *Unión Sindical Obrera* (Syndicalist Workers Union)

UV   *Unió Valenciana* (Valencia Union)

A note on sources

In researching for this book I have gleaned information and insights from a variety of sources, mainly in English and Spanish and occasionally in Catalan and Galician. Full references for many of the books, journals, periodicals, government reports and newspaper articles etc. used in the book are given in the Further reading sections at the end of each chapter. Also useful have been some of the Spanish websites devoted to aspects of contemporary government and politics in Spain, though they vary in the range and quality of information they provide. Useful website addresses include the following:

The Spanish Constitution at http://alcazaba.unex.es/constitucion/
Spanish Government Institutions at http://www.la-moncloa.es/
Political parties e.g. PP (*Partido Popular*/The Peoples Party) at
    http://www.pp.es/
Trades unions e.g. UGT (*Unión General de Trabajadores*/General Workers'
    Union) at http://www.ugt.es/
Autonomous communities e.g. Generalitat de Catalunya at
    http://www.gencat.es/

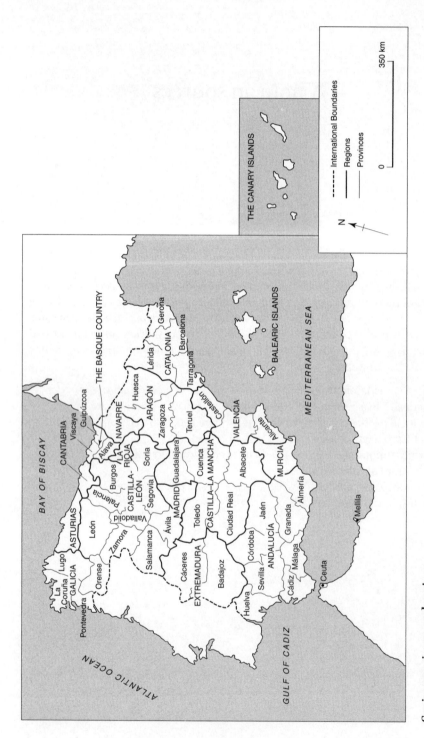

Spain: provinces and regions

Source: Hooper, J., *The New Spaniards*, London, Penguin, 1993.

1

Introduction: from dictatorship
to democracy

Spain, the travel guides never tire of informing us, is a 'land of contrasts'. An excursion into the past reveals that contrasts punctuate its political history, as much as its landscape. Thus, the Spain that was led by Franco's regime into economic protectionism and international isolation is markedly different from that which, on 1 January 1999, moved to abandon the peseta in favour of the euro. And the mood in Spain on 6 December 1998, when 20 years of the Constitution were celebrated, was very different to the sinister atmosphere of 23 February 1981 (known as '23F'), the date of an infamous and doomed coup attempt. Moreover, the deep-rooted attachment of the political Right in Spain to centralism and national unity was very much at odds with the pragmatic approach of José María Aznar and the PP (*Partido Popular*/People's Party) to forming a (minority) government of the Right in May 1996, with the support of Catalan and Basque nationalists, hungry for more self-government.

The central aim of this book is to discuss the ways in which contemporary political élites at regional, national and EU[1] levels of government have arrived at political and policy changes in Spain's democratic project. Later chapters explore the pressures they have faced, their powers, constraints and the strategies they have adopted in the pursuit of sectional and collective interests. This chapter begins with a brief background account of the construction and demise of the previous regime.

Franco's dictatorship

Following victory in the Civil War in April 1939, General Francisco Franco became supreme authority in Spain. The various facets of his power were personified in the title of *Caudillo* (war lord or leader) which he chose for

---

[1] The term EU (European Union) is generally used in this book, except in historical contexts where the terms EEC (European Economic Community) and EC (European Community) are used.

1

himself, and expressed through the many posts that he held. Among them were: Head of State, Prime Minister, leader of the Falange (the only party) and *Generalísimo* or Head of the Armed Forces. Franco used this power to protect and advance the interests of various élites, who provided the bedrock of support in his regime. By balancing their ambitions, he maintained control of his New State (*Nuevo Estado*), virtually up until his death in November 1975 (only relinquishing the post of prime minister in 1973). He did so by a policy of 'divide and rule', encouraging strong rivalries between the élites, especially those within the main institutional 'families' or factions (*poderes fácticos*), namely, the military, the Church and the FET (*Falange Española Tradicionalista*/Spanish Fascist Party). The latter consisted of fascist parties who supported the Nationalist cause in the Civil War and who were united by a decree of unification declared by Franco in 1937.

Franco's rule was initially imposed by a series of repressive measures and actions which aimed to obliterate the opposition forces (mainly drawn from the urban and rural lower classes) which had formed the Republican side during the war. The army provided the swiftest and bloodiest methods of repression but legal instruments, such as the 1939 Law of Political Responsibilities, created an equally effective, if more circumspect, means of achieving the same ends. It established a specific criminal category aimed at punishing those who were supporters of the Republican cause. The Church also was enlisted to help formulate a state ideology incorporating a new national identity, consisting of a re-Christianised Spain, delivered from the evils of communism and atheism by the victorious intervention ('by the grace of God') of Franco. The propaganda machine of the New State also created positive images of the *Caudillo*, evolving with the circumstances of the times. Thus the brave soldier and visionary leader of the Civil War metamorphosised into the skilful politician, who steered Spain through the Second World War, and who ultimately, in his twilight years, became the grandfather of the nation.

Social control was reinforced by the adoption of a corporatist model of labour relations. Unlike the (neo-)corporatism which evolved as a policy strategy in most western industrialised states in the 1970s in response to the economic turmoil caused by the OPEC (Organisation for Petroleum-Exporting Countries) oil crisis, this was (classical) corporatism imposed by the New State. The OSE (*Organización Sindical Española*/The Spanish Syndical Organisation) aimed to unify the officially recognised employers and workers unions (others were banned) into a representative structure across the whole economy. Economic élites forfeited the opportunities for the competitive risks (and profits) of the liberal market economy in favour of the more stable, collective corporatist model which, under the authority and regulation of the state, would protect their fundamental interests and also tend to favour them in periodic disputes with their workforces.

The conduct of international relations during the Franco era was dominated by economic nationalism, in which self-sufficiency (or 'autarky') became the main goal. It was also coloured by the sense of loss of empire and international status, felt especially in military circles since the calamities of the Spanish-American War of 1898. An ideological and political affinity with the Axis powers during the Second World War created a brief window of opportunity for Spain to become, once again, a big player in international affairs. Luckily for Spain, neither the Axis powers nor Franco coincided in their judgement of when the time was ripe for Spain's widely anticipated intervention in the conflict. So when the military fortunes of the Axis powers went into reverse, Spain was still sufficiently uncommitted to be able to back-pedal into a more diplomatically neutral position.

The construction of the New State

The construction of the New State was undertaken with the help of regime élites. The bureaucracy of the Republic's government was dismantled by the removal of its employees and their replacement by supporters of Franco's Nationalist cause. Recruitment operated on a personal basis of recommendations, contacts and favouritism involving the élites closest to the New State. This method of creating the new bureaucracy served to institutionalise an extensive network of patronage and a culture of policy-making driven by factional interests, above the collective interests of the New State. Top civil service posts continued to be filled from the traditional civil service corps (see Chapter 5). Tensions and fragmentation characterised the new bureaucracy, as élites competed to colonise key ministries with their various cohorts of supporters.

The Army was the most powerful group in the early stages of the New State, commanding the key ministries of Defence and Foreign Affairs. But Franco also ensured that, although its officers permeated throughout virtually all state institutions, the Army as an institution did not present a threat to him or the New State as a whole. The Church, too, was allowed to play a key role especially in ministries such as Education, but Franco did not show great interest in transforming Spain into a theocracy.

Many of the tensions which existed between the élites of the New State revolved around the role and direction of the Falange. Franco skilfully played off pro- and anti-Falangists against each other for much of his period of office. By the 1960s, the representative function of this outmoded and inflexible regime-party was eclipsed by the emergence across Spanish society of new social movements and opposition groups. Monarchists also were played off against each other by Franco, who declared Spain a kingdom in 1947 but delayed making a final decision on his successor until 1969. The Bourbon heir, Juan Carlos, the son of Don Juan (who did not renounce his dynastic rights until 1977) was nominated by the Succession Law of that year. (Cagey to the end, Franco ensured that the law contained a clause still enabling him to revoke his decision in favour of an alternative.)

The post-Second World War era necessitated the regime to change if it were to survive. Franco realised that the international politics of the time required that a democratic veneer be applied to its institutions. Accordingly, Spain was officially dubbed an 'organic popular democracy' and dressed up with a parliament – the Cortes – to which (highly restricted) elections were first held in 1946. By this means, Franco hoped to establish the New State on a more legal footing, purportedly resting on popular support.

Economic stability was a more difficult task to achieve, but equally important for the regime. Without economic prosperity, containment of the inherent social and political tensions would become difficult. The economic élites continued to benefit from the existence of the regime through good times (by legitimate means) and bad (by using their privileged access to official sources of supply of scarce resources for black market profit-making), but their patience began to wear thin as the economic crisis deepened in the late 1940s and early 1950s. The Falangist party élites who controlled economic policy for much of the dictatorship waned in power in the 1950s as their vision to transform Spain into a prosperous but predominantly rural society became increasingly anachronistic and outmoded. Cabinet reshuffles during the 1950s symbolised the impact that economic changes were having on the politics of the regime.

Economic policy under the dictatorship

Much of the history of the Spanish economy up to the 1960s was dominated by the weak performance of its agricultural sector. Poor yields, high costs and low incomes were its persistent traits, produced within the confines of a geographically and socially unbalanced land-tenure structure. In the centre and north of the country, there was a preponderance of often uneconomic, medium and small holdings: *minifundio*. Typical of the south were the large estates – *latifundio* – of Andalusia and Extremadura which offered intermittent employment to a large rural proletariat.

The wealth generated by these estates placed their owners at the centre of political and economic power in Spain. This élite was surrounded by the protective arms of the military, which helpfully suppressed any rebelliousness among the workforce, an ideologically privileged position afforded to them by the Catholic Church, and an accommodating bureaucratic élite, experienced in the art of survival through centuries of political upheaval. In such a static environment, industrial development in Spain was a piecemeal and very slow affair. Industrial expansion on a large scale did not take off until the 1960s because the regime's stagnant economy was incapable of giving birth to an industrial or entrepreneurial élite. A few regions, for locally specific reasons, provided exceptions to the rule, such as Catalonia (where they manufactured textiles), the Basque Country (which became important for steel and shipbuilding) and Asturias (where the coal-mining industry was based).

By the 1930s, the Spanish economy and its vested interests had been protected by a vast array of tariffs, dating from 1891, 1906 and 1922, which cocooned it in an environment that was inefficient, unproductive and corrupt. The arrival of Franco in power reinforced the protectionist trend. Indeed, protectionism became a key component of the Falangist economic and social doctrine of national self-sufficiency and rural development. Protectionism served the survival instincts of the new regime too, by strengthening the state's grip on the weak and the defeated in the populace, but at a cost of returning Spain's economy to nineteenth-century levels of economic performance.

The economic stagnation which persisted throughout the 1940s was exacerbated by the damage done to Spain's industrial and transport infrastructure, caused by the Civil War. Persistent drought conditions made recovery in the rural economy more prolonged and difficult. These factors made more remote the Falangist ideal of a society founded on a stable and prosperous rural economy. Spain was also rebuffed by the international community in the aftermath of the Second World War. Resentful of Franco's affinity with the defeated Axis powers, the Allies excluded it from the European Recovery Programme and Marshall Aid. Only the regime of General Perón of Argentina proved to be a 'friend in need' to the Spanish dictator, providing him with much needed credits to purchase food supplies between 1947 and 1949.

That aid notwithstanding, and starved of essential raw materials and export income, the Spanish economy continued to spin further and further downward, with enormous human costs, as near famine conditions prevailed in many areas.

Effective policy action to deal with these problems was hampered by a multiplicity of institutional and structural weaknesses. First and foremost, was the dictator's own inability to comprehend the economic task that lay before his government and his preference for military-style solutions to policy problems. The advice of the few pragmatic economists who had access to élite decision-makers in the regime, was passed over in favour of the ideological doctrine of the Falange which, in turn, was modelled on the fascist systems of Italy and Germany. A corrupt administration made economic enterprise and the procurement of credit and new materials under the Falange a hazardous activity for potential entrepreneurs. Import substitution and the goal of self-sufficiency (via currency controls and a range of import-quotas and licences) lay at the heart of their philosophy of autarky. The INI (*Instituto Nacional de Industria*/National Industrial Company) which was established in 1941, based on the Italian equivalent (the IRI – *Istitutio per la Ricostruzione Industriale*/Industrial Reconstruction Institute), was the focus of Franco's industrial policy and was run up to the 1960s by his childhood friend Juan Antonio Suanzes. Its objectives were to achieve self-sufficiency in Spain and to provide the basis for national defence by way of industrial development. Engineering, chemicals, transport and energy were the major economic activities embraced by its companies.

The failure of these policy initiatives to achieve economic recovery in Spain was all too patently obvious by the end of the 1940s. However, the regime was provided with some face-saving relief by the opening up of international credit lines by the US government and banks from 1949. The UN (United Nations) also lifted its ban on member-states trading with Spain. The threat posed by the Soviet bloc to Europe and communist advances in south-east Asia induced a degree of amnesia in America government circles concerning Spain's dictatorship and its unsavoury allegiances during the recent past. Strategic defence issues began to drive international policy on Spain. It was strategically located in an important part of the defence map, not least because of its proximity to North Africa and the naval entrance to the Mediterranean. Agreements with the USA to locate military bases on the peninsula in 1953 served as some compensation for economic leniency towards Spain. This shift in the international climate of political opinion towards Spain gave the dictatorship another chance to pursue the Falangist economic aim of national industrial self-sufficiency through import substitution. The appointments of Manuel Arburúa and Rafael Cavestany to the government in 1951 led to the introduction of a new set of policies aimed at achieving this end. Their policies rested on the idea of using foreign borrowings to provide credit to industry to purchase technologically advanced industrial machinery. This, it was hoped, would kick-start domestic manufacturing and reduce food-price inflation (and a burgeoning black market) by importing large quantities of foodstuffs.

Although agriculture enjoyed something of a boom, the anticipated expansion of the industrial economy in Spain failed to occur. So, too, did the means of repaying these loans, namely, the anticipated expansion of exports of industrial exports. Instead, inflation was rampant and Spain moved closer to bankruptcy as a balance of payments crisis made loan repayments more and more difficult. With regime élite groups increasingly riven by internal tensions and conflicts, and, in the case of the economic élites, a growing loss of faith in its capacity to deliver economic policies appropriate to their interests, a further cabinet reshuffle was reluctantly made by Franco in 1957. Appointed were two economists who were closely linked to the Catholic lay organisation the Opus Dei, Alberto Ullastros Calvo and Mariano Navarro Rubio, who together with Laureano López Rodo (already in government) forged a new economic policy direction for the regime.

Although politically conservative these were economic liberals to whom the failure of the Falangist self-sufficiency model was patently obvious. Together with other economists, the so-called 'technocrats' challenged the old economic orthodoxies promoted by the Falangist élite and ultimately replaced the Falangists as the main architects of economic policy in Franco's Spain. In short, they set about opening up the Spanish economy to market forces.

The Stabilisation and Liberalisation Plan of 1959 was the first fruit of their efforts to convince Franco of the merits of their strategy in a language that he could understand, namely, that the only chance of political survival for the near bankrupt regime lay in liberalising the Spanish economy. The plan aimed to facilitate inward investment into Spain by a change in the law and to encourage the export trade by reducing tariff and other barriers to trade. Spanish membership of supranational organisations such as the OECD (Organisation for Economic Co-operation and Development), the IMF (International Monetary Fund) and the World Bank gave added legitimacy to the ideological shift in the parameters of economic policy being implemented by the new technocratic élite running economic policy in the Franco regime. The economic timing was also right for this shift of policy. A buoyant international economy benefited Spain in a number of different ways. Foreign investment flowed in, especially to Madrid, Catalonia and the Basque Country. Migrant workers from Spain found employment across western Europe and on the other side of the Atlantic, and their remittances helped to boost family incomes and expand the domestic consumer market. The Spanish tourist industry also took off as higher standards of living among northern European workforces, and advances in air transport, continued to enhance the appeal and accessibility of Spain's (hot) Mediterranean coastline, over traditional (and colder) domestic resorts. Large-scale investment in hotels and other facilities (much of it inward investment) generated further domestic economic spin-offs and benefited from an abundant, and cheap, indigenous labour force.

Though these economic developments undoubtedly prolonged the life of the dictatorship, they did so at a price. The social, economic and ideological authority of the regime was increasingly undermined by the influx of new money, new cultural values and new levels of social awareness. These changes undermined the political authority of the regime and in effect challenged its élites to respond. They did so in sometimes contradictory ways, vacillating between repression and accommodation of the forces that challenged their authority. Social unrest was one of the important catalysts for change. A general strike in Barcelona in 1951 was particularly significant because it was called not by illegal underground unions but by the official unions. Another important moment occurred in 1956, when student demonstrations demanding democratic control over student unions forced the liberal Catholic intellectual and Minister for Education, Joaquín Ruiz Giménez, out of office (he later became disenchanted with the regime and joined the growing opposition movement on its fringes). Labour legislation changes reflect the impact that social unrest was having on the regime. From the late 1950s, new laws were introduced covering collective bargaining, the election of employer representatives in the workplace and the right to strike. They facilitated the emergence of social forces independent of the regime. Economic élites were discovering during the 1960s that the old methods of social control, such as reliance on the army for putting down labour disputes, did not necessarily lead to increases in productivity. Instead, they began to see the wisdom of negotiating directly with the unofficial labour organisations that were emerging across the economy.

The response of the regime to most challenges to its authority continued to be repressive and reactionary. This was considered acceptable, even by the technocrats who believed that such measures were necessary until economic prosperity reduced social tensions and made the regime more popular. Political executions continued to be approved by Franco's Cabinet up to September 1975, two months before his death. The rise of the Basque separatist movement – ETA (*Euskadi Ta Askatasuna*/Basque Freedom Movement) – during the late 1960s produced the most violent challenges to the regime and were responded to by police violence and by the use of 'emergency powers' in the Basque Country. International protest mounted, as state violence against its opponents escalated, especially between 1969 and 1973. For hard-line Falangists and many in the military, the movement towards economic liberalism had been a huge mistake and they advocated a return to the old certainties of economic nationalism and political repression.

Others within Franco's regime began to arrive at the opposite conclusion and to plan a way of reaching an accommodation with the forces of opposition that would better preserve their interests. But until Franco passed away, change was not expected.

Democratic transition

It is possible, with the benefit of hindsight, to identify some pre-existing conditions and factors which facilitated Spain's transition to democracy between 1976 and 1979. These include the following:

1 the economic and social transformation which took place in the 1950s and 1960s;
2 the international pressure for political change and the examples of democratic transitions in Portugal and Greece;
3 a public mood well disposed towards democratic change;
4 the fact that the political power of the regions still rested on the personal authority of the ailing Franco;
5 the assassination by ETA in December 1973 of Admiral Luis Carrero Blanco, Franco's trusted deputy and prime minister.

It was patently obvious to most in Spain that Franco's death would herald in a new era but it was by no means certain what shape that would take. There were a number of possibilities, represented by what became the key political groups and movements of the transition process. The option of continuity advocated by the *continuistas* had been dealt a serious blow by the death of Carrero Blanco. His replacement, Carlos Arias Navarro, recognised that some changes were necessary; however, he was committed to maintaining power in the hands of the old élites and perpetuating the Francoist regime in its essentials. In contrast, the *rupturistas*, mainly consisting of those defeated in the Civil War, advocated a rupture or a complete break from the past, led by political groups committed to democracy. They envisaged establishing a provisional government made up of democratic forces, which would go on to create what they envisaged to be proper democratic structures appropriate for post-Franco Spain. Between, these two extremes lay the *reformistas* who had evolved politically within the Francoist regime, and who recognised the need for political change towards democratic structures. They proposed doing so, by using the narrow room for constitutional and legal manoeuvre available in the Fundamental Laws of the regime.

Arias Navarro's brief reign as prime minister, after the death of Franco on 25 November 1975, foundered on his inflexibility and failure to produce creative responses to the political and economic crises facing Spain. He was replaced by Adolfo Suárez, politically one of the least likely and most certainly the least experienced of the three nominees presented to the king from which to choose a prime minister. Secretly, in fact, Suárez had been under observation by the king for some time and both before and during the selection process was his first choice. His name had been placed on the nomination list by the persistent pressure on key members of the old Cortes by Torcuato Fernàndez Miranda, President of the Cortes and Council of the Realm, and long-time confidante and adviser to the king.

Despite the outcry which his appointment in July 1976 drew from *continuistas* and *rupturistas* alike, Suárez moved quickly to advance the process of political reform. A Law of Political Reform (*Ley para la Reforma Política*) was steered through the Cortes (with the assistance of Fernandez Miranda) in November 1976, paving the way for democratic transition. The left-wing opposition remained sceptical and distrustful and called for abstention by the public in the referendum on political reform. Until all political parties were fully legalised, the PSOE (*Partido Socialista Obrera Español*/Socialist Workers Party of Spain) and PCE (*Partido Comunista de España*/Spanish Communist Party) leaderships felt that they had no other option but to register dissatisfaction with the process (Chapter 3). Moreover, élites in the opposition parties were very wary of making tactical errors which might undermine their efforts to become a major democratic party.

The referendum of December 1976 resulted in a massive public endorsement of Suárez's reform process. In favour of the reforms were 94 per cent of the turnout. Opposed were only 2.5 per cent. It was a remarkable achievement, not least because under the reforms, the élites of the higher civil service, the army and the judiciary would continue in their positions of authority, moving seemlessly from dictatorship to democracy, without challenge.

The success of this referendum gave the *reformistas*, led by Suárez, the initiative. The main opposition groups were required to enter what, by now, they saw as an inevitable process of negotiations leading to some form of compromise. The legalisation of the political parties – the PSOE in February and, most particularly, the PCE – on what became known as '*Sabado Santo Rojo*' (Red Easter

Saturday) – cleared the way for the first elections of the transition period, on 15 June 1977. Emerging with a large majority was the UCD (*Unión de Centro Democrático*/Union of the Democratic Centre) an alliance, belatedly, forged out of many small parties and groups, led mainly by élites from the Franco regime who were attempting to realign themselves into politically advantageous positions in the newly evolving political system. The victory of the UCD and Suárez was helped by an electoral system which he had the power (under the Political Reform Law) to adopt without negotiation and which favoured the forces of conservatism. However, the PSOE under González also did well, emerging as the main opposition group, while the two more hard-line parties of the left (the PCE) and the right (AP – *Alianza Popular*/People's Alliance) did poorly. The nationalists parties in the Basque Country and Catalonia also had an impact.

In the aftermath of the 1977 elections the most important task in the process of democratic transition was the drafting of a new Constitution. A seven-member group, representative of the main Spanish and nationalist political parties (except the Basques), and appointed by a constitutional committee of the newly elected Cortes, undertook the task of negotiating this document. The most controversial debates revolved around the role of the Church, education and the question of regional autonomy. The negotiations on these and other matters highlighted how much the transition process had become a matter of bargaining and consensus-seeking between party élites. Public participation was very limited. Sometimes the Constitutional Committee of the parliament was used merely to rubber-stamp compromises worked out between key negotiators. On one occasion AP withdrew from that committee in protest at the secret negotiations reached between Alfonso Guerra (for the PSOE) and Abril Martorell (for the UCD) which were pushed through the committee (without debate) by their combined majorities. In one such agreement the PSOE compromised on its opposition to private education. The negotiations also took place against a background of economic crisis and labour unrest. Public demonstrations in Catalonia in favour of regional autonomy also affected the atmosphere of the constitutional negotiations. And there was an ever-present danger that a right-wing backlash might prompt elements in the military to seize power and turn on the democratic process.

The need for urgency in reaching agreement was apparent and so also was the need for compromise by those groups pressing the new government with regional and social demands. An important breakthrough was the signing of the Moncloa Pacts. These were agreements between Suárez and the parties of the left. In exchange for a programme of social reforms, the unions and those opposition parties would co-operate in stabilising the economy by keeping wage demands below the level of inflation. For the PCE and its leader Santiago Carillo, the Moncloa agreements provided an opportunity to demonstrate their capacity to help make policy in a responsible manner. To the PSOE, the agreements offered less. The PSOE's leadership resented Suárez for stealing its 'clothes', i.e. the use of a corporatist labour market strategy. In the aftermath of the agreements being signed, labour market conflict declined, giving the constitution-writers some breathing space. For the Spanish business élites the agreements provided a tangible reward for supporting democratic change.

In October 1978, the text of the Constitution was finally approved by both houses of Parliament and in December it was accepted by 87.9 per cent of those voting. Significantly, in the Basque Country the turnout was considerably lower than elsewhere. The Basque abstention signalled the fact that the issue of Spain's 'historic nationalities' (*nationalidades históricos*) and regions would continue to arise in Spanish politics in the foreseeable future. The Basque Country provided the most deep-seated difficulties for Suárez. Despite these, he and the PNV (*Partido Nacionalista Vasco*/Basque Nationalist Party) leader Carlos Garaikoetxea, negotiated the Statute of Guernica in July 1978, which paved the way for the Basques to win some degree of self-government. It was a major success for Suárez, but did little to impress ETA (see Chapter 2).

The collapse of the Moncloa Pacts in December 1978 marked the beginning of a new phase of opposition politics from the left-wing parties who were becoming increasingly hungry for power. Under siege, the UCD began to crumble, but not before winning the elections of March 1979, the first under the new Constitution. Internal divisions presented ongoing threats to the UCD. The party was in fact an alliance of various groups that had emerged out of the collapse of Francoism and sought refuge under the UCD umbrella. It had few roots in society at large and little membership or social base in the way that democratic parties normally have. It was a party consisting of highly competitive élites – the 'barons' – whose factions, now that major constitutional question was settled, increasingly disagreed with each other over the policy directions of the UCD, leading to poor parliamentary discipline and defections. Moreover, one potential source of UCD votes – the industrial and commercial élites of Catalonia and the Basque Country – tended to support nationalist parties there.

In January 1981, Suárez resigned and, on 23 February 1981, in the midst of the parliamentary conflict that surrounded the inauguration of his successor as prime minister, Leopoldo Calvo Sotelo, came a reminder of the continued fragility of the recently democratic Spain. This was the attempted *coup d'état* by a group of civil guards (*Guardia Civil*), led by Lieutenant-Colonel Antonio Tejero Molina, who took control of the Cortes and held its members for 36 hours. This action was intended to serve as a rallying point for the forces of the far right, to reverse the transition to democracy. The prompt action by the king in conveying to the military and the public his condemnation of the action against parliament, together with widespread public and political revulsion, led quickly to it being quashed.

The elections of 1982 were of enormous importance to Spain's fledgling democracy leading, as they did, to the formation of a new government. They brought about the transfer of power from the UCD, that coalition of groups whose leaders had begun their political lives at the heart of the dictatorship, to the PSOE, whose leadership was a part of the underground opposition to that dictatorship. The consolidation of Spain's democracy was reinforced by this peaceful transfer of power. There still remained many unresolved issues, the debates about which dominated politics up to the end of the 1990s. The most important of these was the nationalities and regions issue.

Further reading

Aparacio, M.A. (1989) *Introducción al sistema político y constitucional español*, Barcelona, Editorial Ariel.

Carr, R. and J.P. Fusi (1979) *Spain: Dictatorship to Democracy*, London, George Allen and Unwin.

Gilmour, D. (1985) *The Transformation of Spain: From Franco to the Constitutional Monarchy*, London, Quartet Books.

Grugel, J. and T. Rees (1997) *Franco's Spain*, London, Arnold.

Pérez-Díaz, V.M. (1993) *The Return of Civil Society: The Emergence of Democratic Spain*, Cambridge, Mass., Harvard University Press.

Powell, C. (1996) *Juan Carlos of Spain: Self Made Monarch*, London, Macmillan.

Preston, P. (1986) *The Triumph of Democracy in Spain*, London, Routledge.

Preston, P. (1993) *Franco: A Biography*, London, HarperCollins.

2

Towards a federal Spain?

A prominent feature of the political history of Spain has been the failure of various regimes throughout the centuries to create a single nation, under the strong rule of a central government. Most recently, the authoritarian and centralised machinery of the Franco regime began to disintegrate after the *Caudillo*'s death in 1975. The new constitution, adopted in 1978, set the scene for a Spain consisting of 'autonomous communities' *(comunidades autónomas)*, which attempted to chart a course for unity within the diversity of nationalities and regions. In so doing, it fell short of creating a full federal state. Up to the late 1990s, the outcome of Spain's autonomy process was still being hotly contested. It continued to be a key constitutional question in political life there. But the debates focused mainly on the level and forms of autonomy and decentralised government. No one in the mainstream of party political life in Spain had the temerity to contend that the existing system should be replaced by a strong centralised state: a predominant assumption for much of the nineteenth and twentieth centuries. Few could comfortably predict if Spain would evolve into a federal state in the twenty-first century, yet the concept of federalism continued to have a tantalising appeal as a strategy for managing ethno-regional differences there (Smith 1995: 24).

Historical background

The failure of Spanish centralism is as intriguing a subject of enquiry as the success of its decentralisation. It is, in part, a product of the legacy of rule by the House of Hapsburg which allowed local autonomy to kingdoms and principalities. These were arranged in loosely connected political and economic structures that eventually contributed to the undermining of Hapsburg rule in 1714. The Bourbons countered these prevailing trends in the eighteenth century and tried instead to erect a strong modern Spanish state. After some success towards the end of that century, their efforts eventually came unstuck

13

with the first Carlist War of the 1830s (Carr 1982: 184–95). Thereafter, the nineteenth and early twentieth centuries are scattered with the political corpses of advocates of both centralised and decentralised forms of government, who attempted to pick up the pieces left by the Bourbons and Hapsburgs (Keating 1993: 343–50).

Advocates of centralist models spanned the political spectrum. They included monarchists (who favoured the authoritarian certainties of a Catholic, Castilian-speaking state), a liberal republican grouping (which was dismayed at the humiliating defeat of Spain by America in 1898) and, a faction of the socialist party, the PSOE (which advocated centralised solutions to socialist development in Spain).

Decentralised and regional solutions were also promoted by a disparate band of political groupings (*El Mundo*, 6 December 1994: 4–5). These included Carlists (who supported a return to the loose conglomeration of principalities of the Hapsburg epoch, together with the return of traditional privileges, particularly to areas where support for Carlism was strongest such as the Basque Country, Navarre and parts of Catalonia); federal republicans (who promoted a campaign to create a modernised, democratic and decentralised federation); and some socialists (who also favoured a confederal solution and succeeded in getting a PSOE conference resolution to this effect adopted in 1918). Peripheral nationalism, which started in Catalonia and the Basque Country in the late nineteenth century, and spread fever-like to Galicia, Andalusia and other regions shortly afterwards, had a variety of sources. In Catalonia, it was primarily sponsored by the local industrial bourgeoisie (Balcello 1996: 18–27). They resented the involvement of a Madrid-based political and administrative élite of Andalusian landowners in their economic affairs and also vigorously campaigned for the defence of the Catalan language. In the Basque Country, it was a reaction against the industrialisation there, which was sponsored by the Madrid banking and commercial élite. Basque nationalism was traditionalist, agrarian and Catholic in character. The Basque nationalists also made the promotion of the Basque language a key battleground (Fusi 1989: 763–5). Galician nationalism as a political force mainly developed in the 1930s. It too was based on the existence of a distinct language and culture. As a political movement it did not have the popular support-base and initiative of the other two 'historic nationalities' and was more dependent on their example for political direction.

Andalusia also had a movement for regional autonomy in the early twentieth century. This grew out of the demands for land reform by those who opposed its landowning élite. That élite was doubly disdained because it presided over the centralised political apparatus in Madrid, and the impoverished regional economy of Andalusia (see Chapter 1). Even Aragón, Mallorca, Valencia and Asturias, spurred on by left-wing republican ideas, displayed growing regional stirrings by the mid-1930s. Out of all of this regional political manoeuvring, the First and Second Spanish Republics (1873–74 and 1931–39 respectively) provided two brief, but important, respites from centralist rule in the nineteenth and early twentieth centuries.

The Constitution of 1978, which outlined the principle of a state of autonomous regions and nationalities, was to be the next attempt to square the circle of a single nation of Spain (Monreal 1986: 60–1). It envisaged separate 'historic nationalities' (for Catalonia, the Basque Country and Galicia) and regions (for the rest), each with various degrees of autonomy and home rule. In the interim period, the Francoist regime sought to obliterate cultural diversity for the sake of Spanish national unity and looked back to a heavily embroidered and propagandised notion of Spain as an imperial and great Catholic power. It challenged what it saw as atheistic and communist threats coming from the 'separate areas', by imposing political centralism and anti-autonomism (Giner 1984: 86). The exception to this was Catholic, traditional and Carlist Navarre which was rewarded for siding with Franco during the Civil War by being allowed to retain some of its traditional privileges, or *fueros* as they were called. For the others, press restrictions, the ban of minority languages in schools, the stamping out of regional cultural organisations, and the peremptory arrests of suspected political activists, followed in many cases by disappearances and executions, were all part and parcel of a machinery of repression aimed at 'national homogenisation'. This process had unintended consequences in that it actually served as a stimulus to the widespread growth of underground movements for autonomism, separatism, regionalism and independence. The alliance between these movements and the democratic opposition to the Franco regime took place mainly in the peripheral nationalities of Catalonia and the Basque Country, and in the economically impoverished regions of Andalusia and Galicia. The existence of this alliance meant that the transition to democracy after Franco generated a solemn commitment by democratic forces to a degree of regional autonomy. For some political organisations this involved a shift of policy.

In the 1960s the PSOE opposition in Spain was committed to federalism. This commitment was reinforced by the international publicity attracted by the infamous Burgos trials of Basque militants in 1970 (Hollyman 1995: 12). However, during the transition to democracy, the PSOE agreed to abandon its federalism and to embrace the concept of the autonomy state in exchange for concessions on a new electoral system, to be adopted for Congress. By 1977, all the main parties contesting the first democratic elections of that year had made a pledge for at least some sort of regional autonomy in Spain.

The end of Francoism, therefore, served up the opportunity not just to establish Spain as a democracy but also to give some measure of autonomy and home rule to the nationalities and the regions, many of whom were already showing a degree of political awareness and distinctiveness.

The evolving constitutional debate

In retrospect, the creation and evolution of the Spanish system of autonomous communities can be divided into four stages:

1 from the first moves towards establishing democracy and recognition of the
   regions and nationalities in 1976 to the approval of the Constitution in
   December 1978;
2 lasting from the approval of the Constitution, to the threatened reversal of it
   by the coup attempt in 1981;
3 an era of cautious and legally contentious change from the first PSOE
   government in 1982 to the re-election of PSOE to a minority government in
   1993;
4 an era of political uncertainty and opportunity for the regions and nationalities from 1992 to the present.

1976–1978

The regional question was a priority for Adolfo Suárez, the prime minister
appointed by King Juan Carlos to initiate democratic reform in Spain. He moved
quickly to deal with pressing political demands of the Catalans and Basques.
Catalan nationalism was easier to formulate a response to, as it was multi-class
in character. Basque nationalism was more class based. So, while economic
élites in Catalonia were advocates of decentralisation, in the Basque Country
they had supported the policies of the dictatorship (Grugel and Rees 1997:
186). After some equivocation, Suárez sought out and reached agreement with
the historic Catalan leader – Josep Taradellas – then residing in France, enabling him to return from a long exile in June 1977 and making him, with the
blessing of a royal decree, president of its restored *Generalitat* or regional
government (which, for the moment, had very limited powers). In making this
inspired and symbolic gesture, Suárez avoided direct involvement in potentially
explosive inter-party negotiations in the region. He also set a precedent for
constitutional developments in the regional sphere for the next few years.
The central principle of the agreement for Catalonia was to recognise not
only its right to self-government, but also its simultaneous integration
within Spain. It was an agreement based upon a principle of mutual trust
(Pérez-Díaz 1993: 199).

Such an agreement was more difficult to achieve in the Basque Country
against the background of ETA violence, the demand by the PNV for the release
of political prisoners, the failure to reach agreement with the Basque leader-in-
exile José María de Leizaola and the complexities surrounding the position of
Navarre (which was a part of the historic Basque Country but also was politically distinct). Suárez pressed on. After the 1977 election, deputies gathered in
what became pre-autonomous regional assemblies in both Catalonia and the
Basque Country and set about formulating statutes of autonomy. In return for
recognising these bodies as legitimate governments-in-waiting, Suárez gained
the support of the historic nationalities for the extension of autonomous
powers to the other regions of Spain and lowered the temperature of nationalist demands for a time. He also won grudging acceptance from centralists

within his party, the UCD and the regime at large. They were persuaded to believe that by creating a general system of regional governments, the claims of Basques and Catalans could be submerged within a general process of regional (administrative) decentralisation, taking place over a long time. In short, it would be a divide-and-rule policy. Therefore, a contradiction lay at the heart of the autonomy policy. The nationalists regarded it as leading to real and separate decision-making and discretionary executive powers, while the UCD and Suárez meant to introduce a limited system of devolved executive powers only. From this contradiction arose later difficulties which contributed, not least, to internal conflict in the UCD and its eventual electoral decline.

By September 1978 many more pre-autonomous bodies[1] had been set up, following a series of negotiations with Manuel Clavero, the minister without portfolio appointed by Suárez's government (who was, in fact, a minister for the regions as yet without any regions, as he ruefully pointed out) (Hollyman 1995: 13). Acting as precursors to regional governments, these pre-autonomous bodies with part-legislative and part-executive powers were constituted from a mixture of parliamentary and provincial representatives. They served as a partial response to the clamour for regional powers which had swept across Spain during the era of democratic transition.

What was the basis for the constitutional formula for regional autonomy adopted in 1978? At the time of the Second Republic a formula called the *Estado Integral* had been devised to depict a state which lay somewhere between federal and unitary extremes and drew from both federal and unitary theories of the state (Keating 1993: 347). On the one hand, in line with unitary theory, it asserted the sovereignty of the Spanish people and the right of their national Parliament to pass the statutes of autonomy for the regions, and to ensure that central government interests were protected in the regions by their representatives the civil governors (*gobernadores civiles*) and government delegates (*delegados del gobierno*). On the other hand, it took from federalist and contractual theory the notion that the regions should frame their own autonomy statutes in negotiations with the centre and gain regional approval by means of a local referendum. The Constitution of 1978 expressed a blend of these principles and created a state that was neither federalist nor unitary, but *un estado de las autonomas* (i.e. a state consisting of autonomous regions or communities each of which was to have a legislative assembly [*asamblea regional*] elected by universal suffrage, a regional government [*consejo de gobierno*] headed by a president [*presidente*] and a High Court of Justice [*Tribunal Superior de Justicia*]). Following federalist principles, the autonomous communities from the outset also had representatives at the national parliament (the Cortes) level: some members of the Senate (*Senado*) or upper house were to be chosen by regional assemblies (Giner 1984: 90). Moreover, regional assemblies were given the power to

---

[1] Galicia, Aragón, Valencia, Canary Islands, Andalusia, Extremadura, Castille y Leon and Castille-La Mancha.

propose bills in the Congress of Deputies (*Congreso de los Diputados*) or lower house. In the 1990s, the extension of these powers was to become a vexed issue.

In the constitutional referendum of December 1978, the PNV abstained on the grounds that it did not need to seek approval for a position which was already defined in the ancient *fueros*, granted to Basques in medieval times. Apart from that significant abstention, the Constitution won widespread support and the autonomy state came into existence. There were two main routes to autonomy status embodied in the Constitution:

1 The 'fast route', detailed in Article 151, which applied to the three 'historic nationalities' which had voted for autonomy by referendum in the Second Republic. According to Transitional Provisions 2 of the Constitution, they needed to attract just a simple majority in a regional referendum to have a statute of autonomy approved.
2 The 'slow route', detailed in Article 143, allowed a lesser degree of autonomy to other regions and held out the prospect of changing to full autonomy after five years. To initiate the autonomy process by this route required the backing of all the provincial councils (*diputaciones provinciales*) and two-thirds of the municipal councils (*ayuntamientos*) in any aspirant autonomous community. These councils would then draw up a statute of autonomy, which would have to be approved by the Cortes as an organic law (*ley orgánica*, the highest type of parliamentary law). For at least five years such 'slow route' regions would have limited powers.

Other routes to autonomy also existed, but these are given separate treatment below. The two main routes were distinguished also by the extent of powers and functions (*competencias*) they accorded to the regions concerned. Not only did they include the activities for which all autonomous communities could take responsibility, but they also set out the powers exclusively reserved for central government. In some policy areas shared responsibility was possible, a feature which created much opportunity for negotiation and debate between the regions and central governments – both the inside and outside the courts. Competition for greater powers and status amongst regions was also a contentious topic in subsequent years.

Powers of the autonomous communities

1 Power exclusive to autonomous communities. According to Article 148 of the Constitution there were a range of powers to which the regions and nationalities could accede, though the speed at which they did so depended on whether they were defined as 'fast route' or 'slow route' regions. These sorts of powers involved control over town planning, museums, the regional language (where applicable), tourism, social welfare and others.
2 Powers shared between autonomous communities and national institutions. In the final analysis the state had ultimate authority in areas of shared

power but this still gave considerable scope for manoeuvre to the regions. Legislation was necessary to transfer these powers from the centre. Shared powers included those that enabled regions to make policy for agriculture and economic development but within the broader frameworks of national laws and policies. Shared powers are referred to in Articles 148 and 149 of the Constitution.

3 Powers exclusive to the central state. Article 149 of the Constitution identified four areas which were, in theory, exclusive to the central state. These were taxation; policing; foreign affairs and justice. In practice some regions gained control over aspects of policing and taxation. They also engaged in external relations.

Ambiguities of this nature have fed into the debate about how the autonomous community system in Spain should evolve.

1978–1981

The Constitution left in a vague and flexible form the interpretation of a number of key elements:

1 The definition of a region was not clearly outlined. This gave rise to a number of conflicting claims. For instance, while the Basque Country claimed the province of Navarre, the Navarrese, whose medieval *fueros* were still considerably intact, would have none of it, at least for the time being. They opted instead for separate autonomy status (Asturias, Cantabria, La Rioja, Madrid and Murcia also formed single province regions rather than join multi-province regions).

2 In practice, there were a number of optional routes to greater autonomy. The Constitution enabled the Cortes to devolve extra powers to regions by means of organic laws, without previously having to reform their statutes of autonomy. This happened in the case of Valencia and the Canary Islands which gained a higher level of autonomy by this means. Navarre also, was given its own special route. Andalusia surprised Suárez and the UCD government by almost succeeding in following the 'fast route' to autonomy via an 'exceptional route' contained in Article 151 of the Constitution. Under considerable political pressure, the government had set out the exceptional conditions which Andalusia was required to fulfil if it was to be allowed to join the 'historic nationalities' in the 'fast track' route to autonomy. The main condition involved winning the support of a majority of the electorate in each of the region's eight provinces. Just one province, Almería, failed to fulfil that condition. Eventually, faced with uproar in Andalusia arising from such a marginal defeat and with the agreement of the PSOE opposition, the UCD government conceded full autonomy status to the region in 1980. The effect of these controversial and widely publicised events was to heighten regional consciousness, not only in Andalusia, but across the other regions

of Spain, leading to the hastening of the whole autonomy process, dubbed 'autonomy fever' or the so called 'demonstration effect' (Solé-Villanova 1989: 332).

3 The level of the 'shared' autonomous powers which regions wished their new regional institutions to exercise was left up to regions to define through their own statues of autonomy. The Basques and the Catalans took full advantage of this discretionary feature and forced Suárez to include a formula in their statutes by which the upper limit of the powers of the auton-omous communities could be decided ultimately by the Constitutional Court (*Tribunal Constitucional*). This loophole led to many legal wrangles in the 1980s. Also gained were important and symbolic concessions, such as a Basque-recruited police force and the restoration of Basque traditional eco-nomic rights, the *conciertos económicos*.

A growing sense of instability in Spain and frantic competition between regions to gain more powers, all of which had the potential to engulf not just the UCD but all democratic forces in the country, led Suárez, in 1981, to seek agreement with the PSOE on a series of formal regional pacts. These would recognise the need for special concessions in the Catalan and Basque cases, while simultaneously trying to dampen down expectations in the other regions. During 1979–80, bits of the state machinery had collapsed in some areas of the province of Guipúzcoa and Vizcaya, as police and members of the judiciary were intimidated by extreme Basque nationalists (Pérez-Díaz 1993: 202). As if to confirm the delicacy of the times, the attempted coup of '23F' had also erupted and concentrated the minds of the UCD and PSOE negotiators more than ever. By the end of that year the autonomy statutes for the three historic nationalities and Andalusia were approved and the remaining 13 statutes were in place by February 1983. The first elections to the new regional parliaments took place between 1980 and 1983. (Catalonia and the Basque Country had their elections in 1980; Galicia's took place in 1981; Andalusia's in 1982 and the rest in 1993.)

1982–1993

Central to the pacts forged between Suárez and the PSOE after the 1981 coup attempt was the LOAPA (*Ley Orgánica de Armonización del Proceso Autonómico*/Organic Law on the Harmonisation of the Autonomy Process), the objective of which was to harmonise and limit the various types of autonomous powers that regions and nationalities could exercise. This amounted to impos-ing state restrictions on some of the new statutes of autonomy. Angered by LOAPA, Basque and Catalan nationalists took an appeal against it to the Constitutional Court. It ruled, in 1983, that while the government was correct in holding that the Constitution required all Spaniards and groups within Spain to be treated equally, and that social and economic privileges such as the *fueros* in some regions should not enable discrimination against other regions, insti-

≠ asimetría

tutional uniformity, as proposed in some sections of the LOAPA, was not constitutionally compatible with the autonomous process. New legislation to replace the LOAPA was passed by the PSOE government in 1983. It recognised that while restricting the spread of regional powers by means of a uniform, harmonised regime (the LOAPA way) was out of the question, a set of common guidelines was necessary, with the aid of which regions would draft their laws, regulations and timetables for the assumption of powers.

The LOAPA was therefore put to one side and the question of how far state and autonomous government powers and institutions might extend towards each other, or even overlap, was moved into the jurisdiction of the Constitutional Court to ponder over, case by case, for much of the 1980s. Between 1981 and 1993 there were 847 cases, the vast majority of which emanated from Catalonia and the Basque Country. The findings of the Constitutional Court were binding and final, and revolved around decisions about which competences were 'exclusive', or 'shared'. The Constitutional Court, therefore, played a fundamental role in the evolution of the autonomous state in Spain (Hollyman 1995: 17).

In the 1990s, and especially after 1993, the extra political leverage available to nationalist and regionalist parties in the face of electorally weakened Spanish governments meant that the political route to constitutional change was more open than hitherto. This contributed to a sharp fall in legal actions by the regions, which increasingly chose the political path to greater autonomy.

While the ten 'slow route' regions, by 1987, were beginning to complete the statutory five-year period before a reassessment of their powers was once more constitutionally permissible, it was not until 1992 that the PSOE acted on the matter. In February of that year, González reached a series of agreements with José María Aznar, leader of the PP, by then the main opposition party, under which, in exchange for gaining 32 new areas of responsibility, an overall maximum level of responsibility, a ceiling or *techo*, for the *autonomías* was defined. This covered aspects of the relationships between the ten 'slow route' regions and the government and aimed to bring the powers of the 'slow route' regions into line with the others. The expansion of co-operative links among the regions was also contained in the 1992 Agreements. For example, the activities and coverage of such joint administrative bodies as 'sectoral conferences' (*conferencias sectoriales*) expanded in the 1990s. Fifteen were established under the 1992 Agreements. They consisted of personnel from regional and central government, as well as officials meeting to discuss and make decisions on some sectoral issues of common concern to various regions, such as agriculture or tourism.

1993–

The most important constitutional issue of the 1990s in respect of its regions was, however, the question of what to do with the Spanish Senate, for years languishing in the half-light of unfulfilled ambitions. Described in the Constitution as a House of Territorial Representation, the Senate was, strictly speaking, a chamber of provincial representation. Its members were predominantly elected at provincial level: four from each of the 52 Spanish provinces. Only 20 per cent of its members were actually appointed by the regional parliaments from amongst their members. Moreover, in its proceedings, the Senate had never functioned successfully as a chamber for the regions and, in general, was rather ineffective as a legislative body.

In December 1993, this situation began to alter with the setting up of the General Committee for the Autonomous Communities in the Senate to deal specifically with regional matters. Furthermore, in 1994, a symbolic gathering took place of all the presidents of the autonomous regions (with the exception of the PNV, which was in the run-up to regional elections and repeated its wary abstention from the event as it had done in the referendum of 1979) and the Prime Minister, Felipe González, who addressed the Senate. To mark the occasion Jordi Pujol of Catalonia and Manuel Fraga of Galicia chose to speak to the chamber in Catalan and Galician respectively (Brasslof 1995: 6). Working parties were also set up, with all-party support (including that of the PNV), to examine inter-regional relations and the development of a new institutional framework to deal with European Union initiatives in the regions. A second symbolic gathering of the regional presidents in the Senate took place in 1997.

Advocates of change envisaged that ultimately the Senate could become a genuine chamber of territorial representation, ostensibly along the lines of the German *Bundesrat*, organised along quasi-federal lines and reporting to the regions and nationalities of Spain rather than to its provinces. The government of *Partido Popular*, however, is unlikely to move in this direction with great haste.

The impact of *Euskadi Ta Askatasuna* (Basque Homeland and Liberty)

Founded in the early 1960s, ETA is a radical movement for Basque separatism and independence, whose tactics of violence have provided a major challenge to the Spanish state (Núñez Astrain 1997: 32). The suspension of this violence through a cease-fire declaration in September 1998 has presented to all sides of the conflict new obstacles, as well as opportunities, in the making of a peace process.

In the early years ETA drew support from nationalist idealists, many of whom were inspired by the cultural and linguistic revival of the 1950s and 1960s. In the 1970s, ETA broadened its support-base to include the interests of working-class immigrants from across Spain. It adopted a Marxist-Leninist ideology and rhetoric and attacked the external (to the Basque Country) sources of capitalist and political power. In the 1980s and 1990s newer generations of members and supporters have been willing to carry the fight on. The *Jarrai* (the youth wing) has engaged in civil disruption which has served as a form of training for more violent tactics.

By assassinating Carrero Blanco in 1973, ETA speeded up the transition to democracy in Spain (see Chapter 1). However, unlike the PNV, it did not accept the concept of a Spain consisting of various nationalities and of autonomous communities, which were intended by the Constitution-writers to settle the nationalities and regional question. The high abstention rate and the low level of support for the 1978 Constitution in the Basque Country served as a warning of the level of disaffection from democratic Spain that existed there. ETA attempted to channel this disaffection into popular resistance to the Spanish state and a movement for Basque independence.

It used bombings, kidnappings and assassinations in its campaign to force Spanish élites to recognise its claim to the right of self-determination for Basques. It anticipated that the introduction by the Spanish state of repressive measures in the Basque Country would fuel popular resentment there and increase further the momentum, in the long term, towards the recognition of its demands by the Spanish state. In the short term HB (*Herri Batasuna*/Basque Homeland and Freedom Party), its political wing, provided a channel by means of which ETA support could put pressure on the Spanish state; in short, a Basque version of the IRA tactic of 'an Armalite in one hand and a ballot paper in the other'.

From the late 1960s to 1998, ETA killed around 800 people, 93 in one year (1980) alone. It targeted figures at all levels of the state and from various institutions such as the police, the judiciary and political parties. In 1995, the head of the PP in the Basque Country, Gregorio Ordóñez, and the former head of the Constitutional Court, Francisco Tomás y Valiente, were killed. An attempt on the life of PP leader, José Maria Aznar, failed (and, ironically, increased his electability to government).

Responses by the state to the violence of ETA have ranged from the repressive to the conciliatory. The anti-terrorist legislation introduced in 1977 by the UCD government suspended detainees rights, including the right to see a lawyer. Abuses of this law by the police were widely recognised to have taken place in the Basque Country and were used by ETA to attract sympathy for the cause and to justify its ongoing campaign of bombings. Likewise the use of the GAL (*Grupos Antiterroristas de Liberación*/Anti-terrorist Liberation Groups) by the Spanish state to wage a so-called dirty war against ETA in the early 1980s continued to create difficulties for government into the 1990s and did not bring the defeat of ETA any closer (see Chapter 4).

During the 1980s and 1990s a number of factors came together to create the conditions for ETA to declare a cease-fire. Brief cease-fires in the past have shown the capacity of the ETA organisation and its volunteers to maintain millitary discipline but they have not been part of a long-term change of tactics. The cease-fire of September 1998 seemed to amount to such a shift.

The example of the Northern Ireland peace agreement is cited by ETA as one of the factors behind its decision to call a cease-fire. Having close contact with the IRA (and HB with Sinn Fein), ETA has been able to observe the rationale for the IRA cease-fire and to judge the progress that has been made during the negotiations leading up to the Good Friday agreement. They see the possibility of similar progress in the Basque Country. However, the Spanish government has pointed out that the Basques already have more autonomy than Northern Ireland will get under the Good Friday Agreement. ETA however, views the official recognition of the republican aspiration for a 32-county republic as a model for its aspirations to be recognised by the Spanish state in any agreement in the Basque Country.

The circumstances which led to the ETA cease-fire are as follows:

• The presence of the PP in government supported by the PNV, and CiU (*Convergència i Unió*/Convergence and Union) has created the possibility of some progress being made in negotiations with the representatives of the Right in Spain. Movement of ETA prisoners to prisons more accessible to their Basque families is one issue about which the PP government has made positive statements and which ETA has been presented with as a possible reward for entering negotiations and dialogue.

• The growing public revulsion against ETA violence culminated in the massive public demonstrations across Spain and the Basque Country after the death (following the kidnapping) of Miguel Angel Blanco, a young Basque PP councillor, in July 1997. The purpose of violence, for example to gain public support from the repression that follows in its wake, was not producing the desired effect, from ETA's perspective, therefore its efficacy was increasingly in question.

• Political isolation of ETA and HB increased in the Basque Country since the Pact of Ajurea-Enea was signed on 12 January 1988 by the main Basque parties. It expressed the signatories' opposition to violent tactics. The decline of the HB vote in the 1990s also provided evidence of the marginalisation of ETA's cause.

• Police successes in capturing and imprisoning ETA members and sympathisers and closer co-operation between the French and Spanish governments on extraditing suspects made the pursuit of the ETA campaign more hazardous for its volunteers.

In the negotiations and dialogue that are expected to follow the cease-fire, ETA's central demand is for the right of the Basques to self-determination to be recognised by the Spanish state. The starting position of the Spanish government is that this does not exist for any of the Spanish 'historic nationalities' and therefore cannot be conceded to the Basques. It is likely that prolonged negotiations will produce a formula that bridges the gulf that lies between these two positions.

Whatever their final outcome the ETA cease-fire and the subsequent negotiations are sure to lead to a further expansion and redefinition of the powers of Spain's nationalities and regions.

Political and administrative developments

Party politics in the regions[2]

Regional and nationalist political parties have had an important impact on political development in Spain, not just at autonomy level, but also at the centre. Most prominent in the 1990s has been CiU, the coalition which was led by Jordi Pujol from its formation in 1979. It espouses a Christian democrat, centre-right philosophy, and supported the minority government of PSOE between 1993 and 1995, and that of PP, after 1996. In the autonomous parliament of Catalonia, CiU has had a solid majority since 1980. It has engaged in promoting Catalan interests economically, politically and culturally in a variety of arenas. Its tactics have had more political impact than those of more extreme Catalan groups, such as the left-wing nationalist party, ERC (*Esquerra Republicana de Catalunya*/Republican Left of Catalonia). In Congress, while the CiU has lost seats since 1989 when it held 19 (dropping to 17 in 1993, and to 16 in 1996), it has played a crucial role in government formation during much of the 1990s (see Chapter 4). The ERC recovered the one seat it held in the early 1980s in 1993, and retained it in 1996.

As a group, Basque nationalist parties have tended to attract a higher percentage of the Basque regional vote than Catalan or other nationalists and regionalist parties in their respective areas. However, the nationalist vote has been largely split between the PNV, a Basque nationalist and Christian democratic party, EH (*Euskal Herritarrok*/Basque Nation) (or as it was known from 1978–98 HB, a Basque separatist coalition linked to ETA), and EA (*Eusko Alkartasuna*/Basque Solidarity), a breakaway group from the PNV. There are also a few smaller parties. Consequently the PSOE which has also done well in the region, usually attracting the second largest percentage of votes, has had a strong influence on the regional government, generally forming coalitions with the PNV. The HB tended to refuse to take up seats won in the Cortes, except in 1995 when it tried to exploit the PSOE's weak electoral position by doing so. It regularly participated in local and regional assemblies. While the PNV won five seats in Congress in the 1989, 1993 and 1996 elections, HB dropped from four to two seats and EA from two to one seat between 1989 and 1993. The HB and EA held two seats each in 1996.

In Galicia, the big Spanish parties have been predominant. From 1989, after defeating the PSOE in the regional elections, Manuel Fraga presided over the

---

[2] Further treatment of political parties is contained in Chapter 3.

Galician regional government *(Xunta de Galicia)* with a significant majority for the PP. (As a former government minister under Franco and founder-member of PP, his victory marked the return of the Right as an electoral force to be reckoned with in Spain) (Gibbons 1990: 31). The nationalist vote in Galicia tends to be split between various left- and right-wing groups, the largest of which is the left-wing BNG *(Bloque Nacionalista Galega*/Galician Nationalist Bloc) led by Xosé Manuel Beiras. In the 1996 general elections, the BNG won two seats in Congress.

Regional and nationalist parties contest and are represented in the parliamentary assemblies of many of the other regions, for example PAR *(Partido Aragonés Regionalista*/Aragonese Regional Party), UV *(Unió Valenciana*/Valencian Union) and CC *(Coalición Canaria*/Canary Islands Coalition). However, Spain's national parties tend to dominate the regional parliaments in those areas too, not least because they have the resources of patronage at their disposal with which to attract the votes of electorate. In Andalusia, despite PSOE's historical grip on the electorate of the region, the PA *(Partido Andalucista*/Andalusian Party) gained a significant tranche of votes in the regional elections of 1994. That said, the PSOE still managed to limp into power in the regional government (called the *Junta*) there, but by a very tight margin, and mainly due to the inability of the opposition parties to form a coalition. In 1996, the PSOE won a more convincing victory in a repeat election in Andalusia. In the general elections, the PA did not manage, in 1993 and 1996, to recover the two Congress seats won in 1989.

In terms of their broad strategies, regional and nationalist parties have tended, to some extent, to copy each other. This was illustrated during the Second Republic as, one after another, the historic nationalities sought autonomy status. As we have also seen, 'autonomy fever' spread across the land-mass of Spain in the late 1970s and early 1980s, when regional consciousness even surfaced in areas of Spain such as Extremadura and Murcia, not known previously to have had any special claims to regional separateness. In the early 1990s, a similar ripple-effect was generated in the historic nationalities when the ERC, inspired by the successful fight for independence in dissident republics of the USSR such as the Baltic states, introduced a motion in 1993 in the Catalan parliament reiterating the Catalan nation's 'right to self-determination'. Aided by the CiU (which protested that it was not going so far as to seek independence), the motion was passed.

The motion was based on a UN concept developed in the 1960s for the worldwide decolonisation process. It reignited the question of the ultimate direction and outcome of the autonomy process, at a time when, thanks to the 1992 Agreement, the gap between the powers devolved to the historic nationalities and the other regions was closing (much to the irritation of the nationalists, who wished to open up that gap again). A similar motion was passed in the Basque parliament, promoted by HB and the PNV, but that introduced by Galician nationalists in the parliament in Santiago fell foul of Manuel Fraga's PP majority. These events reveal the ambiguous position of nationalists, who at times offer crucial support to the Spanish governing parties (e.g. CiU support for the PSOE and the PP in the Congress and PNV pacts with the Basque branch of the PSOE in the Basque parliament). Despite protest actions, such as PNV's abstention from the 1994 Senate meeting of the presidents of the autonomous communities, the mainstream nationalist parties work well within the system. At times, most noticeably before elections, they sound more extreme than usual and occasionally behave like a protest group rather than a political party. Also, the regional party system seems to be only partially successful in helping to absorb both moderate and intense regional feelings. The case of the Basque Country and the violent actions of ETA (before its cease-fire in 1998) serve as some evidence for this. In Catalonia and Galicia, the party system appears to have been much more successful in channelling nationalist demands. Even the presence of the main Spanish opposition party in power in some of the regions may sometimes absorb local frustration with central government (e.g. Felipe González barely canvassed for PSOE in Galicia in the 1989 regional elections, giving rise to speculation that he was not unhappy to see PP installed there, to face some of the pressure from nationalists.)

During the era of the first four PSOE governments (1982–96), bargaining between the centre and the regions has tended to be characterised by two distinct 'styles'. First, in the autonomous communities run by regional and nationalist parties or the PP, relations have been overshadowed by constitutional conflicts, sometimes resolved only after long drawn out political negotiations and legal action. Second, in the autonomous communities run by the PSOE, such relations have been largely a matter of internal party negotiations with conflicts arising from internal party power struggles.

Regional government and administration

The institutions of the autonomous communities are, mirrored, to a large extent, on those of central government. Thus, for example, although they consist of just a single chamber and have between 33 and 135 delegates (*diputados*), the system of election adopted for the regional assemblies is much the same as that for the national Congress (see Chapter 3). Their powers and procedures, although on a smaller scale are not much different either. These include:

- legislation (albeit, only for one region);
- scrutiny of the activities of the regional government;
- nomination of the regional presidents;
- election of a number of senators to the Senate;
- presentation of bills to the Cortes (national parliament);
- making appeals to the regional high court and to the Constitutional court.

Variations in the legislative competences of the autonomous communities arise from the individual statutes of autonomy which have been negotiated with central government. The members of regional governments are chosen by the regional president to whom they are in turn individually accountable. Regional governments approve bills which are then submitted to the parliaments. They also issue decrees and resolutions, and regional ministers may issue orders on appropriate ministry matters.

The structure of the executive varies from region to region, so whereas in Galicia fisheries is an important part of the regional administration, in Castilla-La Mancha, it is of minor significance. Also, nomenclature varies. The regional government is called the *Xunta* in Galicia, the *Generalitat* in Catalonia and the *Diputación Foral* in Navarre. But, in many ways the administrative bodies are internally similar in structure to national ministries with under-secretaries, director generals etc. (see Chapter 5). So-called mixed committees (*comisiones mixtas*) of bureaucrats taken from central and regional levels of government, have co-ordinated the transfer, from the central to the regional layer of government, of those functions and resources upon which the policy initiatives of the autonomous communities largely depend. Since the 1992 Agreements, the sectoral conferences have reinforced the inter-regional and centre-region dimensions of the policy process.

The creation of this (regional) layer of 'meso-government' has also led to a large expansion in the number of public employees: rising from 44,475 in 1982 to 565,460 in 1991. The corresponding reduction in central government employees has been markedly less: while 400,000 posts were transferred to the regions between 1982 and 1991, only 300,000 were lost at the centre (Hollyman 1995: 20). In 1992, the PP president of Galicia, Manuel Fraga, proposed the development of the concept of a single administration (*administración única*). It was founded on ideas similar to the 'subsidiarity' principle (popularised in EU (European Union) debates by Jacques Delors) and involved central government handing over all appropriate administrative responsibilities to the autonomous communities and thereby minimising administrative duplication and unnecessary cost. However, apart from the impact that opposition to the idea encountered from the then PSOE government, the continuing necessity to maintain bilateral relations between central government and each of the 17 autonomous governments made it difficult to foresee how a substantial reduction in the size of the administrative machinery, required to manage these relations, could be achieved. Also, the importance of bureaucratic resources as a way of rewarding supporters of the parties in power, regionally and nationally, cannot be ignored in explaining its size: clientelistic networks (especially of the PSOE) undoubtedly expanded with the autonomy process.

A key driving force behind the expansion of regional powers was the continued competition between the regions for more powers. As early as 1984, the Basque Country, Catalonia and Navarre had control of policies such as education, health, policing and (regional) television broadcasting. The Basque Country and Navarre also had tax-raising powers. For a time, such powers sharply distinguished these 'historic nationalities' from the other regions. But when those 'other' regions were given a major boost to their 'exclusive' powers through the 1992 Agreements, the appetites of the 'historic nationalities' for more concessions were whetted. The response to their demands for such concessions, aided by the precarious electoral state of the PSOE and the PP governments, was impressive. It ranged from the establishment of the Catalan police force (the *Mossos d'Esquadra*) to special measures to promote the Catalan language. The 'historic nationalities' have stressed their distinctive traits (*hechos diferenciales*) to justify their special demands, but it is their votes in Congress that have made the crucial difference to the response of government in the 1990s (Brasslof 1995: 1). The concept of shared sovereignty (*soberanía compartida*) was launched by Jordi Pujol in 1997, to give expression to the distinctive character of Catalonia as an autonomous community and to justify CiU's demands for additional powers beyond those laid down in its statute of autonomy (*Estatuto de Sau*) (*El País* Anuario 1998: 86). Meanwhile the other regions have achieved a comparatively effortless enhancement of powers, as central government has sought to find a balance in its concessions to all the autonomous communities. The PP commitment, in 1996, to concede control of over 30 per cent of personal income tax to all regions, is an example of this trend.

As for the future of this process, the evidence points to a continuing shift of power from the centre to the regions, a process driven by the seemingly insatiable desires of the 'historic nationalities' for greater control over their own affairs. This manifests itself in two main areas of policy: fiscal and budgetary policy and external relations. Ultimately, any region or nationality which acquires a wide capacity to raise taxes, plan expenditure policy and develop autonomous external relations may be self-governing, in all but name.

Local government and administration

The present system of provincial and municipal government dates from the early nineteenth century and has altered little since then, despite the passage of a major law on local government in 1985, which was heralded at the time as a fundamental reform. Municipal government (the *ayuntamientos*) consist of elected municipal councils and also (in the bigger towns) commissions made up of senior councillors (*concejales*) who advise the mayor (*alcalde*). The latter is a figure of considerable importance in Spanish political life and is elected by a meeting of the full council. On occasion – as in the cases of the mayor of Málaga, Jesús Gil, and the mayor of Barcelona from 1979, Pasqual Maragall – they attain national prominence (notoriety, in the case of the former).

The provincial governments[3] have served chiefly as a conduit for central government rule, the basic unit of which is known as the *administración*

---

[3] Apart from 6 which have become single-province autonomous communities, there are now 44 provincial governments.

periférica (delegated state administration). This was an important agency of state control, particularly during the Franco era, and still has significance today. Vivid proof of this is the existence of the role of civil governor in the provinces. He is appointed by the prime minister on the recommendation of the Cabinet (*Consejo de Ministros*) and is responsible for the implementation of the policies of the central government at provincial level. He has particular responsibilities in the area of public safety (e.g. during major forest fires) and public order (e.g. rioting). In Catalonia and the Basque Country he has been considered by many nationalists as a figure of opprobrium, a symbol of state power and of past repression.

In provinces which are also autonomous communities (e.g. Cantabria), the government delegate undertakes the responsibilities of the civil governor (see Chapter 5). Moreover, while in most multi-province autonomous communities there are provincial councils (*diputaciones provinciales*) made up of a number of provincial councillors (*diputados provinciales*) elected by municipal councillors from each province, in the single-province autonomous communities, the provincial council, commissions and departments have been replaced by the autonomous parliaments, governments and administrations respectively.

Provincial powers and functions are largely directed at co-ordinating the activities of the municipalities and administering special services such as the *fueros*, where appropriate. Like municipalities, provincial councils do not have significant law-making powers. Their more important tasks include the annual approval of a municipal works and services plan for each province. Since Spain's EU membership commenced, provinces have been increasingly collaborating on joint public-works projects.

Tension has dominated the recent history of relations between the different levels of government: first, tension between the regions and central government over the desire of the former to have greater autonomy from the latter; second, tension between the regions and the municipalities over a suspected municipal 'pact' forged between local authorities and government in the 1990s, which threatened to hamper the ambition of the regions to fully control local authorities; third, tension over the future of provincial government, which is generally less well regarded than the municipality in Spain (to the point where in Catalonia, a replacement system of counties [*comarques*] has been devised to reflect more accurately local communal contours and boundaries). Financial relations are a major factor in such tensions.

Financing the regions

The right to the financial autonomy of the regions was formally recognised in Article 156 of the 1978 Constitution. It was balanced in the Constitution by the overall responsibility given to the Spanish state for taxation and for the general economic well-being of all its peoples. Arising from this somewhat ambiguous beginning, a law on the financing of autonomous communities (*Ley Orgánica de Financión de las Comunidades Autónomas* – LOFCA) was passed in 1980, which, among other arrangements, made provision for a consultative council, the Council for Fiscal and Financial Planning (*Consejo de Política Fiscal y Financiera*).

Council members were the economy ministers of regional and central governments (Newton 1997: 125). They have engaged in debates on questions of public investment, service costs, public debt and the distribution of resources to the regions. Here, and in the various political arenas, the question of how much financial accountability should be devolved to regional government and with what political and economic costs, served as a major bone of contention during the 1980s and 1990s. The many bilateral negotiations and disputes which also took place between the centre and the 17 autonomous regions, concerning their separate financial regimes, added to the fractious nature of their relations.

Regional government finances derive from a number of sources. The most important of these sources are:

1 An annual block grant paid to each of 15 autonomous communities (the Basque Country and Navarra for historical reasons, have a separate system based on the ancient *fueros*) after complex negotiations worked out in special bilateral committees. This block grant is a tax-sharing grant which means that it transfers from central budget a proportion of the amount of national taxation revenue in accordance with the specific regional competences and ensuing services costs encountered by the various regions arising from their specific statutes of autonomy.

2 Specific transfers directly finance the particular services of health and social services under a separate arrangement.

3 The FCI (*Fondo de Compensación Interterritorial*/Interterritorial Compensation Fund), since 1984, has diverted 30 per cent (35 per cent after 1992) of public investment funds into the regions. This is calculated by reference to a needs formula reflecting population density, emigration, unemployment levels and per capita income, and is particularly intended to give help to less developed areas, such as Galicia, or areas of manufacturing industry in decline like the Basque Country. Critics argued that it was less to the benefit of the poor 'slow route' regions, where public investment plans were not as well prepared as in the 'rapid route' regions. In the 1990s, the allocation of the FCI has been more closely co-ordinated with EU regional development funds and such anomalies have been addressed.

4 While the regions have been able to raise money by means of taxation, the main funding source has been central government. Death duties, stamp duties and gambling taxes are collected by the regions acting on behalf of central government. The parliaments of the regions may add a surcharge to such taxes, but are reluctant to use this facility as it poses a threat to their

electoral popularity. They have also lowered taxes. In autumn 1996, the Basques unilaterally lowered company corporate tax from 35 per cent to 32.5 per cent. This generated outrage from other regions which complained of unfair competition and issued law suits against the Basques. Regions can also impose service charges.

5 Raising funds through the money markets is another possibility for the regions and nationalities, though not without some controversy. In 1989, the Basque government created a furore when it offered bonds to investors at a higher rate of return than similar bonds offered for sale by the Spanish Central Bank. This threatened an embarrassing if not destabilising rush of funds from Madrid to Bilbao. Despite claiming that the right to undertake such action derived from the *fueros*, the Basques were eventually forced to bow to pressure from the Central Bank on the matter. Some regions also have generated large borrowings, most notably Andalusia, Catalonia and Valencia. This has been a source of tension between such regions and the austerity-minded finance ministers in central government.

Under special economic agreements based on their traditional rights – the *fueros* and *conciertos económicos* – the Basque and Navarrese special financial regimes enabled those communities to collect their own taxes at rates set centrally. Exceptions to this arrangement were customs duties and petroleum and tobacco taxes, which were collected by central government. In compensation for services provided by the Spanish state such as defence, these autonomous communities have had to forfeit a *cupo*, that is to say, a fixed amount of the total tax income that they collect. They convey this *cupo* to the central treasury in Madrid.

While provincial government was for many years financed by a share of business turnover tax, the introduction of VAT (value added tax) in 1986 led to its replacement by a system of direct grants. (Metropolitan government such as that in Barcelona has been similarly financed.) Provincial governments continued to have powers to add a surcharge to municipal business taxes. Municipalities raise revenue mainly from property taxes, business taxes and a vehicle tax, all of which are set by central government, but, in some cases, are surcharged by the municipalities (Solé-Vilanova 1989: 221). Fees and user charges (e.g. for water, sewerage, planning permission) are especially important sources of municipal finance to the point that they have been abused by some municipalities due to the relatively wide discretion they have in this area. Municipalities also get an annual grant from central government which is administered through the regional governments.

Following the 1993 election, after pressure from the CiU on a severely weakened PSOE government, a system of 'tax co-responsibility' was introduced by the Council for Fiscal and Financial Planning. This gave the regions responsibility for the retention and disposal of 15 per cent (increased to 30 per cent by the PP government, elected in 1996) of personal income tax. It provoked criticism from the poorer regions (e.g. Galicia) which argued that wealthier regions, with their greater tax-generating capacity, would benefit more than poorer regions, thereby generating wider economic cleavages in Spain. However, the policy also reflected the criticisms of those who argued that strengthening the fiscal responsibility of regions would actually lead to more fiscal accountability and efficiency. The higher tax-collection rates which prevailed in the Basque Country and Navarre (which already had fiscal co-responsibility), provided supportive evidence for this latter argument.

The outcome of the 1996 elections brought more fiscal autonomy to the regions and nationalities. In 1997, the PNV leader, José Antonio Ardanza, won the right to set and collect almost all taxes in the Basque Country in exchange for supporting the PP government. This policy represented a U-turn for Aznar. The PP was criticised by the PSOE which claimed it would lead to 'tax dumping' if lower tax rates (such as the 1996 reduction in corporate tax) attracted high tax payers into the Basque Country.

Increasingly, pressure from the European Union has forced change in regional financial regimes, such as in the areas of regional debt and regional development funding. Indeed, the relations between the regions and external agencies and organisations have increasingly become important.

External Relations

EC (European Community)–EU emphasis on the regions in recent years, embodied in such concepts as 'subsidiarity', 'partnership with the regions' and a 'Europe of the Regions', create the idea that the position of regions in member-states such as Spain has been enhanced during the 1980s and 1990s. However, the absence of a comprehensive agreement on co-operation between Spain's autonomous regions and central government on EC matters has meant that, in some respects, the constitutional and statutory position of the regions may actually have been undermined by these trends. So, are the regions in Spain really advancing their interests in the reformed EU?

During the negotiations at the Maastricht Summit, the Spanish government opposed proposals by the Dutch to give Belgian and German Regional Representatives official status at some Council of Ministers meetings. Spain feared that this would lead to its own regions receiving similar status (Molins and Morata 1994: 121).

Some evidence is available to suggest that the nationalities and regions are strengthening their position in the EU:

1 In 1994, the Constitutional Court ruled (during the run-up to the European elections) that the 'historic nationalities' could operate their own 'consulates' in Brussels and elsewhere. The 'consulates' would have the right of direct negotiation with EU officials on policy issues of specific concern to

their regions. Fifteen of the 17 autonomous governments now have such representation.

2 Regional organisations such as *Patronat Català Pro-Europa*, *Interbask* and *Fundación Galicia* have also successfully filtered information to and from the EU, Catalonia, the Basque Country and Galicia for many years.

3 Many regional development programmes such as those for the transfrontier zones between Galicia and Portugal have generated some verifiable economic spin-offs.

4 In the EU Committee of the Regions, Spanish regions are represented by a strong team. Of its twenty one initial Spanish members, seventeen were regional presidents who offered some possibility of influence at the higher levels of EU decision-making for the regions. German and Belgium regional representatives already had even more clout, for example, in the EU Cultural Affairs Council meetings, where they had the status of observers.

5 An agreement reached between the regions and the government in 1990 established the rules of procedure on a variety of matters concerning the implementation of EU law. A policy co-ordinator was to be appointed in each autonomous community.

6 Another agreement signed in 1994 obliged the Spanish government to take into account the 'common positions' of the regions views on the negotiating strategies. The impact of the regions views on the negotiating strategy would vary in strength according to whether the policy related to 'exclusive' or 'shared' competences (Jones 1997: 50).

It is possible to extend this list of benefits to the regions arising from EU membership, but, there is also evidence of some weakness in the positions of the nationalities and regions of Spain in the EU.

Most importantly, perhaps, the shift of sovereignty from Spain to the EU has affected in a negative way the constitutional position of the nationalities and regions. By and large, they are not separately represented in EU decision-making bodies. Efforts since 1986 to forge a binding agreement between the regions and the government aimed at co-ordinating the views of the autonomous communities as well as appointing regional 'observers' as members of such bodies have fallen down. The chief obstacle in the way of agreement has been the insistence of the 'historic nationalities', especially the Basques and Catalans, that they should have more status than other regions in such matters (Morata 1995: 122). Nevertheless, regional representatives have been allowed to attend some committee meetings alongside central government representatives, to discuss issues of relevance to their areas. Through the various committees of the *Conferencia para Asuntos Relacionados con los Comunidades Europeas* (the special 'sectoral conference' forum for EC Relations created in 1988), EU policy implementation is overseen at a sectoral level. This was initially an interim body, and a fully agreed and constituted body was established in 1992. Although in theory this forum gave regions a vehicle by which they could influence EU matters, it also revealed the difficulties in finding agreement between such a variety of regional interests.

Tensions have been apparent in the distribution of regional funds which Spain has received since 1988 through the Community Support Frameworks. Spain–EU Commission tensions were evident from the outset in the preparation of the plans for these funds, as Spain initially rejected the idea of its regions participating in the process: it eventually backed down. The allocation of funds received through the Community Support Frameworks has also provoked tensions between the Spanish government and the regions, as central government retained control of a considerable tranche of the funds and denied the regions a role in allocating these funds.

At the heart of the issue of regional relations with the EU lie the constitutional and statutory ambiguities of external relations and foreign affairs. Under Article 149 of the Constitution, the autonomous communities are required to conform to the over-riding principle that the Spanish state is sovereign in the matter of international relations. However, the various statutes of autonomy and some region-friendly judgements of the Constitutional Court, especially since 1989, have given the autonomous communities greater freedom in the conduct of international relations. This freedom has been taken advantage of with some flair and intensity, especially in Catalonia under the Presidency of Jordi Pujol, and in Galicia under Manuel Fraga (García 1995: 130–1).

Catalonia has actively projected itself on to the international stage on a number of fronts: economically (e.g. by using 'consulates' in the major international industrial and financial centres to attract investment to the area); culturally (e.g. actively promoting Catalan cultural identity abroad) and politically (e.g. advancing its interests through representation on the Committee of the Regions). In Galicia also, external relations have been incorporated into day-to-day political realities: culturally (e.g. contributing to the development of the pan-Celtic movement and fostering links with other Celtic nations); economically (e.g. advocating the case of Galician maritime interests during the tuna fish 'war' with France in 1994 and the halibut 'war' with Canada in 1995); socially (e.g. in its contribution to emigrant centres in Latin and Central America); politically (e.g. in the condemnation of the US blockade of Cuba in September 1994 by the President of the *Xunta de Galicia*, Manuel Fraga, who had earlier hosted a visit of fellow *galego* [Galician], Fidel Castro). All regions have promoted their interests abroad. In 1992, 16 out of 17 presidents of autonomous communities made 124 visits abroad (Gibbons 1999).

The growth of horizontal institutional links between the regions and nationalities of Spain and other European regions, reflect the development of some 'independent' external relations beyond the Spanish multinational state. The most significant is the so-called 'Four Motors of Europe', formed in 1988, which is a lobby group made up of the regions of Baden-Wurtemberg, Rhône Alpes, Lombardia and Catalonia. Galicia is a member of the Regional Conference of Peripheral Maritime Regions (*Conférence des Régions Périphériques Maritimes*) which includes regions of EU and non-EU states. The purpose of this organisation is to counter handicaps suffered by peripheral maritime regions in Europe. Catalonia belongs to other organisations concerned with cross-frontier issues such as the Trans Pyrenean Working Groups (*Comunauté de Travail des Pyrénées*). The city of Barcelona is a member of C6, a group of six French and Spanish cities with common interests (Molins and Morata 1994: 126–7). The significance of such organisations, though, is limited by their comparative lack of direct and specific influence at either central government or supra-national levels.

The autonomous process has also allowed the development of some policy initiatives directed externally (e.g. Galicia has developed a number of aid pro-grammes for the Galician emigrant communities in Latin America including pensions) (*Xunta de Galicia* 1990: 12). While some superficial freedom of action may be apparent in these external links, the underlying constitutional relation-ships ensure that such actions take place within the parameters of the 1978 Constitution, the autonomy statutes and Spain's 1986 Treaty of Accession to the European Community. These form the bottom line of such trends.

Conclusion

The question of what to do with Spain's regions and nationalities has domi-nated constitutional and political debate there since the demise of Franco and the transition to democracy. The way in which that transition took place meant that while the Franco regime and its ideology of a centralised and uniform Spain were transformed quite speedily in the 1970s, the reform of state institu-tions and policies was a slower, incremental or even sporadic process which continued throughout the 1980s and 1990s. The absence of true and fixed parameters to the degree of autonomy and self-rule a nationality or region might aspire to or attain, whetted the appetite of Spain's self-defined autono-mous communities and generated a degree of competitiveness, especially between those nationalities whose claims to autonomy had considerable his-toric and cultural legitimacy and the regions whose claims for autonomy were more functional and territorially based. Consequently, the autonomy powers debate was driven by an internal dynamic consisting of 'historic nationalities' continually striving to stay ahead of the rest of the regions, some of whom seemed determined efforts to catch them up.

The constitutional formula which enabled such a diversity of nationalities and regimes within a unified Spain generated the problem of how far the concept of a unified nation-state could be stretched before it snapped and came asunder. The degree of home-rule dealt out to the nationalities and regions in Spain suggests that the unified nation-state was indeed quite a pliant object. Ceding control over key aspects of revenue and expenditure policy and the capacity to develop external relations policies and initiatives were also accom-modated, albeit sometimes reluctantly, by the guardians of Spanish unity: its central government and the Constitutional Court. Attempts to draw a line under the autonomy process or to place a ceiling on transferable powers have tended to be undermined by political parties at the centre, desperate to win or to stay in power in Madrid. One solution might be to transform Spain into a federal state. The ultimate commitment to a unitary state in the 1978 Constitution makes this impossible in theory, without a change to the Constitution as Jordi Solé Tura has observed (Guibernau 1995: 250). However, in practice Spain might well attain most of the characteristics of a federal state, for example, by transforming the role of the Spanish Senate, and by re-evaluating the relationships between the different layers of its government at local, provincial, regional and central levels. The growth of federalism in the European Union would also have a benign impact on the emergence of a federalised Spain, if not in constitutional theory, then in the actual practice of government.

References

Balcello, A. (1996) *Catalan Nationalism: Past and Present*, London, Macmillan.

Brasslof, A. (1995) 'Spain's Centre and Periphery: Is the Tail Wagging the Dog?' Conference Paper, Salford University.

Carr, R. (1982) *Spain 1808–1975*, Oxford, Oxford University Press.

El Mundo (6 December 1994) 'Documentos: Una España Federal', Madrid.

El País Anuario (1998), Madrid.

Fusi, J.P. (ed.) (1989) *Espana: Autonomías*, Madrid, Espasa-Calpe.

García, C. (1995) 'The autonomous communities and external relations', in R. Gillespie, F. Rodrigo and J. Story (eds) *Democratic Spain: Reshaping External Relations in a Changing World*, London, Routledge.

Gibbons, J. (1990) 'Political Change in Galicia in the Regional Elections of December, 1989', *ACIS: Journal of the Association of Contemporary Iberian Studies*, 3:2.

Gibbons, J. (1999) 'Spain: A Semi Federal State', in D. McIver (ed.) *The Multinational State*, London, Macmillan.

Giner, S. (1984) 'Ethnic Nationalism, Centre and Periphery in Spain', in C. Abel and N. Torrents (eds) *Spain: Conditional Democracy*, London, Croom Helm.

Grugel, J. and T. Rees (1997) *Franco's Spain*, London, Arnold.

Guibernau, M. (1995) 'Spain a Federation in the Making', in G. Smith (ed.) *Federalism: The Multiethnic Challenge*, London, Croom Helm, p. 250.

Hollyman, J.L. (1995) 'The Tortuous Road to Regional Autonomy in Spain', *Intellect: Journal of the Association for Contemporary Iberian Studies*, 8:1, pp. 12–23.

Jones, R. (1997) 'Institutional Mechanisms for the Participation of Spanish Regions in EU Policy-Making: A Threat to State Autonomy', *Intellect: Journal of the Association of Contemporary Iberian Studies*, 10:1.

Keating, M. (1993) *The Politics of Modern Europe: The State and Political Authority in Major Democracies*, Cheltenham, Edward Elgar.

Molins, J.M. and F. Morata (1994) 'Spain: Rapid Arrival of a Late Comer', in M.P.C.M. Van Schendelen (ed.) *National Public and Private EC Lobbying*, Aldershot, Dartmouth Press.

Morata, F. (1995) 'Spanish Regions in the European Community', in B. Jones and M. Keating (eds) *The European Union and the Regions*, Oxford, Clarendon Press.

Moreal, A. (1986) 'The New Spanish State Structure', in M. Burgess (ed.) *Federalism and Federation in Western Europe*, London, Croom Helm.

Newton, M.T. (with P.J. Donaghy) (1997) *Institutions of Modern Spain: A Political and Economic Guide*, Cambridge, Cambridge University Press.

Núñez Astrain, L. (1997) *The Basques: Their Struggle for Independence*, Wales, Welsh Academic Press.

Pérez-Díaz, V.M. (1993) *The Return of Civil Society: The Emergence of Democratic Spain*, Cambridge Mass., Harvard University Press.

Solé-Vilanova, J. (1989) 'Spain: Developments in Regional and Local Government', in R. J. Bennett (ed.), *Territory and Administration in Europe*, London, Pinter, pp. 205–29.

Smith, G. (1995) *Federalism: The Multiethnic Challenge*, London, Longman.

Xunta de Galicia (1990) *Planes de Ayuda a la Galicia del Exterior*, Santiago, Lunta de Galicia.

3

Parties and elections

In May 1996, Prime Minister José María Aznar welcomed Manuel Fraga Iribarne to the Moncloa Palace as his first official visitor. The occasion was steeped in symbolism, marking a major success for the conservative right in the PP, of which party the former Francoist minister, Fraga, was a founder member and first secretary general. However, even in victory, the difficulties which have beset them throughout their history could not be fully shed: the PP was unable to capture sufficient votes to command an overall majority in the Cortes, much to the surprise and dismay of its supporters (pre-election opinion polls had forecast a comfortable majority for the PP). It was only able to form a government with the support of Catalan and Basque nationalists: a rather ironic turn of events for a party whose history began as a leading advocate of the virtues of a strong and centralised government system for Spain. Small wonder that Felipe González, finally relinquishing power after 14 years in government, was moved to say that there never was 'a defeat as sweet' as this.

Partido Popular (People's Party)

Founded as the AP in October 1976, the PP was, initially, a coalition of seven small parties headed by former ministers, including Fraga. Shortly after the first National Congress of the new party, the 1977 elections took place. The AP confidently anticipated that it would capture a large proportion of the right-wing vote, which its leadership expected lay waiting to be tapped. In reality, it won the support of just 8.23 per cent of the vote, amounting to 16 seats in the Congress and two Senate seats: Adolfo Suárez's UCD, the main claimant to the right-of-centre vote, emerged with 35 per cent of the vote.

It was evident that the AP had misjudged the mood of the electorate. Its subsequent history, between the late 1970s and the 1990s, was dominated by various attempts to reposition itself within the party political spectrum, to try to command as large a proportion of right-of-centre votes as was necessary to form a government. First efforts in this respect were unsuccessful. Although the AP eventually accepted the 1978 Constitution, its well-known antipathy towards the autonomous state, and its support for the death penalty, generated a public perception of it that was closer to the right-wing extreme than to the centre of the party spectrum, which was where the UCD lay (Medhurst 1982: 308). Thus, while the AP remodelled itself by forming part of the CD (*Coalición Democrática*/Democratic Coalition), which included some Christian democrats who had not joined UCD, the electorate was not impressed and dealt a further blow to its vote in 1979, bringing it down to 5.96 per cent which translated into nine seats in the Congress and three in the Senate. Municipal results a month later were even more dismal.

Staring oblivion in the face, the decisions of the next National Congress (in December 1979) would be crucial if the AP was to make any impact on a still evolving party-system. The party adopted a three-prong strategy. First, it focused its attentions on the so-called 'natural majority' of voters in Spain, whom it believed to lean towards the right-of-centre (Montero 1988: 148–9). Second, it redefined itself as a liberal conservative and pluralist party with a catch-all programme like the Gaullists in France and the Conservatives in Britain. It also put an emphasis on traditional values – the family, an anti-materialist morality and a strong state – aimed at stamping out social dissension and lawlessness. Third, it created a strong presidential party structure under the leadership of Fraga. Subsequent elections in the early 1980s seemed to bear out the wisdom of this strategy: the AP won a majority of seats in the Galician elections of November 1981 and took over the regional government: the *Xunta de Galicia*. The AP also pushed the UCD into third place in the Andalusian elections, which the PSOE won overall. More significantly, it reconstituted itself again as the AP–CP (AP–*Coalición Popular*/AP–People's Coalition), embodying not only disgruntled ex-UCD Christian democrats but also the liberals (from the *Unión Liberal*, a constituent party) and some regional conservatives namely, PAR, UV (*Unió Valenciana*/Valencian Union) and UPN (*Unión del Pueblo Navarro*/Navarrese People's Union). The AP–CP won 25.4 per cent of the votes in the 1982 general elections, giving it 106 deputies and 54 senators, amounting to a spectacular rise in fortune from just a few years previously. More importantly, it was now the largest right-of-centre party group, the UCD having virtually imploded.

However, if its supporters thought that the AP–CP would quickly transform itself into a party of government they were very misguided. Instead, during the 1980s the coalition stagnated, went into temporary decline, and even threatened to pull itself apart as the fissures between its internal components occasionally opened. But first there were some further successes as the AP–CP won majorities and formed regional governments in Cantabria and the Balearic Islands, and increased its support in Galicia. The party also gained some international gloss by joining British and French conservatives in the International Democratic Union in 1983.

Much of the success of the AP–CP in the early 1980s can be attributed to the collapse of the UCD and the migration of a proportion of disaffected voters to the next party-political option available on the electoral menu. It was not due to a transformation in the public perception of the AP–CP as the true heir to right-wing government in Spain. Despite the upsurge in support, the AP–CP faced internal divisions, most notably over its ambiguously phrased position (amounting to a barely concealed 'No') on Spain's continued membership of NATO (see Chapter 7). It seemed that the AP–CP was a coalition without a clear ideological direction and when internal debate did occur it had no way of channelling it effectively. The 1986 election showed the AP–CP to have failed in its attempt to become the party of the 'natural majority' in Spain. Not only was there no such right-wing natural majority in evidence – if anything it existed on the centre-left of the spectrum – but the party actually lost a deputy in the 1986 elections (though it did gain three extra senators) and made only marginal gains in its overall percentage of the vote.

There followed a period of turbulent debate, division and leadership change which continued up until April 1990 when José María Aznar became party president. He began to steer what from January 1989 was called the *Partido Popular* in the direction of government, a process which culminated in the partial success of the general elections of May 1996. This period before 1990 saw the reshaping of the AP–CP through the temporary loss of its Christian democratic group, which joined the independents in the Cortes in 1986, and the liberals *(Unión Liberal)*, who left in 1987. None the less – keeping its ideological options open – the newly launched PP preserved its claim to be the legitimate home of Christian democracy in Spain (but then so also did González occasionally claim it for the PSOE), while it also advocated neo-liberal policies of economic modernisation.

The resignation of Fraga as AP–CP leader in December 1986 had, to some extent, drawn a line under the less savoury memories of the party's association with the Francoist past, which were identified as an electoral liability. It also unleashed a bitter struggle between the leadership challengers, leaving the party temporarily weakened. A brief reign as leader by Antonio Hernández Mancha saw the AP–CP continue to slip in the electoral polls and in 1988 Fraga returned briefly to relaunch the party for the forthcoming European elections. In this, he was helped once more by some Christian democrats who had been led into the PP (so-called following the Conference of the Refoundation in January 1989) by Marcelino Oreja Aguirre (who has had the unique distinction of having been defence minister under the UCD, PSOE and the PP). The PP, once more a broad-based coalition of conservative as well as some Christian democratic and liberal groupings, also attempted to draw into the fold the small band of Christian democrats who made up Adolfo Suárez's CDS (*Centro Democrático y Social*/Social and Democratic Centre).

In late 1989, Fraga stood for and won the Presidency of the Xunta de Galicia and was replaced as leader of the PP by Aznar, his nominee (though he still held

the honorary title of founder-president) (Colomé and López Nieto 1993: 355).
A meeting of Fraga's closest allies held at Perbes, near his home in Galicia, convinced Fraga that Aznar should succeed as leader of the PP (Palomo 1990: 98–107). A national conference in Seville later formalised this choice. Aznar was the president of the autonomous community of Castilla-León: a former tax inspector who was recognised for the efficient management of that region. He focused the attention of the PP on the waning popularity of the socialists, who were increasingly beset by corruption scandals. He also sought to further distance the party from its ancestral roots of right-wing extremism, emphasising its respect for democratic institutions. He promoted the PP as a 'catch-all' party, offering the electorate a recipe of sound economic management, market liberalism and clean government. He paid close attention to party matters. New Generation *(Nuevas Generaciones)*, the party's youth section, expanded rapidly. Party membership also increased dramatically under the PP's general secretary, Francisco Alvarez Cascos. Most important of all, Aznar quickly asserted his control over the party itself to avoid the ignominy suffered by his predecessor Hernandez Mancha, whose power-base was too fragmented. Party central office became the hub of all major PP initiatives, with Aznar in firm control. Strong leadership was seen as necessary if PP was to emerge as a serious contender for government office.

The Spanish public were slow to accept the new face of the right in Spain, but accept it in substantial and growing numbers they eventually did. In the 1993 general elections, the PP won 141 seats in Congress, 18 less than the PSOE. In the 1994 European elections, the PP won more votes nationally than the PSOE. By the end of 1995 it had won sweeping successes in the regional and municipal elections. After the general election of May 1996 the PP was the party with the largest number of seats in the Congress (i.e. 156 to PSOE's 141), though it lacked an overall majority. This outcome required the PP to show that it really did accept the diversity of nationalist opinion within the frontiers of Spain. It was obliged by electoral mathematics to enter negotiations on the formation of a government with the Catalan party, CiU, and others. Sceptics argued that the PP approach to this enterprise would test the real instincts of this, the latest party political manifestation of the Right in Spain. But if the PP had learnt anything from their many years in the political wilderness it was, surely, the art of reinvention. Could it be possible that they would find the elusive 'natural majority' of the right, in an alliance with nationalist and regional parties?

Policy orientation

Despite initial reservations about the 1978 Constitution from among their ranks – some factions called for more explicit references to the role of the Catholic Church – the predecessors of the PP fully supported the Constitution. This acceptance of the constitutional settlement also extended to the autonomous regions, another concept initially difficult for some in the PP to agree, committed as they were to the idea of a 'strong' state. Indeed, the PP under Aznar have sought to bring the debate about the autonomous regions to some sort of conclusion by ring-fencing a set of non-transferable powers, while finalising and speeding up the transfer of the remaining transferable ones. They have also encouraged the strengthening of the local layer of government and emphasised the need for a balance to be struck between citizen's rights and responsibilities.

On the economy, the party has advocated market-friendly policies, including a reinforcement of privatisation trends and greater emphasis on a more flexible labour market. The 1996 election programme promised prudent tax reductions, and a reorganisation of the taxation system. The PP has a strong element of free marketeers but Aznar did not give them control of the key economic positions in the 1996 government. Moreover, he has trodden carefully on the controversial pensions reform issue, where even the PSOE accused him of being soft towards the unions. Public expenditure cuts were also a feature of the PP's policy programme, to be achieved by sharp reductions in the number of senior office-holders, and by savings gained from greater efficiency in the delivery of services, particularly social services. On social issues, PP's traditionalists can still make their voice heard: in 1996 the party opposed giving same-sex partners identical rights to married couples.

Commitment to EMU (Economic and Monetary Union) produced for the PP, as well as the PSOE, a strong incentive for cutting back on public expenditure to help Spain qualify for participation in the first wave of member-states joining the single currency project. However, in opposition the PP was more critical of the impact on Spain of meeting EMU convergence criteria than the PSOE (or at least its leadership) (Camiller 1994: 264). After the 1996 elections its first appointee as Foreign Minister was Abel Matutes who held the highest European qualifications, among them some time spent as Commissioner and as MEP (Member of European Parliament). On NATO (North Atlantic Treaty Organisation), despite its opposition to the 'Yes' campaign of the PSOE in 1986, the PP was in fact a strong supporter of membership of the alliance: its opposition in the 1986 referendum was based on its conviction that the PSOE did not go far enough to accommodate NATO.

The party has advocated a tough line on law and order and terrorism. ETA showed its antipathy towards PP in 1995 by assassinating Gregorio Ordóñez, the PP leader in the Basque Country, and attempting to do the same to Aznar in the same year. In July 1996 it killed the local PP councillor – Miguel Angel Blanco – and provoked spontaneous anti-ETA demonstrations across the country. In government, Aznar and Jaime Major Oreja, the Interior Minister (also a former PP leader in the Basque country), clashed with the PNV, who tended to take a more conciliatory line towards ETA violence. However, having initially met ETA's cease-fire declaration – in the autumn of 1998 – with a sceptical and lukewarm reaction, the PP, as we have seen, began to make some positive responses to the ETA gesture (see Chapter 2).

Partido Socialista Obrero Español (Spanish Socialist Workers Party)

Founded in 1879 by a Madrid printer – Pablo Iglesias – the PSOE's first electoral successes were registered in the local elections of 1891. From then until victory by the Nationalists in the Civil War, the party was an active political force in Spain, albeit initially dominated by Iglesias, up to his death in 1925. He won for the PSOE its first parliamentary seat in 1910 and by the time of the Second Republic, its parliamentary presence enabled it to play an important role in government formation.[1] The parallel evolution of the UGT (*Unión General de Trabajadores*/General Workers' Union), the socialist-dominated trade union, from its formation by the PSOE in 1888, helped the development of the socialist party.

In the aftermath of the Civil War, the leadership of the party was severely weakened by executions, imprisonment and exile. Until the 1960s, the PSOE was, in fact, a party-in-exile as far as its organisation was concerned. (The first party congress abroad took place in 1944 in Toulouse, where Rodolfo Llopis was elected secretary general). The ensuing remoteness of the leadership from events at home, together with the growing influence in the labour movement of the Communists and their union, CCOO (*Comisiones Obreras*/Workers' Commissions), led to disaffection among socialists within Spain, especially those groups in the area encompassed by the so-called Seville–Bilbao–Asturias 'triangle'. Opposition to Llopis and the older generation of socialists crystallised in a series of challenges to the leadership between 1972 and 1974, led by *sevillianos* (Sevillians) Felipe González, a lawyer, and Alfonso Guerra, a theatre director. This culminated in González winning the party leadership at the thirteenth Party Congress-in-exile at Suresne (near Paris). The young 'pretenders' also gained recognition from the Socialist International at this time, as well as strong support from the German SPD (*Socialdemokratische Partie Deutschlands*/Social Democratic Party of Germany), which wished to see a social democratic party emerge in the eagerly anticipated post-Franco era. Funds from German parties (even the Christian democrats contributed) helped to establish a network of PSOE offices across Spain by the time Franco died.

Through *Coordinación Democrática* (referred to as *Platajunta*), the political front mounted by the PSOE and PCE in March 1976 to advance progress towards democracy, the party strengthened its hand in the negotiations over democratic transition. Commitment to Marxist ideology and a clean constitutional and political break, or *ruptura*, with the francoist past were still firmly on its agenda at this stage. The 1976 party programme of PSOE's first party congress held in Spain since Franco died described it as a 'mass party with a mass character, Marxist and democratic'. In this way, it was seen to offer a fundamental challenge to the old francoist regime, equal to the PCE in its command of strong language. But division among socialists in the late 1970s was still prev-

---

[1] It won 115 seats in the 1931 elections, falling to 58 in 1934.

alent in Spain and this affected the PSOE's chances of winning an overall majority in the 1977 elections (until it merged with the PSOE in 1978, Enrique Tierno Galvàn's PSP – *Partido Socialista Popular*/People's Socialist Party – presented an external challenge). Eventually, growing divisions within the PSOE between radical and reformist wings prompted González (a 'reformist') to resign from the leadership at the Party Congress of May 1979. The PSOE Left had blocked his efforts to remove Marxist-influenced sections from the party programme, which he and his allies regarded as undermining PSOE's electability. His speedy reinstatement as leader in September of the same year, at a special party congress, reflected the ultimate inability of the PSOE Left to sustain its challenge and the acceptance by the party grassroots of a more moderate centre-left position on the party spectrum in Spain. Gillespie attributes the rightward shift of the *sevillianos* in the 1970s to a number of factors, including 'the experience of consensual policy making during the early transition years and a greater pragmatism and sense of national responsibility as office drew near'. Their position was also strengthened by the expansion of party membership and the influx of more moderates (Gillespie 1989: 78).

The PSOE's policy shift and González re-election were assisted by reforms – advocated by party vice-president Guerra – to the method by which delegates to Congress were selected. It was also won by González's investment in a personal tour of the party up and down the country during 1979, in between congresses. In truth, it can be said that there was also no other credible alternative to González as leader of the PSOE, a fact which was to continue to be true into the 1990s, albeit by then because he stood head and shoulders above the rest of the party as a proven national and international statesman. However, it could also be said that the cultivation of the image of González by the PSOE as the strong leader ultimately made his replacement all the more difficult (Sinova and Tusell 1997: 193).

The year 1979 marks the point when the PSOE became fully committed to being a catch-all party rather than what Share calls a 'mass movement', which was its previous orientation (Share 1985: 409). The resounding electoral victory in the general elections of 1982, won with 48 per cent of the vote, confirmed the effectiveness of the strategy of the party moderates and the widening of its electoral support-base across the centre ground. Doubtless, the task was made somewhat easier by the self-destructive tendencies of the UCD party which, around the same time as the PSOE was undergoing internal transformation, was crumbling away beneath the feet of its hapless leader and (until January 1981) prime minister, Adolfo Suárez. The challenge of the communist PCE, too, was blunted by its own internal turmoil at that time.

Internal dissension within the PSOE was by no means erased after 1982, despite the formidable strength of the González–Guerra leadership. This was apparent in 1986 when there was considerable internal dissent over the PSOE government's advocacy of support for Spanish membership of NATO (see Chapter 7). However, the formula which produced the general election victory of 1982 worked decisively again in 1986 and 1989, albeit with reduced majorities of 42 per cent and 40 per cent respectively, In 1993, mustering 39 per cent of the vote, the Socialists were forced to seek the support of other parties to form a minority government. That task fell to the CiU, which saw some benefit to be won from an arranged 'marriage' for Catalonia until, no longer able to turn a blind eye to the infidelities and calamities befalling the PSOE, it withdrew its support in 1995. The ensuing election in 1996 took González and the PSOE out of office, but with a commendable 38 per cent of the vote still intact, despite pre-election opinion poll predictions of the meltdown in store for the party. In truth, the PSOE's resilience was partly due to the shift of its support-base in the 1980s and 1990s from the urban working class (except in Andalusia where it was traditionally supported by rural labourers) to the middle class and middle-aged, including a substantial percentage of the female vote. The PSOE was also helped by the extension of its clientelist networks into every crevice of the public sector during its long period in office (see Chapter 4).

Towards the end of the 1980s and in the early 1990s portents of future ills began to appear in the PSOE, undermining its demeanour of electoral invincibility and the self-assuredness of its leadership (Heywood 1992: 4–5). In the first place, there was a build-up of allegations of influence-peddling or 'sleaze' to augment party finances or, worse, for personal gain (see Chapter 4). Most notoriously, the case of Juan Guerra led to the fall of his brother Alfonso from the office of party vice-president, the rupturing of the González–Guerra partnership and the discrediting of the party among many actual and potential supporters (Esteban 1992: 105–8). Second, the difficulties in the relations between socialist governments of the PSOE and the socialist trades union, UGT, became so pronounced over economic and social policy, which was increasingly influenced by the growing international vogue of monetarism, that a general strike was held in 1988 followed by further intermittent bouts of hostility between them in the 1990s, including a one-day strike in 1994. Third, conflicts over economic policy within the PSOE between market liberals epitomised by Carlos Solchaga (when he was finance minister) and more populist Leftists or *guerristas*, so-called after Guerra, became more marked in the early 1990s, following the latter's departure from Government in 1991. After the defeat of the PSOE in 1996, the party seemed to be initially inclined to wait for Aznar to miscalculate in government and to await a recall by the electorate. By mid-1997, the PSOE seemed at least to be moving towards a review of this strategy. In Catalonia, the formation of a new left-wing alliance between Catalan socialists, the IU (*Izquierda Unida*/United Left) and other smaller parties of the left pointed in one direction for the PSOE to follow, nationally. The resignation of González as party leader in June 1997 suggested that he was not going to be the one to persuade the party to change, although the possibility could not be excluded that he would return to leadership after the party had conducted an exercise in self-analysis.

Joaquín Almunia, a Basque lawyer and trade unionist, took over as party secretary general in 1997. A loyal supporter of González and former minister of Public Administration he initially failed to win the party's nomination as candidate for prime minister for the general election of 2000. This resulted in the confusing public impression of a party with two leaders rather than one. However, Josef Borrell, a Catalan, who won that nomination, was to become embroiled in corruption allegations emerging in 1999 and stood down as party candidate in May of that year. Almunia later became the PSOE nominee for prime minister in the forthcoming elections.

Policy orientation

While the PSOE has had a historic attachment to a federal republic embodied in its early manifestos, it acquiesced in the constitutional concept of the autonomous communities. With its large majority after 1982, the PSOE in government worked to put the machinery of regional government in place. The party's own federal structure, which prevailed despite González's and Guerra's firm grip on it, allowed regional parties in the historic nationalities to have autonomy over their own regional party programmes. Despite such evidence of commitment to regions and nationalities, the manner in which the PSOE actually made government policy for these entities, in the mid-1990s especially, led to widespread and perhaps somewhat unfair comparisons with the metaphorical 'tail wagging the dog', notably in its relations with the Catalan party, the CiU. Be that as it may, the PSOE contrived to advocate and support the transfer of more powers over finances and services to the regions and nationalities, and such initiatives as the enhancement of the role of the Senate. In doing so, it also warned, sporadically, of the dangers of excessive fragmentation and the need for an overall ceiling (*techo*) on transfers, as the PSOE put it, to preserve the integrity of the state.

On the economy, the socialists shifted from a pre-1979 Marxist-based ideology of interventionism and nationalisation to a much more market-friendly approach. Too much should not be made of its shift to the right: the PSOE did not embrace ideologically-driven wholesale privatisations and the labour market and social sector continued to benefit from PSOE's overall protective approach despite the party's clashes with the unions. In fact, the PSOE's approach to the economy was pragmatic and involved an awareness of the significance of both the public and private sectors in its development. This was evident in the reforms introduced for the public enterprise sectors, where readiness for market competition if not privatisation became the guiding principle, and minimal cost to the state an overriding goal (see Chapter 5). The PSOE's approach was a catch-all strategy, *Felipismo* rather than neo-liberalism or Marxism, aimed at maintaining or enhancing PSOE's electoral advantage (Holman 1989: 14–15).

Influential in guiding state expenditure policies in the mid-1990s was the desire to ensure that Spain qualified in 1997 for membership of the single currency club. This was in line with the PSOE's strongly pro-European policies which were carried into the government which successfully negotiated Spain's membership of the EC in 1986 (see Chapter 7). The PSOE generally, and González, in particular, very openly fought to place Spain among the leading member states of the EC/EU despite the high economic and social costs involved (Kennedy 1996: 97). It also committed itself strongly to many inter-national alliances and organisations. The party's conversion to NATO in the mid-1980s, although internally divisive, was ultimately successful and rewarding in terms of allied member-state plaudits, most significantly the appointment of Javier Solana as the NATO Secretary General in 1995 (see Chapter 7). The PSOE policy also accommodated Spain's active partnership with the American-led allies in the Gulf war while allowing occasional dalli-ances with Central and South American regimes (e.g. Cuba), which were dip-lomatically at odds with the USA, but culturally close to Spain. Such investments in a foreign policy for Latin America gradually paid political and economic dividends to Spain.

Izquierda Unida (United Left)

The IU is the left-wing alliance of various parties which emerged from the cam-paign against Spanish membership of NATO in 1986. Thereafter, it took part in elections with steadily growing support, so that by the mid-1990s, benefiting mainly from growing disenchantment among many socialists with the rightward drift of the PSOE, the IU was on course to establish itself as a third force in Spanish parliamentary politics.

The IU is now a federation of various parties, among them, the PASOC (*Partido de Acción Socialista*/Party of Socialist Action), *Izquierda Republicana* (Republican Left Party), *Nueva Izquierda* (New Left) and the PCE, the latter forming the main body of the alliance.

Old communists and the New Left

The PCE has engaged in a process of change and transformation through the IU. This change has been necessitated by a number of factors, most importantly, the slump in support for the old communist party in the early 1980s, and the changing international climate for European communist parties, heralded by the collapse of the Berlin Wall in 1989 (*El Mundo*, 21 April 1995: 8). This re-evaluation and repositioning of the PCE has probably saved it from oblivion, despite the contingent growing pains it has experienced. The PCE was founded in 1921 from groups which had broken away from the PSOE over the question of whether that party should join the Third International. It grew significantly in membership and influence during the Civil War and afterwards, especially through the work of the communist trade union movement, the CCOO. During the late 1950s and early 1960s it gained in reputation by its efforts to improve conditions in the workplace.

After the death of Franco, the party was the main promoter of left-wing opposition to the then old regime through the *Junta Democrática* (Democratic Committee) and, with PSOE in *Coordinación Democrática* (Democratic Coalition), was expected to play an important role in democratic Spain. It also moderated its strategy in 1977 in return for legalisation, after which it won 9.2 per cent of the vote and 20 seats in the Cortes. In the 1979 general election, the PCE slightly increased its vote, winning 24 seats but thereafter it began to go into decline, partly as a consequence of internal conflict revolving around the authoritarian and centralised leadership style of Santiago Carrillo, who had been its secretary general since 1956. (Whereas his background was the clandestine world of opposition in the Franco era, the new era of democratic elections demanded other skills.) The party became racked by divisions, splits, desertions and a lack of clear direction, especially in the early 1980s. Question-marks began to hang over Carrillo's position. Following the sharp decline to 4.1 per cent of the vote and four seats in the 1982 elections, Carillo was replaced as secretary general by Gerardo Iglesias.

The fractiousness was not halted by this change. Distrust between Eurocommunist and pro-Soviet wings of the PCE continued. Electoral support and membership continued to ebb away. By 1986, the PCE had broken into three parties at national level, or five, if we include schisms in Catalonia and the Basque Country. Its results in the elections reflected a sorry state of affairs. In 1986, it won only 4.61 per cent of the vote, although it raised its presence in the Congress to seven seats.

The NATO opposition movement and the participation of the PCE in an alliance campaigning for 'No' to Spain's continued membership of NATO opened new doors for the party and allowed it to develop ideologically through the IU. It was able to accommodate all sorts of radical thought, ranging from green environmentalism to pacifism, while staying true to communism. The IU enabled it to grow out of its obsession with the 'Moscow question', that is to say, how the party should view Soviet communism.

Since the 1950s, the divisions between pro-Moscow and more independent elements within the PCE had been evident. In the 1970s and 1980s, the party adopted a Euro-communist line, encouraged by Carrillo but not without alienating some of its pro-Soviet supporters and leading activists in the process. Over the question of the Soviet invasion of Afghanistan, for example, divisiveness led to the creation of some splinter groups such as the pro-Soviet *afganos* (Afghans) (Keating 1993: 330). In the 1990s, the question of how to respond to the collapse of Soviet and central European communism divided both the PCE and the IU.

Despite these difficulties, the PCE and IU have enhanced their image and political standing in Spain since the late 1980s. This has been reflected in electoral terms by a progressive rise from 8.99 per cent of the vote and 18 seats in 1989, to 10.58 per cent and 21 seats in 1996. A number of factors help to explain this. First, the leadership of Julio Anguita of the PCE and IU, since he replaced Iglesias in 1988, simultaneously reinforced the communist identity of the PCE and accommodated the various other strands of opinion and groups within the IU. Second, the policies of the IU attracted support from a much wider cross-section of society. Third, the PCE-IU enhanced its image and political standing by serving as a major critic of the PSOE, as the latter moved to the centre ground of Spanish politics. In this, it was helped by the disenchantment with PSOE among socialist trade unionists in the UGT and their convergence with the CCOO in various campaigns against the PSOE government's economic and social policies. However, Anguita's intransigent opposition to the PSOE was criticised by the *Nueva Izquierda*, a faction in IU led by Diego López Garrido, which favours a left-wing alliance, including the PSOE. Anguita in response contrived to exclude the *Nueva Izquierda* from winnable positions on the Madrid election list (Hopkin 1996: 113). In December 1998, Anguita was replaced as secretary general of the PCE by Francisco Frutos, a Catalan who immediately called for a pre-election pact with the PSOE before the 2000 election. This marked a major shift in PCE policy (*El País* 8 December 1998: 1). However, Anguita continued as co-ordinator general of IU until after the European elections of June 1999.

Policy orientation

Formally, the IU (and the PCE) has advocated a federal republic for Spain but it has not overtly campaigned for the end of the prevailing system of a parliamentary monarchy. The party's own federal structure reflected its desire to be ideologically in tune with what its constitution calls 'the pluralistic nature of the Spanish Left and its people' (Newton 1997: 194). For Spain, it has advocated an enhanced role for the Senate, more power for the regions leading to federalism and reform of the electoral system and other institutions, to enhance the level of participation in public life.

On the economy, the IU has advocated a mixed economy with an emphasis on the goal of full employment, and more public investment to create employment opportunities. In this sense, it has perceived a more active interventionist role for the State than that advocated by the PSOE. Its social policies have contained a broad range of proposed initiatives, directed both at its old and new support-bases. The party itself has embodied the principles of the sort of society it envisages for Spain, that is to say, one that is consensus driven, pluralistic, supportive of equality of the sexes and the needs of young people, and achieved by a leadership committed to a policy style involving collective decision-making.

On Europe, the IU has been supportive of Spain's EU membership but critical of the terms of that membership. Anguita was outspoken on the conditions of the Maastricht Treaty, although there was some antipathy toward this attitude within the IU itself. The party, perhaps unsurprisingly given its internal structure, has also been in favour of enhancing the democratic powers of control and scrutiny of the European Parliament. Unlike the PSOE, the IU has been opposed to NATO. It was, after all, born out of opposition to that alliance. It has also been more critical of US influence on international security and strategic issues and Spain's role therein (e.g. during the Kosovo war).

Nationalist and regional parties: the *sopa de las letras* (alphabet soup)

The outcomes of the 1993 and 1996 general elections have offered irrefutable evidence, if such were needed, of the extent to which nationalist and regional parties have become an important part of the Spanish party political system, in addition to their role in the various autonomous regions' indigenous party political systems. The pivotal role in government-making and shaping, especially of CiU in the 1990s, reflects a trend which has been prevalent at regional and local levels throughout the 1980s, following the establishment of the new layers of government there. In Chapter 2 the impact of regional party systems at the regional level was outlined. Below they are discussed in relation to Spanish politics generally.

Convergència i Unió (Convergence and Union)

Apart from the strong presence of PSOE (or the *Partit del Socialista de Catalunya*/Socialist Party of Catalonia – PSC–PSOE as it is known), Catalan party politics were dominated during the 1980s and 1990s by the CiU coalition which is composed of CDC (*Convergència Democrática de Catalunya*/ Democratic Convergence of Catalonia) founded in 1974, and UDC (*Unió Democrática de Catalunya*/the Democratic Union of Catalonia) which traces its origins back to the Second Republic. Of the other parties in Catalunya, the left-wing ERC has had a high standing due, partly, to its longevity (founded in 1931, it maintained a long opposition to the Franco state).

The two parties which make up CiU have been together since the general election of 1979. Despite different emphases, mainly on social policy matters, the coalition is, broadly speaking, a centre-right group with conservative, liberal, Christian democratic and even some social democratic component parts. Since 1980, CiU has been the dominant party in the Catalan Parliament and therefore, either in coalition or on its own, it has had a firm grip on the *Generalitat*. It has used its position to marginalise other nationalist and national parties in Catalonia. In the Spanish general elections, CiU has performed less successfully in terms of votes won than in regional elections. The impact of those seats it has won in the Cortes has been substantial, enabling it to win large policy concessions for Catalonia. This is true both of its support for the PSOE government between 1993 and 1995, and, for the PP government from 1996 onwards.

The leadership of CDC of Jordi Pujol has played a major part in the success of the coalition. From the 1950s, during which time he founded the *Banca Catalana* and spent periods of time in jail under the Franco regime, he has been at the centre of Catalan politics, not to mention high prominence within Spanish politics generally. He has helped to build the CiU support-base and to cultivate links with the business community in that region. He has championed their concerns, seeing such links as a crucial component of the development of an economically successful Catalonia with international status, and, the delivery of full autonomy to Catalunya from the Spanish centre, or *Pujolismo*, as it is some times referred to in the media.

Policy orientation

While CiU does not advocate outright independence for Catalonia, it has promoted the right of Catalans to self-determination, for example, in a regional parliamentary debate on the theme in 1993. Controversy also surrounds its policy on the Catalan language which has aimed to make it the first language of Catalonia, by raising its status in the educational and administrative system of Catalonia. During the 1996 election campaign and subsequent pact-forming negotiations, CiU presented a range of policy proposals ranging from institutional reforms (most notably, in the Senate, the police force and Catalan local government) to fiscal reforms (giving Catalonia greater control over its taxes). On Europe, CiU has been a strong advocate of greater integration: its proximity to European markets is an obvious incentive. Its European policies have been characterised by demands for a fuller institutional role for regions for example (through the Committee of the Regions). It has also spearheaded inter-regional co-operation in Europe (see Chapter 2). On the economy, it has adopted a pragmatic stance, finding common ground with the PP on calls for wider privatisation, and in advocating neo-liberal market reforms.

Partido Nacionalista Vasco (the Basque Nationalist Party)

The PNV has become the strongest nationalist electoral force in the Basque country, although it has not attracted the spectacular headlines of the nationalist extremists of ETA and its political wing *Herri Batasuna*. The party has been in existence since 1895 when it was founded by Sabino Arana. It achieved considerable but short-lived legitimacy during the Second Republic, when it headed a coalition of parties in the brief rule of the Basque regional government. The exile of that government, to escape from the advancing forces of Franco, reduced the party to gesture politics until the restoration of democracy. While it was invited to participate in negotiating the new constitution, PNV recommended voter abstention from the 1977 referendum on the Constitution. This was due to the limited extent to which the PNV considered Basque historic rights to be recognised in the proposed constitution. Subsequently, the party has registered electoral successes, including a majority in the Basque parliament, set up under its statute of autonomy (the Statute of Guernica). It has also held the presidency, or *Lhendakari*, of the Basque Country, in reward for such achievements.

For much of the democratic period, the PNV has been the strongest party political force in the Basque Country. However, its position was eroded during the mid-1980s. The loss of Carlos Garaikoetxea, its first *Lhendakari*, together with some supporters, to form the more left-oriented secular party, EA, led to sharp damage in the 1986 elections, and a challenge to PNV's traditionalists (Ross 1997: 89). Since then, the party has evolved to become more firmly established as the moderate voice of Basque nationalism, promoting centre-right polices of economic reform, under the leaderships of José Antonio Ardanza and Zabier Arzallus. By securing a pact with the PP on the investiture vote for Aznar in the aftermath of the 1996 general elections, PNV displayed the characteristics of its moderate policy profile. Like the SDLP (Social Democratic and Labour Party) in Northern Ireland, it has to strike a balance between pragmatic co-operation with central governments, while remaining representative of moderate nationalist opposition to those governments. In December 1998, the PNV formed the first Basque government consisting of all nationalist parties. The PNV entered into a minority coalition government with EA supported by EH *(Euskal Herritarrok*/Basque Nation*)*, the successor to HB (see Chapter 2).

Policy orientation

While the PNV has long advocated a conservative nationalism directed at the full expression of Basque national identity, it has, during the 1980s and 1990s, concentrated considerable emphasis on issues of industrial regeneration, employment and the economy. It has underlined the need, not just for a role for the private sector in these areas, but also an active (preferably regional) government role. In this context, it has sought to develop a dialogue with various groups such as bankers and trades unions as well as the other parties in the region, exemplified especially by its pragmatic teaming up with the PSOE in coalition from 1987 in the Basque autonomous government. On constitutional issues, PNV has taken a robust line.

Like CiU in Catalonia, the PNV led the call for Basque self-determination in the Basque parliament. In the same vein, it retains a desire for the reintegration of Navarre (a single-province, autonomous community) within the Basque Country, but acknowledges the free will of the Navarrese to remain outside. It has actively promoted the Basque Country within the European Union, seeing a federal Europe as offering a greater opportunity for loosening the ties with Madrid.

Smaller nationalist and regional parties

Herri Batasuna (Basque Homeland) and Euskal Herritarrok

The HB offered a radical and uncompromising Basque nationalism to the electorate as well as a political conduit for the views of those engaged in armed struggle through ETA. It also refused to renounce or condemn the violent tactics of

ETA. It was founded in 1978 out of the various groups then in existence seeking to express ETA's aims politically. It had some electoral success, winning a seat in the European elections of 1989, but had less than consistent results in the 1990s as it became increasingly isolated. Its organisation consisted of a coalition of political groups, most importantly HASI (*Herriko Alderdi Sozialista Iraultzailea*/People's Revolutionary Socialist Party), which was very close to ETA. Following the ETA cease-fire of September 1998, HB expected to play a role in the peace process in a way that was similar to Sinn Fein in Northern Ireland, with which it has close contacts. However, relations with the PP government were not helped by the imprisonment of the entire 23-strong HB leadership in 1997, for inciting terrorism by showing an ETA propaganda video. In the run-up to the autonomous elections of October 1998, HB merged with other groups to form the electoral coalition, EH, led by Arnaldo Otegi. It took a less extreme stance than HB had done during previous elections. It benefited from ETA's cease-fire declaration. In the autonomous elections of the following month EH gained 17.9 per cent of the Basque vote, representing a major improvement on HB's voting record. In 1999, it won a seat in the European Parliament.

Bloque Nacionalista Galego (Galician Nationalist Bloc)

The BNG has emerged since the late 1980s as the main force of Galician nationalism. It advocates a left-wing ideology and has built up a solid support-base led by its charismatic leader, Xosé Manuel Beiras. It has expanded on regional electoral successes by winning seats in the 1996 general election. In 1997, BNG replaced the PSOE as the second largest party in Galicia, winning 19 seats and 26 per cent of the vote in the regional parliament. On Europe BNG has tended to be suspicious of further integration trends, for example in the Maastricht Treaty (*Cambio 16* 15 April 1996: 30–1).

Esquerra Republicana de Catalunya (Republican Left of Catalonia)

Carrying a degree of prestige in Catalonia due to its long-standing opposition to the Franco regime, ERC was founded in 1931 by Francesc Macià and during the Second Republic became the major force of Catalan nationalism. To symbolise the restoration of the Generalitat to Catalonia, Josep Tarradellas, the old ERC leader, was brought back from exile to be installed as the first president (see Chapter 2). Having had modest success in the late 1970s and early 1980s, the party now has only a small level of support and has co-operated with other nationalist groups (such as BNG) in electoral coalitions. The ERC has previously linked up with CiU. It has argued in favour of an independent Catalan nation-state within a confederal Europe and has sought to extend the usage of the Catalan language.

Partido Andalucista (Andalucian Party)

This is one of the parties which have largely grown on the back of the autonomy movement. It was founded in 1973 by a radical socialist and regionalist, Alejandro Rojas Marcos, and has played a important part in the configuration of regional and to some extent national parliamentary life. Its strong presence in the regional parliament has enabled it to challenge the dominance of the PSOE there, and in the Cortes it has had a presence as far back as 1979. It had its greatest electoral impact in 1989 when it won two seats in Congress.

Unió Valenciana (Valencian Union)
The UV was founded in 1982 as a regional party concerned with the defence of Valencian identity and interests. It has evolved as a critic of the political pacts and the ensuing policy concessions to Catalonia. It has participated in the regional government of Valencia and is a conservative grouping close to PP in its general policy orientation. So also is CC (*Coalición Canaria*/Canary Islands Coalition), a conservative electoral federation of a number of regional parties from the different islands, the biggest of which is *Congreso Nacional Canario*. It has been generally supportive of PP and pledged its vote to that party in 1996 in exchange for some policy concessions.

Unió Mallorquina (Mallorcan Union)
The UM is another centre-right party with a similar ideological outlook to the UV and the CC.

In general, these parties have evolved out of the autonomous community impetus in Spain mainly to put pressure on the PSOE governments from their regional bases. With the election of a PP government in Madrid, their role in the party system has been reduced. One group, the UPN, merged with the PP in 1994 (Ross 1997: 97). Others such as UV may follow.

Background to the elections

Three main phases of electoral politics may be observed in democratic Spain since the mid-1990s. The first phase covered the elections of 1977 and 1979 and was dominated by constitutional issues and the legalisation and formation of a multiplicity of political parties. Of the many competing parties, the UCD, led by Adolfo Suárez, had the strongest parliamentary presence after both of those elections. The second phase covered the 1982, 1986 and 1989 elections and was characterised by the electoral dominance (albeit waning by 1989) of the PSOE. It was also marked by the fragmentation and weakness of right-of-centre parties, and their inability to mount a credible challenge to the Socialists. The most recent phase has involved the 1993 and 1996 elections, in which the two main left and right-of-centre parties (the PSOE and PP) have been more evenly balanced than at any time since the UCD was a force to be reckoned with in the 1970s. This has also resulted in much greater electoral and post-electoral prominence for the smaller parties, especially the main Catalan and Basque nationalist parties (CiU and PNV), whose votes have become crucial in the matter of government formation.

Various factors stood out in the run-up to recent democratic elections in Spain. These may be summarised as follows.

The evolution of the party system

The months preceding the 1977 elections were particularly characterised by party system change, but the process has continued up to and beyond the 1996 elections. Of the hundreds of political party formations which emerged around the 1977 elections, the most electorally significant were the UCD, the PSOE, the PCE and AP. The UCD was a party without a history, mass membership or popular appeal (see Chapter 1). None the less, it was forged into an electoral force by adept media (especially television) marketing (one of Suárez's strengths) and sought to claim the centre-right ground of the political spectrum. In so doing, it was joined by various, small, social democratic and liberal party formations in addition to the odd *franquista* (francoist), to become a coalition of individuals and parties who sought to use it for their own particular ends. It was this lack of roots which was to be UCD's undoing when Suárez became increasingly remote from, and autocratic towards, its constituent factions in the aftermath of his slim 1979 victory. Their disenchantment, together with Suárez's weak leadership, both in the government and the party, eventually led to the UCD's collapse. Even his resignation in early 1981 had the appearance of a tactical manoeuvre, to side-step the critics within his party. Suárez backed the widely supported Leopoldo Calvo Sotelo as Prime Minister, but contrived to keep key party positions in the hands of his own supporters. When the electorate was given the opportunity in 1982 to express its own verdict on this state of affairs, as well as the perilous economic and political circumstances of the country, it savaged the UCD. Thereafter, Suárez attempted to construct various other right-of-centre political formations notably the CDS, without much electoral success before giving up politics in 1993.

The *Alianza Popular*, as we have already seen, was the first in a long series of attempts by Manuel Fraga to forge a party of what he regarded as the natural majority of the right. The fact that Fraga was overlooked by the King when he selected Adolfo Suárez to be Prime Minister, and the architect of political reform in July 1976, was an enormous upset for him, though it did not come as a huge surprise (Powell 1997: 107). However, he soon recovered and set about establishing the AP. Surprisingly, he targeted the far-right *franquistas* for his core support rather than the centre-right. This was a tactical error, and was proven to be so by the poor showing his party registered in the 1977 elections. For the 1979 elections, Fraga dropped much of this *franquista* image, when he moved closer to the political centre with his new coalition party, the CD. The even worse performance of CD in the 1979 elections, however, did not deter Fraga and later Aznar who continued to pursue the objective of an electable right-of-centre party in the 1980s and 1990s, until achieving partial success through the formation of the PP minority government in 1996.

The development of the PSOE as an electoral force was at its most critical stages in advance of the 1977 elections and following the 1979 elections. Despite its history, international links and the talented leadership of González and his close supporters, the party was much less well known than the PCE in the lead-up to the 1977 elections. It also had the smallest membership of the two. The legalisation of the PSOE and the mopping-up of most of the socialist groups across Spain strengthened the support-base of the party. Like Suárez, González benefited much from pre-election television coverage. This continued to be an important electoral asset in subsequent elections.

The failure of the PSOE to make advances in the 1979 elections exacerbated internal party tension about its future direction, which, as we have already seen, led to the resignation of González, followed by his reinstatement four months later, and the reinforcement of his moderate stance at the 1981 conference. By the 1982 election, the process of consolidation of the moderates position in the PSOE under González was complete, a position which, subsequently, did not fundamentally change. This cohesion gave the PSOE a considerable electoral advantage over its opponents.

One of these opponents, the PCE, was also in a state of flux in advance of the 1977 elections, a situation which did not cease until the late 1980s, when the PCE became the leading sponsor of and force within IU. The PCE, which began its electoral life with a dramatic entry into legal status (Suárez made a private deal with Carrillo, while the Supreme Court was considering the PCE's application for registration), a good organisational structure and a considerable membership, did poorly in the 1977 elections (see Chapter 1). It came a poor third place after the PSOE, winning only 20 seats, compared to the PSOE's 118. This outcome gave rise to some soul-searching, and reinforced the party's ideological shift towards Euro-communism.

The economic and social context

While prevailing economic and social conditions provided the backdrop to each of the elections since 1977, they tended to be overshadowed by other more immediately controversial matters during actual electoral campaigns. The aftermath of the 1977 elections witnessed the UCD government forging the Moncloa Pacts with, among other policy actors, the employers federation and the unions, on such matters as price and wage controls (see Chapter 1). The perception that the government failed to protect the workforce from large-scale unemployment and loss of wealth in the wake of this agreement heightened trade union suspicions of government economic tampering. By the 1979 election, the impact of the second OPEC oil price rise made the economic outlook even more glum, and the rise in unemployment and the decline of old industries, relentless. The PCE attempted to identify with the ensuing problems of the workers, and to capture the socialist working-class vote from the rightward moving PSOE. But despite economic crises, constitutional and party political issues were still paramount as, indeed, they continued to be in the aftermath of the '23F' coup attempt.

The PSOE promised 800,000 new jobs within four years of the 1982 election and having being elected, downgraded this objective, concentrating instead on further industrial modernisation and labour law change (the introduction of fixed-term contracts) (Marcus 1983: 283). By 1986, the Spanish economy was experiencing an unprecedented level of growth, spurred on by the socialists' policies. This was just one factor among various others (EC and NATO membership to mention two) which set the overall context of the elections of this year. The 1989 elections saw relations between the socialist government and the unions at an all time low. Moreover, signs of an economic slow-down were apparent. By 1993, the rocketing level of unemployment (officially 21.7 per cent), was adding to the woes of the electorate (Lancaster 1994: 183; Pérez-Díaz 1996: 158–9). However, this was also the election which saw political corruption and the issue of trust begin to dominate Spanish electoral politics. In response, the PSOE parliamentary majority was whittled away. It needed nationalists votes to keep in power.

The PP, under Aznar, sought public approval as an alternative economic manager, but media attention and debate (augmented by private channels and less government control) still revolved around the ever more frequent corruption scandals emerging at that time. The marginal improvements in the economy, recorded by the 1996 election, meant that the media would concentrate on the greater headline-generating debate about the GAL and the question marks surrounding the hitherto unquestionable integrity of the PSOE leader, and Prime Minister, Felipe González (see Chapter 4). Besides, both of the main contenders in the election realised that their concurrence on the desirability of Spain meeting the EMU convergence criteria for a single currency meant that there was little scope for promising more public expenditure (see Chapter 7). Any detailed debate on the economy would reveal that they could only offer more cut-backs in already overstretched public services. Indeed, there was also little to distinguish the PSOE and PP on issues of health, taxation, education and employment policies by the time of the 1996 general elections.

The image of the leader

The personalisation of election campaigns among the main candidates for the presidency has been an important feature in post-democratic Spain. The 1977 and 1979 election victories of the UCD were based on the television-groomed image of Suárez, while González also benefited from a positive media portrayal. As Gilmour notes, 1977 was a victory for 'young men, over old': for Suárez and González, over Fraga and Carrillo. The electoral success of the PSOE leading up to, and including, the 1982 elections had a lot to do with the personality of González, who was regarded as 'honest, *simpático*, moderate and convincing'.

No other leader was ever referred to by his Christian name: Fraga was never Manolo (though supporters talked respectfully of Don Manuel) Suárez was never Adolfo, Carrillo was never Santiago. But they were merely politicians, legitimate targets for abuse. Felipe was different: he was treated as an inviolable part of the national patrimony ... (Gilmour 1985: 260).

An important part of the formula for his successful leadership lay in the activities of Alfonso Guerra. He kept a firm grip of the PSOE party machine, thus freeing González after the 1982 election victory for his role as prime minister. The 1986 election consolidated PSOE's position in parliament (Robinson 1987: 120). The PSOE leader became increasingly remote from his party and parliamentary colleagues: he rarely attended the Cortes (see Chapter 4). As a statesman and president he grew in stature while Spain made its mark on the EC-EU (symbolised by the first Spanish Presidency of the EC in 1989). Despite hinting that the 1989 elections were to be his last, González did not desert the party or the national political stage, as he quite easily might have done in the early 1990s (he was rumoured to be favourite for various EU posts). Instead, as the party became embroiled in scandal after scandal, he put his reputation on the line, began to appear more frequently in the Cortes, where no one doubted his skill at debate. He defied predictions of his demise as prime minister in 1993, and even more incredibly again in 1996, given the media focus on the GAL case which directly challenged González. The less than charismatic leadership of Aznar in the PP was blamed by many for the disappointment of the party's high expectations in 1993. Alongside González, in the second of two television debates, he looked the poorer political player. In 1996, Aznar chose not to allow the electorate the chance to make too intimate a comparison between himself and González. No television campaign debate between the two took place and he was marketed to the electorate differently. He offered to lead a moral renewal in the country and attempted to turn the reputed lack of charisma to his advantage, offering what he presented as more necessary and important traits: efficiency, competence and trustworthiness – in place of glamour.

The electoral system

Of fundamental importance to the outcome of elections in Spain are the rules and procedures of the electoral system. For the Congress elections, a party-list system is in operation in each of the 52 constituencies. These constituencies correspond to the 50 mainland provinces, in addition to the North African coastal towns of Ceuta and Melilla. Each one of these constituencies has a minimum of two seats, with additional seats allocated according to variations in population.

The division of the country's electoral districts lends itself to distortions in representation (Colomer 1996: pp. 174–5). The province of Soria for instance, has four times less eligible voters per member as Barcelona. Moreover, a party with strong roots in rural constituencies can gain a greater number of deputies with less votes than a party strongly entrenched in urban areas. Undoubtedly, this design feature was intended to weaken the electoral impact of the urban-left in newly democratic Spain. However, its authors could hardly have antici-pated the shift of PSOE support away from the big urban areas, which were important to it in 1977, into more rural areas such as Extremadura and Castilla-La Mancha, during the 1980s. One reason for this shift was the intro-duction of rural aid schemes in some regions by PSOE governments in the 1980s, which lent themselves particularly well to the development of clientel-istic networks, producing a political return for policy investment in the form of increased votes (see Chapter 6).

The method of candidate nomination is important to understand too. In it, a party submits separate lists for each of the 52 constituencies with the number of candidates corresponding to the seats in any one constituency. The lists may not be added to, or the order of candidates changed, once they have been sub-mitted. It is a much criticised closed-list system that gives power to the party officials, rather than the electors, to decide in what order candidates may be elected. That this is the case means that individual members of Congress are not personally accountable to individual constituents, but are very dependent on party support.

Whether it be the adoption of a fixed and closed-list system, or the introduc-tion of a 3 per cent threshold of minimum votes for each constituency, the emphasis in the design of the electoral system for the Congress is the avoidance of potentially destabilising factors. The result is an electoral system that benefits the two biggest parties most – especially in smaller constituencies with fewer seats to distribute – and penalises smaller national parties with a relatively thin spread of votes across the country (e.g. the CDS in the 1980s and *Izquierda Unida* in the 1990s). Also, regional and nationalist parties, such as PNV and CiU, with geographically concentrated voting patterns, do well under the system. Only in large constituencies, where the vote is split between many parties, is the system at its most proportional (e.g. Barcelona). Small wonder then that the process of Spanish government formation began to involve the regional parties so promi-nently at the same time (i.e. after the 1993 and 1996 elections) as the two main parties tended to win a more equal share of the national vote.

Analysis of election statistics reveals vividly the extent of the distortion in the Spanish system in favour of big parties. For example in the 1996 general election, the PP won 38.8 per cent of the votes and 44.6 per cent of the seats in Congress while the PSOE won 37.4 per cent of the votes and 40.3 per cent of the seats. The IU, which won 10.5 per cent of the votes, gained only 6 per cent of the seats. Regional and nationalist parties with territorially concentrated support also have tended to benefit from the system. The CiU, for example, won 4 per cent of the seats with only 4.6 per cent of the votes in the same elections, which compared very favourably with IU's experience cited above. The system also carries 'wasted votes' such as the 60,000 nationally spread votes for the Greens, which failed to get any representation in Congress, despite the fact that similar numbers of votes were sufficient to get party candidates elected at electoral district level (Sinova and Tusell 1997: 144).

The main conclusion to be drawn from these statistics, which are broadly in line with those of earlier democratic elections, indicate that seats 'cost' least for the big national parties. In fact, each seat won by the parties in 1996 'cost' the PP 62,000 votes, the PSOE 66,800 votes and IU a substantially greater 125,000 votes.

Elections to the Senate have tended to accentuate the trends already identified for the Congress, though the electoral system used is more open than that for Congress. The fact that 208 out of 256 of its seats are filled by provinces each with a fixed number of senators (four for each of the mainland provinces) means that variations in population density are poorly accounted for. The number of electors per senator in Soria is 45 times less than in Barcelona. This trend is reinforced by the first-past-the-post or majority system of voting also in operation, which favours the biggest parties in Spain.

The Senate does have an additional 47 senators who represent the autono-mous communities and who are usually elected by the regional parliaments. That fact notwithstanding, this chamber is still a far cry from the territorial body it was originally flagged up to be by the Constitution. However, negotia-tions between the parties and other relevant interests for its reform are under way at the time of writing.

The electoral system had a more specific impact on the outcome of the 1989 general elections. On that occasion, three constituencies had their elections annulled because of significant evidence of electoral fraud (e.g. double-voting in the province of Pontevedra). Even so, González managed to win the investi-ture vote, helped along by the four *Herri Batasuna* members who decided to abstain and the support of a Canary Islands deputy offered in exchange for some tax concessions to his constituents.

In the European elections, Spain has operated as one large constituency which elected MEPs in 1994. The system encourages 'federal' candidacies, involving a variety of regional parties. It also enables regional parties to attract votes from outside the region from those who would not normally be eligible to vote for such parties in general elections. So, for example, the Galician nation-alist party, BNG, might therefore attract votes from supporters across Spain in the European elections, whereas in the general elections only its support in the Galician provinces, where it has offered a party list to the electors, actually counts (Gibbons 1996: 159).

Other issues

Each election has produced a set of other more or less prominent issues, the significance of which varies from opinion poll to opinion poll, and from one media analysis to another. A frequent background presence in PSOE rhetoric has been the idea of a threat posed by the election of those it has portrayed as the *franquistas*, that is, the inheritors of Franco's mantle. Up until 1989, the AP was characterised as the home of *franquistas*, and after that, the PP. A PSOE election video associated the PP with the 1981 coup attempt and the Civil War (Hopkin 1996: 111–12). In contrast, Aznar argued in 1996 that the election of PP to government would amount, in fact, to a second democratic transition (the first being that of the political reforms of 1977) by implication, replacing PSOE's unhealthy monopoly on government since 1982, with the modern face of Spanish conservatism: PP.

Corruption, 'sleaze' and the issue of political trust became important, especially after the 1989 elections. Opposition parties portrayed the government as being reluctant to investigate political wrongdoing and, in some cases, of being a party to that wrongdoing itself. The PSOE did not enhance its image by such errors of judgement as including José Barrionuevo – the former Interior minister being linked to the GAL death squads – in its election list for Madrid in the 1996 elections (Amodia 1996: 815) (see Chapter 4). The 'sleaze' issue reached fever pitch in the 1993 and 1996 elections. The PP campaigned with a slogan which advocated 'political renewal' and anticipated a 'New Majority'. But the expected devastation of the PSOE and the new PP majority promised by the opinion polls never occurred. It may be that electors had other, more important, issues on their minds than 'sleaze' when voting. Quite likely, too, PP claims of a corrupt PSOE were, in part, cancelled out by the PSOE warnings of the danger of a powerful right-of-centre PP government. Moreover, in 1996 the PSOE conducted an aggressive electoral campaign to counter the widely reported opinion polls lead which the PP appeared to have accumulated. In contrast, the PP campaign was conducted with a degree of complacency.

On the regional autonomy issue, the PP was seen to have the most centrist policies whereas the PSOE had the benefit of experience of co-operation with PNV in the autonomous government in the Basque Country, and with nationalists in Galicia in the 1980s. However, regions, such as Andalusia and Catalonia, were seen by many voters during the 1980s and 1990s to be absorbing too great a proportion of national resources granted by PSOE governments, for reasons of political expediency. The PP had won control of ten regional governments and the main municipalities by 1995 which gave the party a useful 'fortress' across the country from which to show their skills at ruling and winning it, increasing political credit and public prominence. The 1996 elections were forced on the PSOE government by the withdrawal of support by CiU in November 1996. In these and in other ways the regional autonomy issue manifested itself at election time.

Conclusion

While most commentators agree on the importance of political parties to the transition to and consolidation of democracy, it is a much more courageous task to try to define the precise nature of their contribution (Pridham 1990: 2–41). After all, the history of party politics in Spain in the democratic era has also been punctuated by such unseemly sights as the collapse and disarray of the UCD in the early 1980s, the widespread corruption of party finances and the dominance of party élites in the PSOE, which seem to sully the image of parties as harbingers of democratic stability. However, political parties have also been the main if rather crude vehicles for the expression of political values and ideas in Spain. Thus, through the PSOE, the early 1980s witnessed the emergence of a left-of-centre policy platform that captured the hearts, minds and votes of the largest proportion of the electorate. The PSOE continued to occupy this space, despite strong competition from IU, up to the mid-1990s (the 1996 results confirmed the resilience of this core support and in fact the PSOE actually won 168,517 more votes nationally in 1996, than in 1993). Right-of-centre opinion took a longer period of time to coagulate, various manifestations of the party formed by Fraga emerging in the 1980s until the formation of the PP which overcame the PSOE in the 1996 elections. The 'predominant party system' that had prevailed in the 1980s was under challenge (Caciagli 1984: 96). At the regional level, too, the emergence of party subsystems reflected the adaptability of the new political and institutional framework of autonomous communities to widely divergent currents of political opinion. Despite the instabilities which have attended the evolution of the party system in Spain (Ramírez 1988: 24), the image which comes into focus in the late 1990s was of a growing two-party system at national level, supplemented by a mild level of regional multi-partyism (for further discussion see Padró-Solanet 1996: 451–75). This has enabled a partial alternation of power at national levels in 1996: partial because CiU support is a common component of government formation in 1993 and 1996.

The impact of the party system on political development in Spain is also affected by such factors as electoral and government formation rules and the constitutional status of the regions and nationalities. What does seem clear is that Spain's democracy is still evolving and that the development of the party system remains closely linked to that evolutionary process.

References

Amodia, J. (1996) 'Spain at the Polls: The General Election of 3 March 1996', *West European Politics*, 19:4, pp. 813–19.

Caciagli, M. (1984) 'Spain: Parties and the Party System in the Transition', *West European Politics*, 7:2.

Cambio 16 (15 April 1996) 'Xosé Manuel Beiras', pp, 30–1.

Camiller, P. (1994) 'Spain: The Survival of Socialism?' in P. Anderson and P. Camiller (eds), *Mapping the West European Left*, London, Verso.

Colomé, G. and L. Lopez Nieto (1993) 'The Selection of Party Leaders in Spain', *West European Politics*, 24:3.

Colomer, J.M (ed.) (1996) *Political Institutions in Europe*, London, Routledge.

El Mundo (21 April 1995) '75 Años de PCE', pp. 1–12.

El País (8 December 1998) 'Frutos sustituye a Anguita . . .', p.1.

Esteban, J. (1992) *El estado de la Constitución (Diez años de gobierno del PSOE)*, Madrid, Libertarias.

Gibbons, J. (1996) 'Spain', in J. Lodge, *The 1994 Elections to the European Parliament*, London, Pinter.

Gillespie, R. (1989) 'Spanish Socialism in the 1980s', in T. Gallagher and A. Williams (eds), *Southern European Socialism: Parties, Elections and the Challenge of Government*, Manchester, Manchester University Press.

Gilmour, D. (1985) *The Transformation of Spain: From Franco to the Constitutional Monarchy*, London, Quartet.

Heywood, P. (1992) 'The Socialist Party in Power, 1982–92: The Price of Progress', *Journal of Association of Contemporary Iberian Studies (ACIS)*, 5:2.

Holman, D. (1989) 'Felipismo or the Failure of Neo-liberalism in Spain', Political Studies Association Conference Paper, University of Warwick.

Hopkin, J. (1996) 'An Incomplete Alteration: The Spanish Elections of March 1996', *Intellect: International Journal of Iberian Studies*, 9:2, pp. 110–16.

Keating, M. (1993) *The Politics of Modern Europe: The State and Political Authority in the Major Democracies*, Cheltenham, Edward Elgar.

Kennedy, P. (1996) 'Europe or Bust? Integration and the Influence on the Economic Policy of PSOE', *Intellect: International Journal of Iberian Studies*, 9:2, pp. 87–97.

Lancaster, T.D. (1994) 'A New Phase for Spanish Democracy? The General Election of June 1993', *West European Politics*, 17:1.

Marcus, J. (1983) 'The Triumph of Spanish Socialism: The 1982 Election', *West European Politics*, 6:3.

Medhurst, K. (1982) 'Spanish Conservative Politics', in Z. Layton-Henry (ed.), *Conservative Politics in Western Europe*, London, Macmillan.

Montero, J. (1988) 'More than Conservative, Less than Neo Conservative: Alianza Popular in Spain', in B. Girvin (ed.), *The Transformation of Contemporary Conservatism*, London, Sage.

Newton, M.T. (with P.J. Donaghy) (1997) *Institutions of Modern Spain: A Political and Economic Guide*, Cambridge, Cambridge University Press.

Padró-Solanet, A. (1996) 'Political Parties in Spain . . .', *European Journal of Political Research*, 29:4.

Palomo, G. (1990) *El Vuelo del Halcon: José María Aznar y la aventura de la derecha española*, Madrid, Ediciones Temas de Hoy.

Pérez-Díaz, V. (1996) *España puesta a prueba 1976–96*, Madrid, Alianza Editorial.

Powell, C. (1997) *Juan Carlos of Spain: Self Made Monarch*, London, Macmillan.

Pridham, G. (ed.) (1990) *Securing Democracy: Political Parties and Democratic Consolidation in Southern Europe*, London, Routledge.

Ramírez, M. (1988) 'El Sistema De Partidos En España: 1977–87', *Revista de Estudios Políticos*, 59:1.

Robinson, R. (1987) 'From Change to Continuity: The 1986 Spanish Elections', *West European Politics*, 10:1.

Ross, C. (1997) *Contemporary Spain: A Handbook*, London, Arnold, pp. 74–105.

Share, D. (1985) 'Two Transitions: Democratisation and the Evolution of the Spanish Socialist Left', *West European Politics*, 16:1.

Sinova, J. and J. Tusell (1997) *La Crisis de la Democracia en España: Ideas para reinventar nuestro sistema política*, Madrid, Espasa Calpe.

4

The balance of powers

The study of government requires an examination, not only of its most visible, constitutionally defined aspects, but also of those that are informal and less obvious. Only by this means can an understanding of the delicate balancing act that lies at the heart of a political system be relayed. According to its Constitution, the Spanish system is a parliamentary monarchy (article 1.3) by which is meant, formally speaking, that sovereignty lies with the people through the Cortes. In practice, the position of the monarchy is largely symbolic, and parliament, for much of the democratic era, has been overshadowed by single-party majority governments. These factors notwithstanding, it would be unwise to dismiss the institutions of monarchy and parliament as irrelevant to governance in Spain.

The relevance of the monarchy

In fact, in the era of the transition to democracy and since, the Spanish monarchy has carved itself out a rather significant and influential niche in Spanish political life. While the Constitution defines the functions of the monarchy as including those of Commander-in-Chief of the Armed Forces (article 62b), the sanctioning and promulgation of laws (article 62a) and the issuing of decrees approved by the Council of Ministers (article 62f), such functions are mostly formalities (Heywood 1995a: 85). Potentially more significant are the discretionary roles of the monarchy, for instance, in the procedures for designating candidates as *presidente* or head of government. Thus, in the aftermath of the 1993 and 1996 general elections, when no political party had an overall majority in Congress, the king played a role in helping along the process of inter-party bargaining that led to the emergence of the nominee for prime minister.

The personal qualities of Juan Carlos are frequently cited as giving the restored monarchy an extra degree of legitimacy and authenticity. He is highly respected by the Spanish public, especially since his performance in defusing the attempted *coup d'état* of '23F'. Openly pro-European (he even won the Charlemagne Prize in 1982), Juan Carlos is seen to project a positive image of Spain internationally (Powell 1996: 192). His travels and speeches have tended to serve as a backdrop to the country's political and economic diplomacy (Gillespie, Rodrigo and Story 1995: 202).

Like other institutions of the Spanish state, the role of the monarch is closely defined and limited by the Constitution. This role differs from the one originally envisaged by Franco in 1947 when he issued the Succession Law which antic-ipated the eventual restoration of the monarchy. Neither did Franco have this form of monarchy in mind, in 1969, when he presented Juan Carlos to the Cortes and designated him as his successor (Newton 1997: 33). What he made provision for was an 'executive monarchy' with considerable constitutional powers, not a constitutional monarch with limited powers. When Juan Carlos acted to push along the process of a transition to democracy after Franco's death he was, by implication, rejecting the prospect of continuing to rule as Franco did (see Chapter 1). Formally, the legitimacy of his position was ques-tionable until after his father, Don Juan, publicly gave up his claim to the throne in 1977. Informally, he gained for the restored monarchy considerable legiti-macy by proving that the system of which it was an integral part could be reformed from within (Preston 1986: 53–90).

The fraught circumstances of Spain's recent transition to democracy and the role of the monarchy therein have given added weight to those functions which might otherwise be described as mere formalities. For example, the king's formal responsibility for appointing the presidents of the 17 autonomous com-munities has given extra meaning to his position as the symbol of unity in a Spain consisting of nationalities and regions. More poignantly, his role as Commander-in-Chief of the Armed Forces gave him a unique position from which to call on the armed forces to remain loyal to the democratic Constitution during the '23F' coup attempt.

If there is a question mark hanging over the monarchy in Spain it is whether in succeeding generations it can continue to attract the respect and loyalty that Juan Carlos has earned for it. In the mean time, he is often cited as a role model for other royal families who wish to balance the idea and rituals of a traditional monarchy with the needs of the modern state.

The many weaknesses of parliament

Although Spain, constitutionally speaking, is a parliamentary monarchy, the structure of the Cortes, its rules of procedure and evolution since the Political Reform Law of 1976 (which signalled acceptance by the francoist Cortes of the restoration of democratic institutions and processes), have rendered it distinctly meek in the face of executive (and especially prime ministerial) might. That is not to suggest that the architects of Spain's institutional edifices set out to create a weak and subservient Cortes. Rather, the checks and balances with which parliament was endowed, and which were supposed to work in the face of a strong president, were overridden during the late 1970s and in the 1980s by the unanticipated predominance of parties (first the UCD and then the PSOE) with an absolute majority in both the Senate and Congress. Moreover, these majority parties faced a weak and divided opposition over a long period, following the restoration of democracy. Contrary to expectations, for much of its recent history the Cortes has failed, by and large, to act as an effective scrutineer of government, serving instead as a relatively quiescent channel for government legislation to flow through. The return of a more evenly balanced party system to the Cortes after the 1993 and 1996 elections has not substantially altered this picture, though it has focused more attention on the inter-party negotiations for parliament's crucial vote of investiture of prime ministers.

Why two chambers?

Bi-cameral parliaments are generally of two varieties. In one, the upper house is a legacy of the constitutional past (e.g. British House of Lords), while in the other, it is part of a federal or regional structure. In theory the Spanish case is an example of the latter, but in practice it has been slow to develop in this way.

The **national parliament** *(Cortes)* consists of two chambers: the **Congress of Deputies** *(Congreso)*, the lower house and the **Senate** *(Senado)*, the upper house (Aparicio 1989: 115–26). Both chambers may be used to initiate legislation but the Congress ultimately has a veto over the Senate. The delay in transforming the Senate, as envisaged by the Constitution, into a genuine chamber of territorial representation of the autonomous communities, provides an illustration of the over-riding strength of the institution of government in Spain over its parliament, most especially during PSOE rule in the 1980s. The heightened prominence of regional and nationalist parties in the Cortes in the 1990s pushed the issue of Senate reform higher up on the political agenda. A number of options exist concerning the membership of a reformed Senate. Currently, the majority of senators are directly elected in the general elections (see Chapter 3). It is possible that this chamber could instead consist of appointees of the autonomous communities' governments (as in the German case) or, as is more likely, be elected by the parliaments of the autonomous communities (Paniagua Soto 1998: 420). The inter-party working groups established in 1994 to recommend constitutional charges to the Senate have also led the way towards enhancing the legislative role of the autonomous communities therein. The expectation is that this initiative will result in a more negotiated style of policy-making (see Chapter 6) and justify more fully the existence of an upper chamber which, heretofore, has been a virtual mirror-image of the lower chamber. For example, one possibility is that the Senate would undertake the first reading of bills concerned with the autonomous communities.

Party control of the committees

The parliamentary chambers each have **Presiding Councils** (*Mesas*), which include presidents and vice-presidents responsible for co-ordinating the business of the Congress and the Senate. They also have permanent and *ad hoc* (chiefly legislative) committees (*comisiones*) which conduct the main work of parliament. But it is the parliamentary parties (or groups) and the **Board of Spokespersons** (*Junta de Portavoces*) which exercise most control over the political activities of parliament. Members of both houses must be in a parliamentary group, and state subsidies for political parties are linked to membership of such groups. They will generally have a minimum of 15 members in Congress and 10 members in the Senate (an exception to this rule was allowed in 1995 to CC, the Canary Islands coalition). Other deputies, who are unable to form a party or coalition group, must become members of the so-called **Mixed Parliamentary Group** (*Grupo Mixto*) in each house. Given that it is the parliamentary groups, through the Board of Spokespersons, which control appointments to the parliamentary committees and also, in consultation with the Presiding Councils, much of the agenda and processing of legislation, their significance should not be understated. When a parliamentary group has an overall majority, like the PSOE had for much of the 1980s, party and especially party élite influence in parliament is even greater.

There is little continuity in the membership of particular parliamentary committees, thereby reducing the opportunities for the development of policy expertise among deputies. Backup research and advisory support is limited also, with the result that party groups, and particularly their spokesmen, exercise strong influence over the words and parliamentary actions of deputies. Debate is relatively bland. Deputies read prepared statements, reciting the party line with little or no opportunity for spontaneity. Party discipline is the paramount factor in the behaviour of MPs (members of parliament) and there is little breaking of party ranks (Sànchez de Dios 1995: 13).

The parliamentary group system also serves a similar function to an electoral threshold in other countries. It impedes fragmentation of parliament and enhances government stability. So, for instance, deputies turn-coating or deserting their own party ranks (*transfuguismo*) between elections must join the Mixed Group in parliament rather than simply defect to another party group. Parliamentary groups are also crucial to the legislative process.

Legislation

There are seven categories of law and three of regulations. These may be summarised as follows (based on Newton 1997: 63–6):

1 organic laws (*leyes orgánicas*): the highest form of laws, used only for matters of special national interest. They require an overall majority of Congress members to be passed;

2 ordinary laws (*leyes ordinarias*): the main type of law, requiring a simple majority of both houses of parliament *(Cortes)*;
3 basic laws (*leyes de base*): like ordinary laws, these laws spell out the broad outlines of legislation and give government the power to complete the details of the legislation by means of legislative decrees (see below);
4 framework laws (*leyes marco*): also like ordinary laws, these laws spell out the broad outlines of legislation and give autonomous communities the power to complete the details of the legislation;
5 basic legislation (*legislación básica*): like framework laws but are used for legislation involving shared (centre-autonomous regions) competences;
6 royal decree laws (*reales decretos-leyes*): emergency laws which may be issued by the government in limited circumstances and policy areas. They must be submitted to the Congress within thirty days;
7 legislative decrees (*decretós legislatives*): this is the legislation issued by government under the terms of reference contained in basic laws.

Regulations

1 royal decrees (*reales decretos*): the highest form of regulations requiring the signature of the King;
2 orders (*órdenes*): orders issued by Cabinet Committees;
3 ministerial orders (*órdenes ministeriales*): orders emanating from the Ministries. The regional ministry equivalent is the circulars *(circulares)* and instructions *instrucciones)* resolution *(resolución)*: these emanate from central or regional ministries.

Although autonomous communities, backbenchers and even private citizens (with 500,000 signatures) have been constitutionally entitled to introduce legislation independently, efforts to do so generally come to nothing. If they are to succeed, they require the support of the party groups and an 'urgency procedure' ensures that government initiatives are given priority. Working together, the government and the party groups have closely managed the legislative programme. This was one of the reasons why in the 1980s, faced with a single-party majority in parliament, the autonomous communities tended to direct much of their attention to the legal process to seek clarification of, and advances in, their autonomous powers (see Chapter 2). Parliament proved to be a less than fruitful source of those enhanced autonomy powers and resources to which the regions and nationalities believed they had a constitutional claim. In the 1990s, the success of the nationalities in wringing concessions from government parties led to the description 'the tail wagging the dog' being applied to their relationship with each other.

Parliament in Spain has, however, been a comparatively inactive institution, passing an average of about 70 laws per year between 1983 and 1993. Parliamentary committees have the power to make some laws but they can be over-ridden by the full house (Paniagua Soto 1998: 412). They offer a way for parliament to expand its legislative output. (See Chapter 5 for further discussions on the role of parliament in the policy process.)

Scrutiny

To enable it to perform its functions as a scrutineer of government business, the Cortes has appropriate mechanisms in place, but their effectiveness has been limited. This was particularly obvious during the 1980s when the centre-right opposition was in a state of collapse. Thus, while oral and written questions could be put to ministers by both members of the house (*preguntas*) and their parliamentary groups (*interpelaciones*), the time allocated to such exercises was very restricted. Moreover, advance submission of questions in writing was required, providing little scope for spontaneous debate. The attitude of Felipe González, when prime minister, to the Cortes was not conducive to greater transparency and accountability (Sinova and Tusell 1997: 88–89). His seat in Congress was vacant for long periods of time, despite regular criticism of his absence, most notably, by the opposition parties. Between 1989 and February 1992 he made a total of 11 visits to parliament. When he did make an occasional visit to parliament, he tended to comment on foreign and European affairs rather than be drawn on domestic matters. Eventually, he conceded to Congress demands for a weekly prime minister's question time (except when the prime minister was abroad) but in a tightly controlled format: questions were to be submitted previously in writing, the prime minister could exercise choice over which questions to answer and the period for answering questions was restricted to 15 minutes each week. Other ministers faced similar criticism from parliament. In 1993, Narcís Serra, the vice-president, was forced by a Congress vote (in which CiU abstained) to appear before it and explain the governments handling of the economic crisis. This was considered to be a major victory for parliament, but in fact reveals more about the strength and detachment of the executive from parliamentary control. Under Aznar, the weekly parliamentary question time, instituted under González, has continued but serves as a very weak mechanism of accountability. In fact, media scrutiny and debate have evolved as more effective tools of accountability in Spanish public life, though statistics show that televised and radio broadcasting of debates have limited appeal to the public.

Scrutiny by 'investigative commissions' or committees of enquiry is also limited by the rarity of such bodies. Such commissions may only be established by a vote of a parliamentary majority. In practice, this has given the government party a veto (Carlos Solchaga, for example, ruled out government support for the investigation of the controversial giant private holding company Rumasa, which collapsed in 1983). As a tool for the scrutiny of government action and inaction, parliamentary commissions have been of limited effect (Sinova and Tusell 1997: 87). Curiously, some regional parliaments do allow a minority of members to propose the setting up of such commissions though regional governments still retain a limited veto over their actual establishment.

An overview of the Cortes

The Cortes was designed to counteract a strong executive by encouraging consensus-driven, negotiated, policy decision-making in Spain. The weakness of the centre-right opposition within parliament, together with the considerable electoral strength of the socialist governing party throughout the 1980s, and the internal powers wielded by the party élites, undermined its inherent design (Heywood 1992: 11). To cap it all, the odour of corruption has wafted across parliament, requiring it to remove immunity from prosecution from one of its members (José Barrionuevo, in 1995). Symbolic of its low status in the past is the fact that prime ministers have rarely felt it necessary to attend parliament, despite the fact that parliament is central to the process of their appointments.

The changing patterns of party representation in the Cortes in the late 1990s promises an improvement in the fortunes of that institution as a scrutinising, if not legislating institution. The efforts to reform the Senate are also promising developments. Additionally, it must be remembered that despite all its weaknesses it is just one among the many European parliamentary systems to face such challenges (or worse) in the 1990s. Given that it is in its infancy, comparatively speaking, it must be given due credit for its achievements, not least in generating a high electoral turnout and thus considerable legitimacy for its members, whatever their other failings.

The chief executive

What is the basis for prime ministerial power in Spain? Before answering this question, we should take note of the fact that constitutionally speaking, as Heywood observes, there is no such role as 'prime minister' in Spain, rather there is a **President of the Government** *(Presidente)* who is elected to that position by the Congress of Deputies in a vote of investiture (Heywood 1995a: 88). This procedure requires the candidate, on the nomination of the Crown, to submit a programme of government to the parliament in person, and to win an overall majority of support, or failing that, a simple majority, 48 hours later. Arising from this formula, the *presidente* is not a *primus inter pares* but the pre-eminent figure in government. (However, this caveat aside, we will normally continue to use the term prime minister, if not to avoid, then at least to limit the confusion that might arise from speaking of a 'President' in a political system with a monarch as head of state!) A single post of **Deputy Prime Minister** *(Vice-Presidente)* was formalised by legislation in 1983, though constitutionally more than one deputy may be appointed. So while Gonzàlez had just one vice-president, Alfonso Guerra (1982–91) and Narcís Serra (1991–96), Aznar appointed two in 1996: Francisco Alvarez Cascos and Rodrigo Rato (Ross 1997: 30–1).

Having been elected, the prime minister enjoys considerable powers and security of tenure. He can only be dismissed from office (following the German constitutional procedure) by a constructive censure motion, which requires an alternative candidate nominated by 10 per cent of the Congress deputies and the approval of an absolute majority of both houses of parliament. When he lost his parliamentary majority early on in the 1989–93 parliament, González survived in office for four years, not least because the opposition could not agree on an alternative to replace him. The Spanish system, constructed against a historical landscape which is marred by examples of democratic instability, was well protected by such mechanisms as the constructive censure motion. With Spain experiencing a period of minority governments in the 1990s, the relevance of this mechanism – to maintain executive stability – is more apparent.

The power of Spanish prime ministers has also been affected by the political circumstances that have surrounded their periods of office and the public perception of their personal fitness for the role. So, while Adolfo Suárez (1976–81) eventually succumbed to the disintegration of the coalition of factions that was the UCD and Leopoldo Calvo Sotelo (1981–82) failed to command sufficient political authority for the role (Heywood 1991:100–6), González (1982–96) enjoyed strong backing from the PSOE for much of his reign. Aznar also began his period of office in 1996 with the security of strong backing from his party. But his failure to win a more convincing electoral victory in 1996 was blamed, both by critics from within and without the PP, on the widely held view that he lacked that elusive winning ingredient: charisma. However much the problems in the PSOE government might be said to ultimately lie in his hands, González, in contrast to Aznar, was (as we saw in Chapter 3) widely acknowledged to be a charismatic statesman of international calibre and a good public speaker and debater. The television debates between González and Aznar during the 1993 elections helped to personalise the campaign and make González appear more presidential (though Aznar was widely viewed to have 'won' the first of these debates). Yet media critics, notably in *El Mundo*, queried his judgement and his relations with senior PSOE government figures who were linked to the various sleaze scandals, which unfolded in the late 1980s and early 1990s.

More important than personality to the power of the prime minister in Spain may be the political circumstances that surround his period of office. Suárez in the 1970s tended to be remote from and have rather a loose hold on parliament, preferring to be guided by his advisers (the *fontaneros* [plumbers] as they were dubbed in the post-Watergate era). In the 1980s, secured in office by a large parliamentary majority, González distanced himself from the Cortes and dealings with the party and concentrated on strengthening his office. Through his deputy, Alfonso Guerra, he maintained firm control – albeit indirectly – of the party and parliament. It may also be worth speculating that the tradition of the omnipresent leader in Spain also helped González to cultivate a presidential style, albeit replacing Franco's authoritarian leadership with youthful charisma, and the modern image of a statesmen on the international stage.

The reliance of both González and Aznar on the parliamentary support of the nationalist parties in the 1990s changed their attitude to the Cortes. It shifted the role of the prime minister, in this decade, away from being a rather remote but powerful influence over the general shape of government to being involved directly in hands-on negotiations over the detailed creation of policy initiatives and policy development. That this is how executive–parliament relations have evolved reflects more truly the original expectations of the authors of the Constitution.

The pre-eminence of regional élites or 'barons', such as Jordi Pujol of Catalonia, in these relations may not have been anticipated so fully. Using their parliamentary voting strength cannily, the autonomous communities have emerged in the 1990s as the source of the main political check on prime ministerial power whereas in the early years, after democratic transition, the military, the Church and the bureaucracy exercised more direct influence. The judiciary lies as the ultimate bulwark against a presidential abuse of power. During the last parliament, revelations concerning the GAL provided frequent legal threats to González. He survived such allegations.

A very significant feature of the prime minister's authority lies in his control over the selection and dismissal of his ministers. While there is not a constitutional requirement for these ministers to be drawn from parliament, they generally are but parliament cannot force them to resign. That power lies in the hands of the prime minister. Prime ministers may also choose to appoint ministers who are not party members (González had seven independent members of his Cabinet after the 1993 elections). Generally though, the parliamentary and party strength of the prime minister is reflected in the stability of his cabinet. So, while cabinet reshuffles tended to be rather occasional during the 1980s, after the resignation of Alfonso Guerra as deputy prime minister in early 1991 they were much more frequent (Heywood 1995a: 93). This was due to the growing number of corruption scandals which emerged in the 1990s and the related, forced ministerial resignations. It was also due to the weakness of the PSOE in Congress which undermined the position of unpopular ministers more quickly than hitherto. The growth of dissension within the PSOE was also a factor. It arose from the rupture in the early 1990s of the González–Guerra axis that had for so long controlled the party and government.

Electoral weakness has ironically, provided the PP prime minister, Aznar, with some beneficial side effects. It has reinforced his need to pursue a co-operative rather than a confrontational approach to relations with the regions and the trades unions on two key policy issues of 1990s Spanish politics: the future development of the autonomous communities and labour market flexibility. For this reason as much as any, Aznar was able to boast in 1996 that 'España va bien' (Spain is doing fine). For him, it could have been more difficult if PP had won a big majority in the 1996 elections. Cabinet stability has been a feature of the early years of the PP government. The first major reshuffle, which took place in

January 1999, reinforced Aznar's grip on the government and its policy direction (*El País* 19 January 1999: 1).

The process of government formation in 1996

After elections to Congress have taken place, the king has the constitutional responsibility to propose to the Cortes a candidate for the premiership, following consultations with the Cortes. Parliament then proceeds to vote on the candidate and his programme for government, and if approved by a simple majority, the candidate is in turn named as prime minister by the king. After the elections in Spain between 1977 and 1989, this was a relatively straightforward affair. One party held an overall majority of support in parliament and the procedure was invoked in a relatively short space of time. (An important exception to this pattern occurred after the resignation of Adolfo Suárez in 1981. The poor parliamentary support-base of the incoming prime minister, Leopoldo Calvo Sotelo, created a window of opportunity for the '23F' coup plotters while uncertainty reigned, leading to the infamous assault on parliament.) However, if no party holds a majority, as occurred after the (two) general elections, of 1993 and 1996, a prolonged period of negotiation becomes necessary in order to find agreement on a candidate for the prime ministerial post and a programme for government. The fact that Spain has only recently experienced this style of government formation is perhaps all more the surprising given the type of electoral system that was provided by its Constitution-makers (see Chapter 3), and their apparent intention to construct a system to prevent the emergence of single-party diktat in Spanish government.

What were the sort of options for government formation facing González and Aznar after the 1993 and 1996 elections? Laver and Schonfield have outlined the theoretical options facing parties entering negotiations to form governments (Laver and Schonfield 1990). These include 'a grand coalition', 'minimal winning' coalition, 'surplus majority' coalition and 'minority' government.

After both elections, a 'grand coalition' between PP and PSOE was an impossibility for many reasons: ideological, personal, political and historical. A left alliance between the PSOE and IU (with the support of the small parties in 1996) might have provided a mathematically viable and an 'ideologically compact' formula to return González on both occasions to the Moncloa, but González and Anguita had no time for such an option and did nothing, despite the wishful thinking of those on the left of the PSOE and on the right of the PCE, to encourage it. There was of course, the last resort option of fresh elections, but neither González in 1993, nor Aznar in 1996 would have been thanked for that by an electorate already overwhelmed by the many varieties of elections in Spain. As for Aznar, to let the long-sought after prize of being prime minister slip out of his grasp, just as it was within reach, would have been unthinkable.

So, apart from the possibility of a 'caretaker' government involving some or all of the parties, that left the option of an accommodation between the nationalists and the PSOE in 1993, and the PP in 1996, as the remaining outstanding set of possibilities. In this context, there were the options of formal coalitions: either 'minimal winning' just with CiU, or 'surplus majority', involving, additionally, the smallest of the parties. A 'minority' government either of a single party or a coalition, that fell short of a majority (e.g. the PSOE and PNV), was also an option.

It is perhaps not so surprising then that both González and Aznar began consultations with the nationalist leaders, shortly after the outcome of the 1993 and 1996 elections were known (*El Mundo* 1996: 32). In the case of Aznar in 1996, he began by holding telephone conversations with each of the nationalist leaders, breaking the ice for the negotiations and discussions which were to come over the succeeding weeks. Senior negotiators were appointed by the relevant parties (for the PP it was Rodrigo Rato, vice-secretary general, who had a potentially useful Catalan background). The senior figures were assisted by teams of negotiators drawn from the main parties, who engaged in the detailed discussion of policy.

The negotiations themselves were marked by intermittent advances and setbacks as each side attempted to play to its own strengths and to discover and disclose the others' weaknesses. There was, for example, a lot of distrust among nationalists of the PP's post-election change of heart on the matter of participating in a minority government: Aznar had openly scorned the idea during the election campaign and, in fact, since the 1993 election. But Aznar, who was also a realist, agreed in the aftermath of the 1996 elections to allow flexibility with regard to his electoral programme in negotiations and to pursue the possibility of a minority PP government, supported by Catalan and Basque nationalists and a few other smaller groupings. He explained his apparent sharp change of attitude by simply acknowledging that this was the mandate he had received from the electorate, however much he might wish circumstances to be otherwise, and that he was empowered to form a single party majority government. Warming to the new task of 'bonding' with Catalan nationalists, Aznar even declared that he enjoyed speaking Catalan, albeit in private and in the company of his family at home, a claim that drew not just a little scepticism and scorn from media sources.

Nationalists, especially the PNV, were little swayed by such posturings and wanted written specific commitments from Aznar before they would commit themselves to supporting his investiture. They were very mindful of the turmoil which followed the 1993 negotiations when PNV deputies had given González's investiture their support, only to find that their party's National Assembly had serious doubts about the PSOE programme, following which PNV leaders were obliged to renege on the plan to join a minority coalition government (CiU had earlier rejected the PSOE's proposal for a coalition).

Aznar and the PP were reluctant in 1996 to sign up to anything they might later regret, particularly on the specifics of regional finances, and cited EU convergence criteria as one reason among many for this reticence. However, neither did they wish to enter government with major gaps left in any agreement with nationalists, that could quickly make their minority government untenable.

It took two months of negotiations, including three private meetings between Aznar and Pujol, as well as many hours of detailed team negotiations, to find sufficient common ground for an agreed programme. Pujol was anxious to avoid being blamed for the collapse of negotiations and tried to spread the responsibility across the party system by speaking occasionally of the possibility of a caretaker government. A key component of the negotiations was the request by CiU for the transfer to the *Generalitat* of 30 per cent of Catalonia's income tax. So too, was the abolition of the civil governors, that vestige of central government long despised in the 'historic nationalities' (see Chapter 2). The future of military service in Spain was a topic for debate too. The reform of the Senate was also much discussed, but not resolved in post-election negotiations. In the final days, some specific commitments about privatisation held matters up, as the final price was calculated for CiU and PNV support of Aznar and the PP in government.

What of the outgoing, caretaker-prime minister, González? He conceded to Aznar the role of government-maker and along with the members of his caretaker-government offered to observe a period of silence on the negotiations. He did express a preference for a coalition government as an outcome of these negotiations and promised constructive opposition to a PP-led government. In fact, he was in the best of all positions as the defeated candidate for the presidency. While Aznar engaged in painstaking, and for some in the PP, stomach-turning negotiations with the nationalists, González was able to relax in the Moncloa Palace and appear detached and presidential. As negotiations began to progress, he invited Aznar together with former prime minister Suárez to lunch, to exchange views on developments, and to offer advice to Aznar based on much previous experience of government formation (*El País* 11 April 1996: 17).

The king, too, played his part by formally communicating to the newly elected president of the Congress – after a month of the negotiations – that he had decided to charge Aznar with the responsibility of forming a new government. This was announced *after* his meetings with the various parties to ascertain their views on the investiture vote and the negotiations leading up to it. The regional 'barons', in addition to Jordi Pujol (CiU) and Xavier Arzallus (PNV), also had a part to play in the negotiations. Aznar could not afford to make concessions to those parties of the 'historic nationalities' whose votes he would rely on in Congress, only to cause a backlash from the other regions, a significant number of whom (10 out of 17) were PP controlled. Manuel Fraga, PP president of the *Xunta de Galicia* was somewhat concerned at the marginalisation of Galicia in the negotiations with CiU and PNV (Galicia's two new nationalist deputies from the left-wing BNG were firmly opposed to any sort of deal with

Aznar). Aznar promised equality of treatment to all the regions (he offered dialogue to the three PSOE-controlled regions too), for example in the matter of negotiating transfers of control of 30 per cent income tax. Despite some concerns, Fraga gave his blessing to Aznar's negotiations.

The key interest groups were not be forgotten by the negotiators either. Shortly after the elections, Aznar held telephone conversations with the leaders of the UGT, the CCOO and the CEOE (*Confederacion Española de Organizaciones Empresariales*/Confederation of Spanish Employers Organisations). The CEOE leadership was supportive of Aznar's efforts to form a government, held regular meetings with him, and urged the parties to help him establish a stable administration. The uncertainty of the times was reflected in the economy, with an initial sharp fall after the conclusive victory of Aznar at the polls. Meanwhile, the trade unions expressed concern about the plans for change in social security rules and vocational training proposals discussed between Aznar, the PNV and CiU. Aznar, for his part, tried to be reassuring and promised to begin a dialogue with the unions, to try to ensure social harmony during the period of his government.

Aznar ultimately settled for a tone which was conciliatory if not consensual in the negotiations. The end result was a minority PP government, conditionally supported by CiU, PNV and some of the minor regional groups close to the PP. But all parties to the discussion and negotiations knew that it would be by actions, and not just words, that the prime minister-designate would be judged. And they would be watching his actions very closely.

The rise of the judiciary

The proliferation of allegations as well as proven cases of 'sleaze' and corruption which have bubbled to the surface in Spain, especially since the late 1980s, has given heightened significance to the role of the judiciary in underpinning the framework of political accountability in Spain. If we have formed the opinion that the doctrine of the separation of powers, so coveted in democratic theory, has been rendered rather irrelevant in new Spain by the dominance of the legislative by the executive, what of the independence of the judiciary? Has the legal system served to check abuses of power in the other arms of government? The Constitution provides an interim answer to this question. It is clear from this document that its authors certainly intended that Spain should be a state of law (*estado de derecho*) in which the rule of law and independence of the members of the judiciary (for example from party membership) is held to be sacrosanct. The emphasis on, and provisions for, an open, independent and unitary judicial system in the Constitution of Spain complete with a set of incompatibility rules is, in large part, a reaction to the Franco era. At that time, the domination of the executive over the judiciary was paramount and the existence of 'public order' courts, parallel to and independent of ordinary courts, provided a potent symbol of the concept of unity of powers.

Legislative initiatives, too, reveal the sense of purpose that lay behind the reform of the judiciary in the democratic era. From the actions of Adolfo Suárez in abolishing those public order courts in 1976, to the issuing of a revised law of the judiciary in 1996, which laid down the full set of procedures, structures and range of judicial bodies which had evolved through legislation especially in the 1980s, the emphasis has been on modernisation and democratisation in the judiciary. But has it worked? Has the reformed judiciary been able to serve as an effective check on wrongdoing in government and, moreover, has it been seen to be done by a public still carrying vivid and tragic folk memories of abuses of power from the Franco era?

The (*Tribunal Constitucional*) **Constitutional Court** has played an active role in deciding on matters of constitutional propriety since its establishment under the 1978 Constitution and thereby has assisted in the consolidation of Spanish democracy. (The Court is not formally a part of the judiciary, but it will be treated as such for the purposes of this discussion.) Appeals against allegedly unconstitutional laws have multiplied, especially by the autonomous communities[1] in the 1980s, most famously in the successful appeal of the Basques and Catalans against the LOAPA in 1983 (see Chapter 2). The Court has a total of 12 members, who are appointed by the king on the nomination of three-fifths of the Congress (four members) and Senate (four members), as well as nominees by the government (two) and the **General Council of the Judiciary** (*Consejo General del Poder Judicial* – CGPJ) (two). It is a system of appointment which at least is intended to ensure that the Constitutional Court is broadly supported and well qualified to make pronouncements on the actions of government. In the 1980s it was faced with appeals by conservatives who opposed the PSOE governments policies on education and abortion. It upheld government legislation.

Other institutions of state also owe their existence to the desire of the Constitution's authors to ensure the accountability of the legislature, the executive and the judiciary itself. The first **Ombudsman** (*Defensor del Pueblo*), Joaquín Ruiz Giménez (the former Education Minister under Franco who joined the reform movement in the 1960s), was appointed in 1982 and was quickly swamped by individual complaints of malpractice, which were mainly directed at government departments. The General Council of the Judiciary referred to above was established in 1980 to serve as the 'highest governing body of the judiciary'. Its main function was in some cases to recommend and in others to actually make appointments to the various judicial bodies, from the **Supreme Court** (*Tribunal Supremo*) down to provincial court levels, thus performing this function autonomously from the home affairs department. The Department of the Attorney General of the State (*Ministerio Fiscal*) headed by an **attorney general** (*fiscal general del estado*) oversees the appointments and promotion of

---

[1] The prime minister, MPs, parliamentary president and the Ombudsman also have authority to initiate abstract review of legislation; concrete review may be initiated by individuals.

the **public prosecutors** (*fiscales*), whose investigations have led to many cases of 'sleaze' coming to trial.

The court system serves at various point to reinforce this edifice of account-ability. Thus, one of the divisions (*salas*) of the **Supreme Court**, the **Administrative Division** (*Sala de lo Contencioso – Administrativo*), deals with appeals against 'the actions and decisions of high-ranking public bodies' such as the Council of Ministers, the Congress of Deputies, and the Senate among others (Newton 1997: 295). However, on matters of constitutional interpreta-tion the Constitutional Court is more significant than the Supreme Court and is regarded as the court of last resort (although the Supreme Court has had the greater longevity, dating back to 1834). The **high courts of justice** (*tribunales superiores de justicia*), operating in each of 17 autonomous communities, also have administrative divisions which deal with cases against the decisions or actions of the regional ministries (see Chapter 2). **Administrative courts** (*juzga-dos de lo contencioso-administrativo*) also exist at provincial level to perform a similar function there. All of these institutions and mechanisms serve to convey a picture of a firm judicial restraining hand on the actions of the judiciary's own members as well as on those of the public bureaucracy and its political masters. Events during the 1980s and 1990s have shown that this has not been a true picture and that public confidence in the integrity of the institutions of state has been poor. The inability of the courts to decide on appropriate com-pensation for the tens of thousands of victims of toxic oil poisoning, for 16 years after the tragedy occurred, is just one case that has sullied the public image of the judiciary.

The Constitutional Court has been accused, among others by Jordi Pujol, of being overly centrist in its judgements. Moreover, criticisms have been directed at some of the government nominees to the Tribunal (which have included Rodríguez-Piñero, a former professor and friend of Felipe González) (Heywood 1995a: 108). However, it has to be said that on balance rulings of the Constitutional Court have not shown strong bias towards the government. More severe criticism has been directed at the General Council of the Judiciary and, in particular, the changes in the method of appointment of its members introduced in 1985. Thus, instead of eight out of 20 members to be elected by parliament as indicated in the 1978 Constitution, all 20 members were to be so elected. The measure was seen as an attempt to undermine the independence of the judiciary, to give the Socialist government more leverage over the General Council of the Judiciary, and to eliminate its widely perceived conservative bias.

The feeling that the government, in practice, exercises too much control over appointments to the Spanish judiciary is widespread. In circumstances where regional government and national government are of the same political per-suasion, the system of appointment to high courts ensures that two out of the three judges are party based. Clientelistic practices have also been observed in the lower reaches of the justice system. In 1995, the examination system (*opos-iciones*) for junior legal assistants in Madrid and Granada was the subject of serious complaints and allegations of irregularities. Even the post of Ombudsman has been a source of controversy. In 1985, he was accused by *El País* of submissive reverence' to the government (Heywood 1995a: 113). The Ombudsman post was also a source of conflict in 1993–94 when the main parties could not agree on a candidate to fill the role.

The behaviour of public prosecutors and magistrates is also widely criticised. In 1997, the dismissal by the Aznar government of allegations of professional misconduct against some of these officials has done nothing to boost public confidence in the judiciary. The failure of the newly established jury system to work in convicting a Basque activist, who admitted to killing two police officers while drunk, does not augur well for the possibility of judicial reform.

Over and above allegations of clientelism and irregularity has been the persistent problem of the slowness of the judicial system due, in part, to insufficient resources to deliberate on its business. This combination of inefficiency and impropriety explains why, despite the efforts of its reformers, the judiciary is still held in low esteem in Spain. The weaknesses in the edifice of the judiciary do not serve, however, as a sufficient explanation for the general spread of sleaze and corruption in Spain's politics, especially in the 1990s. In fact, the judiciary, despite its shortcomings, played a key role in challenging the culture of corruption in the 1990s and bringing the perpetrators to book. Through the actions of Baltazar Garzón, the public prosecutor (already famous in Spain for leading the campaign against political corruption) who requested the arrest of General Pinochet of Chile in London in October 1998, Spain had an opportunity to reveal its credentials in international law during 1999.

Political corruption

The scope of corrupt cases or *casos* of 'corruption' and 'sleaze' which emerged during the 1990s is breathtaking. It ranged from comparatively mild activities at the lowest level of the party to top-level ministerial corruption. An acceptable definition of 'corruption' is difficult to formulate (Heywood 1998: 10). A descriptive overview is a simpler task. On the borders of legality were those schemes directed at bringing more funds into party coffers to pay for expensive election campaigns, involving party officials evidently charging commissions on public contracts to construction companies (the *Caso Naseiro*) and the alleged payment by companies of fees for bogus consultancy reports to party front companies (the *Caso Filesa*). Then there were the scandals which revealed improper activities of members of the government. The deputy prime minister, Narcis Serra, fell in 1993 after the discovery that the CESID (*Centro Superior de Información De La Defensa*/Spanish Secret Service) had been engaged in phone tapping King Juan Carlos, among others. More damaging to PSOE in particular was the lengthy list of cases involving high-ranking members of the political élite in allegations of corrupt financial dealing for personal gain.

The alleged 'insider dealing' in the *Caso Ibercorp* focused on the activities of Mariano Rubio, ex-Governor of the Bank of Spain and Miguel Boyer a former Finance Minister (Jiménez Losantos 1993: 441–8). The *Caso Guerra* which raised questions about the sudden rise to wealth of Juan Guerra, the brother of the Deputy Prime Minister Alfonso, was the most notorious, and most widely publicised case which broke in 1989 and began the cascade of scandals which flowed across Spain throughout the 1990s (Heywood 1995b: 726). By 1995, there were more than 20 major cases proven or under investigation. With the *Caso Roldán*, the situation reached a level of farce not previously known, when the head of the Civil Guard police force, Luis Roldán, the first civilian in that post, fled the country, pursued by a wave of accusations of embezzlement of public funds and malpractice. Raising daily speculation in the media as to his whereabouts – a Venezuelan ranch and an African jungle hideaway among the many rumours – he was eventually extradited back by the government from South Korea. To make matters even worse, it later transpired that the extradition documents had apparently been forged by Spanish government officials.

More damaging than the individual cases in themselves for public confidence in the government and the political system as a whole, was the fact that each case tended to spread its tentacles across the political élite. One by one, ministers as well as deputies and other senior members of the establishment were forced to resign, and in some cases faced imprisonment, thus generating an impression that the system as a whole was corrupt.

Incompetence, turning a 'blind eye' and direct implication in some cases, led to the resignation of such celebrated political figures as Carlos Solchaga (parliamentary deputy and former minister for finance), José Luis Corcuera and Antonio Asunción (both ministers for Justice), Vicente Albero (Minister for Agriculture) and Narcís Serra (Vice-President). Even the 1996 election campaign witnessed the spectacle of the former Minister of the Interior, José Barrionuevo, by then a member of the party electoral list in Madrid, being prosecuted for his alleged activities in the establishment of a 'death squad' in the early 1980s to counter Basque terrorism (see Chapter 3). The GAL affair rumbled on throughout much of the 1980s and 1990s. Like a storm approaching from faraway, it eventually threatened to blow the hitherto rock-solid Felipe González into the political rapids (amid rampant media speculation about the identity of the mysterious 'Mr X', who Baltazar Garzón, the public prosecutor, placed at the heart of the affair). González was accused of misleading the public about his true role in GAL, and in May 1996 Luis Roldán (of *Caso Roldán* fame) told the Supreme Court that Barrionuevo had informed him in 1990 that González had been aware of the existence of the death squads. A month previously the Court had cleared González of involvement.

Even the incoming PP government of José María Aznar was not left untouched, as speculation mounted in the media after the 1996 election that a deal had been made with González, which would remove the threat of prosecution from him over the GAL affair after his departure from office. These events offer us a number of insights into the nature of accountability in the Spanish polity:

1 The general weakness of parliament in checking abuses by its members and by government ministers.
2 The absence of effective parliamentary opposition for most of the 1980s. That absence led to the growing arrogance of the socialist administration which saw no potential challenge to its position on the horizon and failed to make a clear distinction between what was in the party interest and that of the State, thereby generating a form of *partitocrazia* or rule by party, usually associated with Italy.
3 The emergence of the judiciary, flaws and all, as the leading institution in making political wrongdoers account for their actions partly occurred by default, as other institutions failed to perform this function.
4 The media took the place of a political opposition. In particular, *El Mundo*, led by its editor Pedro Ramírez, became the scourge of the PSOE administration in the 1990s. It became a source of revelation after revelation, heaping embarrassment on the government. Ramírez started *El Mundo* after being pressurised from the editorship of another journal – *Diario 16* – by the PSOE government. Perversely perhaps, it may be argued that the ability of the media to make such accusations with relative ease, especially in the 1990s, showed the growing maturity of Spanish democracy, though predictably the media was accused by its targets of being close to subversion in its criticisms.

There continues to be considerable problems involved in attempting to define and explain political corruption generally, as observed by Heywood (Heywood 1998: 10–11). Political corruption in Spain in the 1980s and 1990s appears to have been mainly a by-product of the poor quality of bureaucratic account-ability in Spain, the blurring of public and private interests by party élites, the rapidly expanding relations between private business and the public sector, and the paucity of parliamentary control over the executive (Heywood 1994: 12). In short, it has been intrinsically connected to the processes of state and economic development in recently democratic Spain.

Party political responses to corruption

The proliferation of corrupt practices in Spanish politics was, as we have seen, partly due to the absence of real opposition to PSOE rule in government throughout most of the 1980s. A press photograph of González, taken in 1985 while he was having a holiday on Franco's yacht, the 'Azor', symbolises, for some, the moment when private gain from public resources were legitimised by the PSOE administration (Sinova and Tusell 1997: 30). The appropriation of the state for personal ends, it is argued, subsequently became fair game. For others, political interference in the judiciary during the debate about nationalising Rumasa (a large private holding company that collapsed in 1983) was the first public incident of bending the rule of law. Of course nothing in politics is so simple, but what is certain is that public disenchantment with political parties dramatically worsened during the 1980s and 1990s, and the outbreak of corruption cases played a major role in this. Opinion polls showed that while 13 per cent of the public believed that all parties were the same in 1980, by 1992, 63 per cent had a negative image of parties.

The election of 1996 and the elevation of PP to government, albeit with the support of the nationalist parties, did not bring about the radical shift from past practices that was expected by many voters. While no major scandals unfolded in the first years of the Aznar regime (though some minor accusations of malpractice by PP in regional governments gave PSOE light ammunition), neither did that government initiate the process of political regeneration promised before and during the elections of 1996. Political allies and friends of PP secured public sector and media appointments without any hesitation from the new governing party. However, some judicial reforms, notably of the CGPJ, were introduced to strengthen its independence from party influence.

To some extent, PP may be excused for failing to act immediately and decisively on its election promise of political regeneration. Post-election negotiations were overshadowed by the particularistic demands of the nationalist and regional parties. Broader issues such as political regeneration were significantly watered down, and PP could argue that it did not have an electoral mandate for radical reform. Plans for institutional reform, after the 1993 and 1996 elections, focused on changes at the margins. During the 1993–96 period of government, PSOE introduced laws for state contracts and for the incompatibility of high offices, to combat clientelism (*caciquismo*) and 'moonlighting' (*pluriempleo*) respectively. Changes to the Criminal Code introduced in 1995, for example, increased penalties for bribery of public officials. After 1996, PP altered the appointments structure in RTVE (Radio-Televisión Española/Spanish state-owned television station and radio network) to favour management by the most able rather than the most influential officials. It also proposed to modify the electoral law to unblock candidate lists and weaken the control over elected members and candidates by party managers. Both these initiatives indicated a desire by PP and PSOE to redress some of the imbalances of power that were inherent in the Spanish polity. The PSOE has also continued to advocate institutional and political reforms notably in the areas of tax-exempt party donations and the method by which parliamentary (investigative) commissions are established. Some critics have pointed to the persistence of inconsistencies in its approach, citing its refusal to investigate malpractice allegations against Javier Solana, the NATO Chief and former foreign minister, as an example.

Conclusion

Against this background how is overall equilibrium achieved between the various state institutions in Spain? First, the role of the monarchy is constrained by the 1978 Constitution so that the king holds a number of key positions in the state, most of which are largely symbolic. Nevertheless, the monarchy can (and does) play a significant if sometimes informal and behind-the-scenes role as intermediary between conflicting forces in the state. Second, Spain is a parliamentary monarchy giving the parliament a crucial role in the creation of the executive and the passage of legislation. For much of the period up to the 1990s, one party was predominant in parliament giving the executive considerable autonomy from effective parliamentary scrutiny. However, the creation of governments with only minority party support since 1993 has shifted the balance of power towards the parties and especially the party élites in parliament. Moreover, reform of the Senate currently being studied is likely to produce a more effective upper house than heretofore. Third, the relatively unrestrained nature of executive rule in the 1980s and the rise of presidentialism in the Spanish system has given way in the 1990s to a governing style in which the government has to be more mindful of its parliamentary weakness, of the countervailing strength of the regional élite 'barons' and also the scrutinising role of the media. The autonomy of the executive has been further curbed by the necessity to negotiate pacts and give firm policy guarantees to the parties to those pacts before investiture of the prime minister is possible. Finally, equilibrium in the Spanish state system has been achieved by the upsurge in the activities of the judiciary, serving as a check on systemic and individual cases of corruption or abuse, and enforcing, to some extent, compliance with constitutional principles. Despite the initial uncertainty and instability that its revelations create, the media has helped in this process too, by frequently setting in motion the investigative process into private gains from public resources in Spain and in the long run contributing to the raising of standards in public life there.

References

Aparicio, M.A. (1989) *Introductión al sistema político y constitucional español*, Barcelona, Editorial Ariel.

El Mundo (1996) 'Anuario: Elecciones Especial', pp. 1–32.

El País (1996) 'Aznar y Suárez Almuerzan con González en la Moncloa', 11 April, p. 17.

El País (1999) 'Aznar Hace un Cambio Mínimo de Gobierno Para Colocar a Arenas al Frente Del PP', 19 January, p. 1.

Gillespie, R., F. Rodrigo and J. Story (eds) (1995) *Democratic Spain: Reshaping Relations in a Changing World*, London, Routledge.

Heywood, P. (1991) 'Governing a New Democracy: The Power of the Prime Minister in Spain', *West European Politics*, 14:2.

Heywood, P. (1992) 'The Socialist Party in Power, 1982–92: The Price of Progress', *ACIS: Journal of the Association of Contemporary Iberian Studies*, 5:2.

Heywood, P. (ed.) (1994) 'Distorting Democracy: Political Corruption in Spain, Italy and Malta', University of Bristol, Centre for Mediterranean Studies, Occasional Paper 10.

Heywood, P. (1995a) *The Government and Politics of Spain*, London, Macmillan.

Heywood, P. (1995b) 'Sleaze in Spain', *Parliamentary Affairs*, 48:4.

Heywood, P. (1998) 'Political Corruption: A Conceptual Conundrum', *ECPR News*, 9:2, pp. 10–11.

Jiménez Losantos (1993) *Contra el Felipismo: Crónicas de una Decada*, Madrid, Ediciones Temas de Hoy.

Laver, M. and N. Schonfield (1990) *The Politics of Coalition in Europe*, Oxford, Oxford University Press.

Newton, M.T. (with P.J. Donaghy) (1997) *Institutions of Modern Spain: A Political and Economic Guide*, Cambridge, Cambridge University Press.

Paniagua Soto, J.L. (1998) 'Spain: A Fledgling Parliament 1977–97', *Parliamentary Affairs*, 50:3.

Powell, C. (1996) *Juan Carlos of Spain: Self Made Monarch*, London, Macmillan.

Preston, P. (1986) *The Triumph of Democracy in Spain*, London, Routledge.

Ross, C. (1997) *Contemporary Spain: A Handbook*, London, Arnold.

Sànchez de Dios, M. (1995) 'Party Discipline in the Spanish Parliamentary Parties', ECPR Conference Paper, Bordeaux.

Sinova, J. and J. Tusell (1997) *La Crisis De La Democracia en España: Ideas para reinventar nuestra sistema político*, Madrid, Espasa Calpe.

5

The policy labyrinth

The question of what governments do in Spain might quite easily be disposed of by examining party programmes for government and observing how they become legislation through the industry of civil servants, the initiative of ministers and the weighing up of parliamentary opinion. Such a version of events would at least conform to liberal democratic theory though it might seem at odds with the evidence of practices on the ground. Another way of presenting public policy-making, according to Laswell and others, is to separate out its key stages and to depict it as a cycle, involving agenda-setting, policy formulation, decision-making and implementation stages, or variations thereof (Laswell 1951: 3–15). In this chapter we concentrate on the factors which shape key government agendas in Spain and lead to the formulation of policy. In Chapter 6, policy-making strategies and implementation in Spain are explored.

Agenda-setting is the process by which demands are translated into issues and given serious attention by public officials and political decision-makers. The study of how issues get on to agendas, therefore, requires an awareness of the multitude of policy organisations and actors involved, their relative power and a variety of other influential determining factors. There are a number of sometimes competing perspectives on how issues and problems come to be seen to require a policy response to be taken into account. Agenda-types also vary, from society-wide discussion (or 'systemic') agendas, to the more focused government (or 'institutional') agendas, with which we are largely concerned in this examination of the agenda-setting processes of Spain (Hogwood 1987).

Structural constraints

One way of explaining the origin of public policy trends and the prevalence of particular issues on policy agendas is by reference to their economic determinants or constraints. Writers such as Thomas Dye have favoured this approach, arguing that public policies are related more to levels of economic development than to political factors (Howlett and Ramesh 1995: 105). High levels of unemployment in Spain in the 1980s and 1990s, and the resultant political emphasis on this issue in the 1996 election campaign may, accordingly, be blamed on the overexposure of Spain's economy and labour market to international competitive forces, especially in the aftermath of democratic transition. However, such an explanation is very simplistic. Other structural factors, besides those of an economic sort, may also be linked to the emergence of policy issues: population trends, for example (Smith 1990: 37–8). The prolonged baby-boom from the 1960s up to 1977 undoubtedly contributed to the soaring unemployment levels of the 1980s and 1990s. Demands for pensions and the matter of government proposals for them have also become more topical, as the proportion of over-65s in the population of Spain has climbed, from 10 per cent in 1981 to 14 per cent in 1991 and an estimated 20 per cent in the year 2000. Such demographic trends have also accelerated demands for a range of policy resources in addition to pensions, such as for health and education policies.

Economic factors do, however, still form an important part of the defining features of Spain's policy agendas. For example, the combination of weak prices, rising costs and shifting patterns of demand, among a host of other factors, has brought the Spanish mining industry to its knees in the 1990s (Salmon 1995: 103–29). It is sustained only by an array of support and subsidy policies. Food and farming policy also illustrates this point clearly: Spain lives with the reality that it is a net importer of cereals, where it has a shortfall, and is a net exporter of products such as fresh fruit and vegetables, where it has overcapacity. In this way the structure of food production affects the issues its policy negotiators raise and prioritise, their bargaining positions and the allocation of policy resources from relevant decision-making bodies such as the EU (Arroyo Llera 1993). The geographical spread of production in various sectors means that Spain's regional policy agendas are also shaped in different ways. So, fisheries policy may be important to Galicia where most of Spain's deep-sea fleet is located, but policies affecting horticulturalists and livestock producers are more important in Andalucia and Extremadura, respectively.

The rules which Spain abides by as member of supranational and international organisations such as the EU and GATT (General Agreement on Tariffs and Trade) also affect these inputs into policy agendas. Legal obligations inherent in the GATT deal of 1993–94, to which Spain was a signatory, affect what products may or may not be subsidised, regardless of policy demands emanating from a range of anxious sectoral interests exposed to the winds of international free trade. Also, it has long been believed in Spain that legally binding concessions on fisheries policies were granted at the expense of the agricultural sector, by Carlos Romero (minister for Agriculture) and his team, during EC membership negotiations in the mid-1980s (see Chapter 7). Whether true or not, the fact remains that Spain's ability to influence the CAP (Common Agricultural Policy) agenda on prices and subsidies were curtailed somewhat by the ensuing legal constraints, until new negotiations on the SEA (Single European Act) made possible the hastening of full membership of the common market for food products. Despite such examples, the impact of Spain's membership of international or supranational organisations should not be exaggerated. Pridham's study of the EU initiative for sustainable tourism in 1992 shows that policy reorientation at national level also requires as a prerequisite a favourable response from national political élites and the presence of appropriate institutional structures (Pridham 1996: 5–27).

The greater prominence of some sections of the Spanish economy above others has enabled some economic élites to have a more privileged role in setting the agendas in the policy process than others. Historically, the Spanish banks have been such a powerful, albeit secretive, and patriarchal force in driving policy, most notably through the so-called *Club de los Siete* (i.e. the meetings of the presidents of the seven major Spanish banks). The employers federation, the CEOE, which lobbies government, also has a strong banking presence, in the form of the AEB (*Asociación Española de Banca Privada*/Spanish Banking Association) (Heywood 1995: 255–6). In the 1980s, the presidents of three of the main banks began to develop close relations with Felipe González and Carlos Solchaga. PSOE critics of this trend such as Alfonso Guerra claimed that González had been 'kidnapped' by the bankers and needed to be rescued from them (Gillespie 1994: 52). By the late 1980s, about 55 per cent of the financial system in Spain was under the control of PSOE sympathisers.

If the role of the banking élite in shaping economic policy agendas by such proximity to policy decision-makers is fairly clear-cut, that of the industrial élite is less so. The prominent part played, historically, by the State in Spanish industry tends to weaken any attempt to make a case that industrial policies are driven by an industrial élite autonomous from the State. Instead, the Spanish state itself has exercised control of large swathes of industry by means of the public trading enterprises, which are chaired by its own appointees. This fact would appear to give the government considerable freedom to shape 'industrial policy'.

The evolution of the public trading enterprises

The concept of PTEs (*Sociedades mercantiles*/public trading enterprises) dates from the Franco era and is distinguished by the fact that the state is involved directly as a player in the market economy through these organisations, which are run along the same lines as public limited companies. In 1992, it was calculated that they contributed approximately 10 per cent of GDP (gross domestic product), less than similar organisations in other southern European states but significantly more than in the UK. Up until the mid-1990s, these organisations were grouped under large holding companies namely the National Assets Group (*Grupo Patrimonio*), the INI and the INH (*Instituto Nacional de Hidrocarburos*/the National Oil Company). *Grupo Patrimonio* had the widest range of enterprises under its umbrella covering the main economic sectors, and with responsibility for state shareholdings varying from 20 per cent (e.g. in the agricultural company, Tragsa) to 100 per cent (e.g. in the company running the renowned Spanish Parador hotels).

The INI was established in 1941 with the purpose of spearheading the reconstruction of the Spanish economy after the Civil War, especially through indigenous industry and enterprise. It formed a range of mainly industrial companies to carry this task out. These included the iron and steel producer, Ensidesa, and the car manufacturer, Seat. Iberia was also one of the many companies established under the INI. Between 1974 and 1984, INI became the home of a variety of oil companies hit by the recession, and the economic uncertainties of the era of transition.

The PSOE government controlled the PTE's very effectively through its appointees: party élites organised in the so-called *Club de Empresarios*. This was formed in 1982 after the PSOE came to power and included the presidents of Telefónica (telecommunications company), Iberia and Aviaco (airlines), Renfe (railways), Repsol (oil) and many other subsidiaries. It was committed to promoting modernisation and democratic values within state institutions (Holman 1989: 16).

In the second half of the 1980s and during the 1990s, the government began to distance itself from its industrial conglomerates and to allow market forces rather than political motives to dictate their future shape and direction. In 1987, Repsol was formed out of the energy-related companies in the INI and began to establish itself as a major player in the European and international oil sectors. In 1991, a new public limited company called Teneo was set up to take over Iberia, and other currently, or potentially, profitable companies in the INI. By 1995, the INI was being dismantled and its loss-making components transferred to a newly established AEI (*Agencia Industrial Español*/Spanish State Industrial Agency). Repsol and Teneo meanwhile were placed under the SEPI (*Sociedad Estatal de Participaciones Industriales*/State Holding Company).

The main purpose of the reorganisation of these public industries and businesses was to remove from the shoulders of the Spanish Treasury (*Hacienda*) the liability for losses in these companies, and to facilitate privatisation and closure, where appropriate. In short, the state-holding companies have become key vehicles for new government strategies and policies. Such policies have been partly determined by economic exigencies, and also by international trends in economic ideas and ideology.

Privatisation and deregulation

Privatisation in Spain, up until the early 1990s, was a fragmented affair, reflecting the disparate nature of the major state holding companies and the history of many of the nationalisations of firms under their charge. As we have already noted, in the 1970s and early 1980s a range of mostly 'old' industries were nationalised as an exercise in bankruptcy avoidance. Privatisation became the preferred strategy from the mid 1980s. The ideological support for privatisation evident in British and French political discourse in the 1980s was not reflected in Spanish politics. Sales of public sector companies did certainly take place during this period but not as part of a coherent strategy, rather a piecemeal exercise reflecting a variety of motives. Thus, the sales of Seat to Volkswagen and Enasa (truck manufacturer) to Fiat in the late 1980s were aimed at securing the Spanish car industry on a more sound footing. The sales of components of the large holding company Rumasa (nationalised in 1983, when on the point of bankruptcy) reflected the fact that the government adopted a pragmatic approach to such takeovers and sales. The main privatisations were co-ordinated by the key élites at the Ministry of Economy and Finance in co-operation with national and international financial élites. Accountability to the Cabinet and parliament for these actions was minimal (Chari 1998: 177–8).

In the 1990s, there was evidence that governments were motivated in their approach to privatisation by three factors. First, there was a desire to cut back the budget deficit and PSBR (public sector borrowing requirements), in line with single currency criteria. Second, there was some successful experimentation with the concepts of 'popular capitalism' and a 'share owning democracy', as in Britain under Conservative administration in the 1980s and 1990s. Third, by 1994, Spain had committed itself to the EU programme of liberalisation of state industries. The culmination of this trend was the introduction of a co-ordinated and structured privatisation policy in 1996 (Scobie 1998: 98). The range of industries and utilities to be privatised was outlined, together with a timescale. Government policy was less inclined also to favour foreign investors than previously, and in some cases retained a 'golden share' to protect the 'national interest' from adverse actions by privatised company boards. Increasingly, the agenda for privatisation would reflect government policy, rather than the opinion of management in the semi-state sector.

Privatisation of Telefónica revealed some of these trends. Sixty-five per cent of its shares were disposed of during 1993–94. The sale of a further 12 per cent in 1995 was divided into two tranches, one of which (49 per cent of the disposal) was directed at foreign institutions, and the remainder at the domestic market. The popularity of this sale among individual shareholders led to an increased proportion of shares being made available to the general public when SEPI (the owner of the stock) sold its final (21 per cent) share of Telefónica in 1997. Three-quarters were allocated to domestic investors. Simultaneously with those developments, the government also laid down a clear timetable for the liberalisation of the telecommunications market and the opening-up of competition in the sector from late 1997.

Plans to privatise a range of other companies including Argentaria (the banking group), Tabacalera (the tobacco products group), Endesa (the electricity generator) and Repsol were prepared for the period 1997–2000. The success of previous public share offers was likely to lead to a repeat of the Telefónica model. Severe loss-making firms in the mining, shipbuilding and airline sectors made it likely that a significant level of public ownership and subsidisation (e.g. the national coal mining company, Hunosa) of industry would continue into the new millennium, while new debates would arise surrounding the regulation and deregulation of competition in a variety of industrial and utility sectors. In these debates, and the ensuing agendas of policy change, EU competition policy pressures would figure prominently (see Chapter 7).

The impact of ideas

If structural or economic explanations of issue-emergence in Spain have their limitations, then a better way of conceptualising the agenda-setting process might be to focus on the language and ideas which inform the actions of its politicians and their policies. According to this view, public policy is 'constructed' by the language of politics which puts an interpretation on what a policy 'problem' might be. Murray Edelman suggests that: 'Problems come into discourse and therefore into existence as reinforcements of ideologies, not simple because they are there or because they are important for well-being' (Edelman 1988: 12–13).

Thus the predisposition of party élites to give ideological privilege to some ideas and beliefs may have, at the very least, reinforced the emphasis placed on particular issues which arose in Spain. The adoption by the PSOE of elements of the language and ideas of monetarism in its macroeconomic policy might explain the emergence of public trading enterprises reorganisation and privatisation initiatives discussed already. The Medium-term Economic Programme of 1984–87 was also informed by monetarists anti-inflation zeal. It is suggested in some studies that, having learnt from the difficult experiences of the Mitterrand government in France, and the Pasok government in Greece, the PSOE made an ideological shift away from the option of employment-generating, demand-led policies of economic stimulation, in favour of supply-side, neo-liberal policies of inflation control (Holman 1989: 10). Too much should not be made of this shift. Heywood suggests that the evidence points in the opposite direction and that state interventionism under the PSOE actually increased in many policy areas (Heywood 1992: 9).

Media control is a factor in the circulation and reinforcement of bias. (The Franco regime realised its potential when establishing RTVE as a state monopoly in 1952.) There are two Spanish state television channels at national level and a network of regional stations run by the relevant autonomous communities. Since 1989, there has been a greater private sector involvement in broadcasting in Spain and the PP government has promised more privatisation of state channels. Significantly though, the news agency EFE is still under government control. Party political conflicts have arisen over the role of the media, notably during the 1986 general elections. The misfortunes of the PSOE in the 1990s were largely due to revelations about the wrongdoings of its ministers and appointees in the pages of newspapers such as *El Mundo*, despite the party's efforts, at times, to stop such revelations, in the interests of 'national security' (see Chapter 6).

The rush towards economic and monetary convergence in Europe, and the enthusiasm for the ideas and ideals of European integration, especially amongst policy élites in Spain, has given rise to various policy problems generated largely by the desire to qualify 'on time' for early membership of EMU. Controlling inflation and cutting public expenditure are just a few of the policy goals which have emerged from such a background set of ideas, with important consequences for policy and the public. The 1997 Budget, for instance, was dominated by the desire of the political élite to meet the single currency convergence criteria. As a public sector budget deficit of 3 per cent of GDP was one objective, a wage freeze on three million public sector employees became an important option in the 1997 budgetary policy debate and subsequently, imposed by the government.

If it is the attitudes, beliefs and traditions shared amongst policy élites in Spain that are chiefly responsible for the way in which policy issues and problems are identified, then the EU does sometimes help to reinforce them. In farming policy, the historic big-farmer bias of the CAP illustrated by the emphasis on prices policy more than structural policy have made the problems of Spanish smaller farmers and family farms of secondary, if not marginal, importance to EC/EU agendas. The Spanish government has generally tended to reinforce this policy orientation. The MAPA (*Ministerio de Agricultura, Pesca y Alimentación*/Agriculture Fisheries and Food Ministry) has been at the butt of criticisms by farming interest groups such as COAG (*La Co-ordinadora de Organizaciones de Agricultores y Ganaderos del Estado Español*/The Co-ordinating Body for Spanish Agricultural and Livestock Producers), which have accused it of being only interested in the macro-level of policy, and of promoting the interests of the food industry rather than family farmers. The language and policy emphasis were slightly redressed following the 1992 CAP reforms, but the problems of serious inequality in the rural economy are still remote from the important agendas. These issues have remained peripheral and problematic rather than crucial, in the rhetoric and policy proposals of policy actors, in the Spanish government and MAPA. The effect of this has been to leave the raising of such issues to the rather more weak, and relatively ineffective, spokespersons, for example in the European Parliament:

> I come from a country with regions where the implementation of 'set-aside', massive early retirement or cuts in production could create serious social problems because it will increase unemployment in agriculture especially casual workers and those heavily dependent on agriculture . . . there is a need for more effective ways of providing information to farmers . . . to positively discriminate in

favour of small farmers . . . sixty percent of funding goes to large farmers (Segarra 1992: 5).

The presence of key policy actors, at various institutional levels, who will articulate and reinforce the dominant views and biases prevent such protests from
having anything but a marginal influence on the equilibrium of the main
policy agendas. For example, Jesús Arengo, president of IRYDA (*Instituto
Nacional de Reforma y Desarrollo Agrario*/National Agricultural Reform Body),
publicly expressed the view in 1988 that the CAP 'set aside' policy would not
cause problems of emigration and desertification, because lots of other policies
would be available to provide appropriate support for rural Spain. In such ways
the legitimacy of EU policies are reinforced at member state level, with the assistance of state élites.

The emergence of feminist ideas on the government policy agendas of the
1980s is also revealing. Despite a numerically weak movement in Spain, feminist ideas were influential due mainly to the strong foothold given to Spanish
feminists in the state apparatus, especially after 1982. The Womens Institute
(*Instituto de la Mujer*), part of the Ministry of Culture, has served as a hub of
feminist activity. It illustrates that the new Spanish political élite was relatively
open to some ideas informing the modernisation of Spanish society.

The institutional environment of the policy process

The issues which are selected for attention by state officials and government
policy-makers are affected also by the organisational structure of the state
within which they move. Some writers such as Mancur Olsen use the distinction of 'strong' or 'weak' to characterise the extent to which government institutions assist policy actors. 'Strong' states have considerable 'autonomy' or
independence, for instance, from the demands of interests groups. They also
have good 'capacity' to enable state policy-makers to act, due to organisational
unity and coherence. 'Weak' states are prone to interest group pressures and
experience a good degree of inter-institutional conflict among policy-makers.
Spain would seem to be somewhere between a 'strong' and a 'weak' state. It has
a weakly developed civil society and thus is not subject to excessive pressure
from interest groups. It also has a highly complex state institutional structure,
spanning many levels, from municipal to central government, as well as involving varying degrees of autonomy from, and control by, central government.
Apart from the devolved layers of government, the most important aspect of
which is the system of autonomous regions, there are layers of decentralised
administration (i.e. branches of central administration in the regions), which
also shape the environment in which problems and issues are dealt with by
policy actors. One aspect of this is the *administración periférica*, or delegated state
administration, already touched on Chapter 2.

The *administración periférica* has served as the tentacles of central government across the provinces and regions of Spain since the early nineteenth century. Its key officials, the government delegate and the civil governor, have long provided the eyes and ears of central government throughout the land, identifying policy needs by providing statistics and information to central government, and ensuring that the policy responses have been implemented. As representatives of central government, these institutions and their occupants have appeared increasingly anachronistic to those who make demands for Spain to have more devolution. The government delegate serves as the senior figure in the region. There, he is second in status only to the regional president and holds overall responsibility for government. The civil governor represents central government at provincial level, most importantly in the area of law and order policy, having charge of the Spanish police and security forces in his jurisdiction. In regions such as Catalonia, this official symbolised the power of the state and was a long standing focus of controversy. The abolition of the post of civil governor became part of the post-election agreement worked out in 1996 between CiU and the PP for the investiture of Aznar as state president (see Chapter 4).

The tensions which exist between the historic nationalities and the centre in Spain manifest themselves in the overlapping structures of devolved and decentralised institutions of government. These tensions have produced a continuous flow of demands for policy change from the autonomous regions (see Chapter 2). Institutions like the civil governor have in themselves come to represent the demand for a change not just to policy, but to the vestiges of a centralised policy style.

Interest groups are not altogether excluded from state institutions involved in the policy process. According to corporatist theory, public policy is made and delivered under the influence of interest groups formally recognised by the state, and as Philip Schmitter notes, 'organised into a limited number of singular, compulsory, non-competitive, hierarchically ordered and functionally differentiated categories' (Parsons 1995: 257).

Such practices were evident in the Franco era but involved official syndicates which were mouthpieces of the government. In the post-Franco era, voluntary interests groups have found a place on a number of 'quangos' or semi-state institutions concerned with the various stages of the policy cycle, and thus providing a neo-corporatist dimension to the Spanish policy process. However, as Heywood observes, the prevalence of neo-corporation in Spain should not be exaggerated (Heywood 1998: 103). This phenomenon is discussed further in Chapter 6.

Quangos

Quangos (of which there are about 40) are responsible mainly for the delivery of public policy on a day-to-day basis but are also the source of newly arising policy issues. Historically spanning both francoist and democratic eras, they were the subject of legislation in the 1950s as well as in the 1980s. They are present in each ministry and separately titled according to function, such as those for agriculture which cover research, conservation, structural reform, production and marketing aspects of policy delivery. Called autonomous administrative bodies (*organismos autónomos administrativos*) these quangos are run by boards of management which, apart from including senior department officials, may also have appointees of the minister present, for example, from appropriate interest groups such as trade unions.

The INEM (*Instituto Nacional de Empleo*/National Employment Forum) which is responsible for overseeing unemployment benefits and training is one such example. Health and social security policy areas too have very important autonomous bodies. The INSALUD (*Instituto Nacional de la Salud*/National Health Service), established in 1978, is in charge of overall health policy delivery, for instance, through hospitals and medical centres (Newton 1997: 104). The PSOE reforms of the health service in the 1980s and early 1990s aimed at extending its coverage of the population and making INSALUD management more accountable. But these reforms, perceived as representing centralising trends, ran counter to the institutional plans of the autonomous regions, which were also anticipating the transfer of health policy responsibilities. By 1997, the public health-care system had been devolved in the cases of seven of the most powerful regions. The remaining ten regions' health services were still administered from the centre.

The INSS (*Instituto Nacional de Seguridad Social*/National Social Security Service), dating from 1979, is the next largest quango, after INSALUD, in the social policy area. It is responsible for the delivery of the wide range of social security benefits. Of particular note, in the membership of this body, is the fact that provision for the representation of unions and employers organisations as well as the government in the delivery of social security is laid down in the Constitution. They are represented on the INSS general council and executive committee in equal numbers.

Also relevant to this discussion of such policy institutions is the role of the Bank of Spain in the making of monetary policy. Since 1994, it has been given responsibility for interest rate policy on an independent basis, free from direct political manipulation. This initiative was prompted in part by the exigencies of European monetary union preparations.

To summarise, the institutional environment of the policy process, as we have seen, does partly explain why and in what form some issues maintain a high profile on the key policy agendas. State institutions in Spain also wield enormous opportunities for patronage and what Bachrach and Baratz call the 'mobilisation of bias' in favour of the governing élites' policy preferences (Bachrach and Baratz 1962). Institutional mechanisms such as those arising from provisions contained in the Constitution to the impact of the electoral system also affect policy options and policy agendas (e.g. during the

Government formation process – see Chapter 4). Many administrative substructures reinforce the process of agenda-setting. However, we do not go so far as to label Spain as a 'weak' or ' strong' state or draw general conclusions from this about the capacity of state actors to control the flow of issues on to policy agendas. That varies from sector to sector, and may be a product of other factors.

The bureaucratic arena

The importance of bureaucracies in the policy process generally, and in the shaping of policy agendas particularly, has been stressed by many writers, most notably Max Weber (Weber 1957). The growing size and complexity of government is generally considered to enhance the power of bureaucrats whose skills and expertise provide formidable resources for other policy actors to match. However, the powers of the bureaucrats should not be exaggerated, at least in the Spanish case. They do not have the status attached, for instance, to French civil servants. Moreover, the top layers of the civil service have been strongly politicised, for example, by the appointments procedures adopted since the transition to democracy. But there is also continuity from the past, and an inherited tradition of bureaucratic power in the Spanish policy process, not to be lightly dismissed in any account of agenda-setting.

The bureaucratic structure of policy-making in Spain, concentrated as it is on the ministries, dates back to the early nineteenth century. Despite reforms introduced in the democratic era, aimed at rationalising as well as devolving the functions of government, 15 state ministries continue to be at the heart of the policy machinery. Some changes at this level have, of course, been registered. The creation of a ministerial portfolio for relations with the EEC (European Economic Community) in 1978, removed the monopoly of the Ministry of Foreign Affairs in this policy area (Story 1993: 250). Another important change was the establishment of the Prime Minister's Office as a separate ministry in 1992. A role in the preparation of Cabinet agendas, the recording of Cabinet minutes and (through the **Government Spokesperson** (*Portavoz del Gobierno*) the announcement of government policy decisions are all activities, included in its portfolio. The fulfilment by PP of a 1996 election campaign promise resulted in the separating out of the functions of Home Affairs and Justice which had been controversially merged between 1994 and 1996 as part of an attempt by the PSOE government to be seen to be tackling corruption allegations. Likewise, the creation of a superministry of Public Works, Transport and Environment took place after the 1993 election, in line with PSOE's approach to the policy areas of transport and environment. In 1996, Aznar created a separate Environment Ministry to reflect the increasing attention being given to that policy area. These changes have helped to shape and reinforce the policy agendas by emphasising some policies over others, from one government to the next, and have also been politically driven by party and electoral considerations. As a broad rule though, most Spanish ministries have charge over one or more policy areas, in line with practice in Western Europe generally.

Ministries are arranged hierarchically, with responsibility to the Cabinet and parliament lying ultimately in the hands of the ministers, who are responsible for policy proposals and policies emanating from their ministries. They are assisted by a number of key figures. Each minister has a private office headed by a chief, who liaises with the ministry. Next, **under-secretaries of state** (*subsecretarios de estado*) whose office goes back to the nineteenth century, perform the key policy co-ordination and communication functions within and between ministries and their subsidiary bodies. Moreover, they supervise the process of preparing draft laws and through the weekly meetings of the General Committee of Secretaries of State and Under-Secretaries (*Comisión General de Secretarios y Subsecretarios*). They have the exclusive task of preparing the policy agendas for Cabinet meetings. Their involvement also in the distribution of budgets to the ministries gives them a formidable role in the Spanish policy process. Increasingly, the number of **secretaries of state** (*secretarios de estado*, or junior ministers) has increased since their creation in a 1977 public administration law (in 1986 there were nine; by 1995, 15). As their numbers have increased so too has their status, not just in being given membership of the General Committee, but also in being able to take the place of the minister at parliamentary question time. In this sense, they have higher status than under-secretaries. Along with some under-secretaries, a few are also members of the inter-departmental cabinet committees, which co-ordinate policy decisions involving different departments (Newton 1997: 95).

The number of **general secretaries** (*secretarios generales*) has also increased since the introduction of this post in the early 1980s. They have responsibility for large areas of policy within departments but do not have the special responsibilities or status of the under secretaries, or indeed secretaries of state. Beneath these levels of ministerial authority lie the **directors-general** (*directores generales*) and **technical general secretaries** (*secretarios generales técnicos*). The directors-general have a particular responsibility for separate areas of a ministry's work (e.g. in MAPA: livestock production and marketing, food policy, fisheries, human resources, etc.) Their number has increased in recent years as the workload of government has expanded. The technical general secretaries are the heads of the technical experts such as statisticians and researchers, whose task it is to provide a continuous advisory service for the various departments. This role of serving as the source of expert opinion on policy options gives the technical general secretaries privileged access to the ministers and their agendas. They also hold the higher status of the two posts, given that they can request directors-general to provide them with information appropriate to their policy preparation and analysis.

The most senior departmental posts are filled by the Cabinet on the recommendations of the next most senior figures in the departments. Although they are officially protected from changes in government, reshuffles at these levels are the norm rather than the exception in the aftermath of an election. The posts of head of the minister's private office, secretary of state, under-secretary, general secretary and directors-general are political appointments. The director-general acts as a bridge between the political appointees and the civil servants in the ministry (Parrado 1996: 262).

A wide variety of Interministerial Committees (*Comisiones Interministeriales*) perform an important policy advisory role for the government. They include experts from many different sources and are in some cases permanent (e.g. the *Comisión Interministerial para Asuntos Económicos*/Interministerial Committee for Economic Affairs) or temporary (e.g. the Organising Committee for the Spanish presidency of the EU).

The long period of socialist government created an extensive top layer of party-appointed public officials (*cargos políticos*) at these senior levels. In the 1990s, these became a target for criticism by the Partido Popular who vowed to substantially reduce their number if elected to govern. Keeping to that promise would be made easier by the fact that there still remained ample resources in the form of official posts with which to reward PPs closest allies, and the inclination of PP to colonise the ministries with its own supporters would be difficult to curb.

The civil servants

The position of the civil service in Spain was relatively unaffected by the transition to democracy. A natural instinct for survival in times of crisis, had been bred into this institution in past centuries, when the frequent turnover of regimes resulted in the creation of the élite civil service corps (*cuerpos*) (Hooper 1987: 230). Membership of these corps became the channel of entry, and also of progress, in the professional civil service in Spain. Academic or professional qualifications, at least in theory, were required, and by means of this institutional device, the cycle of blatant political appointments and dismissals – or 'spoils' system – that characterised much of the nineteenth century was curtailed. Self-regulation of many of their conditions of service and promotion meant that the corps were, instead, able to develop their own patronage networks, to approve appropriate élite privileges and, particularly during the Franco era, to respond to inflationary pressures on their salaries. This they did, for example, by facilitating corruption, or by such devices as automatically promoting all civil servants to higher positions on the career ladder and the pay scale than their duties implied was appropriate. When this proved to be insufficient to keep pace with inflationary trends, the corps condoned the practice of moonlighting (*pluriempleo*) by civil servants, all amounting to behaviour that would bolster the living standards but reduce the performance of Spain's bureaucracy.

In addition to these factors, the rather hopeless inefficiency of the civil service was a product of the practice of promotion by seniority instead of by merit. Moreover, the existence of a multiplicity of corps (about 290 in the early 1980s) in different ministries gave rise to competition between them, and consequently led to poor levels of co-operation or co-ordination on policy matters. Not all corps have had the same influence. During the Franco era, corps containing legal personnel were the most important. With democracy, regional autonomy and EU membership, corps with economists have also become influential (Parrado 1996: 261).

Various attempts to reform the bureaucracy in Spain, as far back as the mid-nineteenth century, came to little or nothing. During the Franco era, reform efforts concentrated on the appointment of the 'technocrats' during the 1950s and 1960s, to lead the economic modernisation of the century (see Chapter 1). The role of the state in this process of economic change was for it to serve as the main promoter of economic development by means of the French-inspired model of 'indicative planning'. For this role, the civil service needed to be transformed into a modern, rational bureaucracy. Some progress along that road was made. Practices such as automatic promotion were abolished, but the corps still retained their firm grip on the civil service and reform was minimal.

During the early stages of the transition to democracy, other political and institutional reforms took priority. Not until the advent of the PSOE government in 1982 were serious administrative reforms attempted. Emphasis in these initiatives was not just on the structure of the bureaucracy, but also on the behaviour of the bureaucrats towards the public. Thus, such matters as public accessibility to ministry officials was improved, by creating open office structures and abolishing the thousands of 'little windows'. Also, time-wasting and circular procedures for official applications were tackled by more efficient new guidelines for civil service documentation. A major reform initiative, legislated for in 1983, attempted to challenge the grip of the corps system on the bureaucracy, by opening up all civil service appointments to public competition and to encourage the emergence of new public managers at all levels (Parrado 1996: 264). However, as its passage coincided with the rapid expansion of the bureaucracy and the creation of the autonomous government administrative systems, the PSOE were accused of paving the way for an extension of its clientelistic networks, through wholesale political appointments. None the less, such practices as 'moonlighting' and widespread absenteeism in the civil service were curbed by the new reforms such as those contained in the Incompatibility Law (*Ley de Incompatibilidades*). The establishment of the Ministry of Public Adminstration (*Ministerio para las Administraciones*) in 1986 took the reform process further, as did a major study of the public administration of Spain which was published in 1989, and its follow-up, the Modernisation Plan, produced in 1992. Those reform proposals visualised a replacement of the traditional legalistic culture of public administration in Spain – most senior civil servants being lawyers – with a management model (Heywood 1995: 132). Moreover, the public would be regarded from an increasingly consumer-oriented perspective, new controls in the form of devolved budgets would be introduced and objective-led management procedures put in place.

In tune with this trend, ministries were given the opportunity of so-called operational service inspections (OSI) of their administrative processes, with a view to improving their efficiency and rationalising their operations. The majority of ministers had such inspections carried out, covering many of their departments and sections. Further reforms aimed at the professionalisation of appointment procedures to the civil service were introduced in 1990, aiming at reducing the chances of corrupt practices widely linked to the competitive exams system of public service recruitment (*oposiciones*). In spite of these developments, the impact on the civil service was less than convincing. The principal obstruction was the attitudes of the civil servants themselves, notably at senior level, towards reforms, aided as they were by civil service corps who resisted the erosion of their members' privileges. Without their full co-operation the reform process was bound to be slow, but attitudes were changing.

In conclusion, the concept of bureaucratic power does not provide us with a simple and straightforward explanation of the process of agenda-setting in Spain. Historically, the institutional strength of the bureaucracy is incontrovertible and its survival, relatively unscathed into the democratic era, is undeniable. However, it has had to face an increasing number of new public management-type reform initiatives in the 1980s and 1990s, which have challenged many aspects of its way of working, including the corps systems, and therefore its very culture and self-esteem.

Most of all, the plethora of government policy initiatives, especially in the 1980s, have led to the expansion of the public service at all levels, thereby creating opportunity for the merging of bureaucratic and party power in the state apparatus. This was an opportunity not missed by the PSOE in government. It facilitated the promotion of large numbers of young professionals, many of them PSOE supporters in the public sector, amounting also to a generational change. As Gillespie noted, the proportion of office holders who were PSOE congress delegates, and therefore with a potential impact on government and party agendas, reached 70 per cent by the early 1990s (Gillespie 1994: 53).

The Cabinet (*Consejo de Ministros*) arena

The rules and norms which are embodied in the main institutions of government and the procedures for introducing and conveying legislative proposals through parliament also affect the capacity of parties to exercise influence over policy agendas.

Apart from the departmental ministers, the Cabinet in Spain consists of the prime minister, the deputy prime ministers (if there are any in post) and, occasionally, a secretary of state. It is the most senior institution and is normally chaired by the prime minister, but the king may attend, and if he does so will chair the Cabinet meeting in session. Convened weekly (each Friday), in the past there were separate Cabinet meetings for issue-raising and decisions, but now these activities tend to be combined at each meeting. The role of the General Committee of Secretaries of State and Under Secretaries in preparing the agendas for Cabinet meetings (items of which are referred to as the 'red index') is of key importance. This Committee may also deal with routine issues, without prior reference to the Cabinet. These are subsequently rubber-stamped by the Cabinet (such items form what are known as the 'green index'). The Committee may also refer policy proposals back to the ministry they came from for redrafting, and thus delay their progress on to the Cabinet agenda (Newton 1997: 82).

Apart from its role in making laws, an activity we look at more closely below, the Cabinet exercises additional functions such as the implementation of existing enabling legislation, by making appropriate regulations which are then approved by the king. The Cabinet also has overall responsibility for the operation of public services', if necessary, taking emergency charge during the eruption of a crisis. It also oversees the activities and legislation of the autonomous communities, at least in relation to their compatibility with the Constitution.

There are five main **cabinet committees** (*comisiones delegadas del gobierno*). These are the Committee for Economic Affairs, the Foreign Policy Committee, the State Security Committee, the Committee for Educational, Cultural and Scientific Policy, and the Autonomy Policy committee. They serve as discussion and issue-raising forums and advisory bodies to the Cabinet. They also deal with policy co-ordination between departments. Significantly, they have decision-making powers on policy matters for which Cabinet approval is not essential. A variety of other cabinet committees may co-opt a wide membership but may only make recommendations to government (one deals with economic affairs related to the EU, for example) (Newton 1997: 85).

Each of the institutions of central government mentioned combine various aspects of the functions of agenda-setting, decision-making and oversight of policy administration. While such activities are dispersed, the formal position of the minister in the agenda-setting stage is clearly identified, and accountability for actions in his or her name is well defined. However, prime ministers (especially González) have tended to concentrate extensive policy making power in their hands. Not only is parliament diminished by this, but so also is the Cabinet, whose ministers have had little collective power. As Guerra once put it 'The Council of Ministers [Cabinet] does not discuss politics, they are matters for the party leadership'. (Camiller 1994: 260).

The role of ministers

While the ministerial departments prepare the draft bills (*ante projectos de ley*) in advance of legislation, it is the ministers who are individually in charge of submitting such bills to the Cabinet. They also have the power to issue ministerial orders, independent of the Cabinet, as well as the responsibility to propose draft budgets for their departments, which they negotiate independently with the Cabinet. Technically, ministers are accountable to parliament and the Cabinet, and may be called upon to justify their action or inaction, or that of their departments. If a particular minister has failed in his or her duties, then resignation or dismissal may be the only option.

Ministers are usually backed up by a private office consisting of a group of advisers (*asesores*). They are mostly party-political advisers, often with longstanding links with the minister but technically they have civil servant status. Despite their considerable weight as a source of policy initiatives, ministers are unlikely to use them to justify overriding expert advice in policy proposals, for example from senior officials such as the technical general secretary.

The movement of issues from the Cabinet arena into that of parliament has been subject to tight political control by the governing parties and also, after the 1993 and 1997 elections, by those parties supporting minority governments. However, not all issues need to make this journey into policy enactments. Some issues can be dealt with simply by government decrees (*decretos legislativos*) if they are already covered by enabling or delegated legislation.

The legislative arena

Draft parliamentary bills (*ante proyectos de ley*) are prepared, as we have already noted, in the ministries and approved and amended (if necessary) by the Cabinet. (They may, in some cases, be preceded by consultative White Papers.) They are next considered by the Presiding Council (*Mesa*) of the Congress which prepares the Order of Business for each House. They now become proper parliamentary bills (*proyectos de ley*) and the *Official Journal of the Congress* (*Boletín Oficial de las Cortes*) publishes them, thereby making them available for public scrutiny. Parliamentary committees conduct most aspects of the parliamentary business and, in particular, the examination of legislation. Of the 16 that are currently established in the Congress, 13 are legislative committees, reflecting the main policy areas. A similar pattern prevails in the Senate and there are also six joint committees, including the increasingly important joint committee for the European Union.

Committee membership is proportional to the presence of the party groups in the chambers. Ministers may attend and speak in the committees but unless they are members they cannot vote. For the purposes of scrutinising a detailed policy proposal, the relevant parliamentary committee appoints a working party (*ponencia*), which may make recommendations within 15 days for government amendments to the bill. If the amendments are then incorporated into the bill by the government, the parliamentary committee will return again to further debate the legislation – section by section – and either decide to pass the bill on to the plenary session of Congress for debate, or seek to extract further amendments from the government. The legislating and debating programmes for such plenary sessions are arranged by the presidents of the chambers. The government may, however, have emergency items included for priority debates.

Within the Senate, a similar set of activities takes place following the submission of proposed legislation, but with a more restricted timespan. After a spell in the Senate (which has only delaying powers of two months, or 20 days if the government deems the legislation to be urgent), bills are brought back to the Congress where they are presented for final approval or rejection, including any amendments proposed by the upper house. They are then presented by its president to the king for his signature, which is automatic apart from isolated circumstances, for example, if the proper legislative procedures have not been scrupulously followed.

Proposiciones de ley, that is to say, private member's bills, follow much the same procedure for their passage through the houses of parliament. The main difference is that before they are submitted to a parliamentary legislative committee, they must be proposed by either a parliamentary group spokesperson, a regional assembly or a parliamentary deputy with the signatures of 14 fellow members from the Congress, or 25 from the Senate (Chapter 4). Private member's bills must also be given permission to proceed by the government and by the Chamber to which they are to be submitted after a special debate of that chamber. If the private bill is an initiative prompted by the general public with the requisite half a million signatures attached, it has some further limitations on its contents. It cannot, for instance, involve major constitutional changes: they must be exclusively formulated in organic laws.

Norton poses the question 'Does parliament matter?' when examining the British case (Norton 1993). In Spain, it would seem that the Cabinet dominated by the prime minister and party élites in the parliamentary committees have the most impact on legislative agendas. In the 1980s this gave the PSOE government (especially González and Guerra) widespread agenda control. In the 1990s, the PSOE and PP had to negotiate policy agendas with CiU in particular.

The party arena

The power of political parties to control the flow of issues on to the key institutional agendas is helped by the relationship between party and bureaucracy in Spain. However, there is a variety of relevant contingent factors. An important one is that the party in question is able to influence appointments to public posts. Ministerial 'cabinets' consisting of party political advisers help to institutionalise party political influence in Spain over policy agendas. The party in power in central government is able to exercise influence most extensively, but the existence of regional, provincial and municipal layers of government in Spain have extended such opportunities to most of the parties, to some degree or other. As we have also seen, the impact of the electoral system has enabled the smaller regional parties to play a role in shaping policy agendas, most obviously after the 1993 and 1996 elections, when CiU won considerable influence over the main PSOE and PP government agendas for their terms of office (see Chapter 3). In 1998, Aznar also admitted that the regional and general election timetable for 1999–2000 had been negotiated with CiU.

Castles argues that party competition and partisan control of government has a big impact on government (Castles 1983). Political parties lay out their policy priorities in manifestos. For all parties these provide discussion agendas for the period between elections. They also provide a set of both general and more specific policy objectives for a party that is elected to government (or even a party supporting a minority government). But manifestos are living organisms which change and evolve between elections, and Spain has had no shortage of elections. They also reflect the cross-section of views which exists within parties, reminding us that rather than being monolithic structures in which all members think alike, most Spanish parties are in themselves coalitions or alliances of often quite distinct viewpoints. Therefore, the suggestion that the government party or parties have served as the chief 'gatekeepers' for issues entering on to the key institutional agendas in Spain provides a rather mechanistic version of agenda-setting. It ignores the debates and jockeying for position which are evident in the party arena, especially among the party élite and the range of fidelity shown to the party line through disciplined obedience.

The PSOE manifesto, for instance, evolved from a socialist programme in 1982 promising radical change to one in the late 1980s and 1990s which contained many neo-liberal policy strands. Some internal policy debates such as those leading up to the adoption by the party Congress of the so-called Programma 2000 in 1990 served as a means of allowing internal party factions to air their differences while attempting to contain embarrassing rifts. Despite years of consultation and preparation Programma 2000 had little impact after its adoption by the party congress. During the 1980s, PSOE factions included the social democrats with members such as ministers José Maravall (Education Minister), Javier Solana (Foreign Minister) and José Barrionuevo (Interior Minister). Another was the new left IS (*Izquierda Socialista*/Socialist Left), consisting of those neo-Marxist intellectuals who emerged from the defeat of the left wing in 1979 (Gillespie 1993: 86). The IS raised pacifist and ecological issues on the PSOE discussion agenda, and took part in the campaigns against US bases. On the right, a faction made up of neo-liberals or liberal social democrats, most prominently, Miguel Boyer and Carlos Solchaga (Economics and Finance ministers, respectively), pressed for greater flexibility in the labour market, privatisation and monetarist economic policies at the expense of social security. They were given the support of González, despite criticism from some quarters, most prominently by Alfonso Guerra, who at times even resorted to contradicting ministerial statements on policy. Regional wings of the PSOE also pressed for their own policy preferences, which were not always in line with mainstream party thinking. The Catalan socialists, PSC, pressed from within the PSOE federation for the expansion of regional power to the outer limits of the Spanish Constitution, but it was CiU, the Catalan nationalists, who actually pushed PSOE government policy furthest along this path, because of their electoral significance.

The electoral manifestos of 1993 and 1996 were replaced by programmes for government, which were the product of inter-party bargaining. In this process, party policy commitments were rapidly sacrificed, modified or watered down in exchange for promises of conditional parliamentary support for the leading contenders for government. Central to these proceedings was the CiU, which wrung concessions from both the PSOE (in 1993) and the PP (in 1996) on issues highlighted in their respective manifestos. In the 1993 election, these included reforms to the labour market, against the wishes of many in the PSOE, and in 1996, on greater autonomy over regional and tax-raising finance, despite opposition from such PP stalwarts as Manuel Fraga.

Despite such pressures, many manifesto issues have found their way on to government agendas and have been pushed through the decision-making and implementation stages of the policy process despite dogged opposition from elements both inside and outside the party system. The LOGSE (*Ley Orgánica de Ordenación General del Sistema Educativo*/Organic Law on the General Organisation of the Education System) was one such policy, unveiled in 1987, which aimed at reforming the provision of education with implications for religious and ethics teaching, which was fiercely opposed by the Catholic bishops but, none the less, passed into law in 1990.

Notwithstanding their comprehensive coverage of the relevant policies, Spanish European election manifestos have had little influence on policy in Spain. The reasons for this are not difficult to discern. Voters in European elections have tended to be swayed more by domestic policies and issues. Besides, Euro-parties have little power to carry out their manifesto pledges in an EU-dominated by the member states through the Council of Ministers.

The public arena

Many issues do not originate from within government, the party system or indeed the organised interests. The occurrence of a public crisis may shine a spotlight on issues that otherwise lie dormant. The occurrence of a toxic syndrome which killed over 650 people in 1981 from the use of adulterated cooking oil was a major consumer health crisis in Spain which, due to public demand and concern, brought about a rapid scrutiny of policies for the regulation of food products. However, it also revealed the shortfalls in the legal redress available to citizens affected by such calamities, as it took years for the process of compensation to be finalised in the courts. The rapid spread of Aids in Spain was another such issue which brought about a series of policy responses, and followed closely the example of other states. Forest fires too in parts of Spain reached a crisis point in the late 1980s and early 1990s. They prompted the interaction of regional, central and local authorities in developing appropriate policy initiatives.

Despite these examples of issues arising from concerns and crises in Spanish society, the role of party and political élites in controlling the flow of the main policy issues on to key agendas is paramount. This may reflect what Cobb, Ross and Ross refer to as the 'insider initiation' model where those with special access to decision-makers initiate a policy and do not necessarily want it to be expanded and contested in public (Howlett and Ramesh 1995: 114). But in some cases, too, public support can be mobilised by party élites to justify their actions.

Élites and agenda-setting

Following Mosca and Pareto, élite theory reveals that power is inevitably con-centrated in the hands of a few groups and individuals in the policy process. Ministers and leading individuals within the Spanish party system serve as the most important channels and 'gatekeepers' for issues into the key agendas. The most important figure is the prime minister, whose position and power is under-pinned by the requirement of a 'constructive vote of no confidence' by the Cortes to replace him (see Chapter 4). Formally, therefore, the power of the prime minister is immense, though political circumstances may vary from one prime minister to the next (Heywood 1991: 111). Aznar is more constrained by parliament than González was for much of his period of office. The outstanding personal popularity of Felipe González in the 1980s meant that he was able to play a key role in defining government policy initiatives that were of major concern to him. For example, he led the campaign for a major reversal of PSOE policy on the issue of Spain's relationship with NATO (Chapter 7). His referen-dum on this policy was a high-risk adventure, with very serious consequences for the government if it had backfired. Its success gave the policy a legitimacy based on public, over party, support. The key role of Alfonso Guerra in bridging the space between party and government, as Gillespie has noted, meant that the PSOE and its parliamentary group would (until the beginning of the 1990s) loyally echo government policy (Gillespie 1994: 52). Not all areas of policy were within his control. Other élite figures were important too. Guerra's influence, as we have noted did not extend very far into the Ministry of Economy where Miguel Boyer and Carlos Solchaga, for a time, held greater sway over policy in that sphere. Although enjoying much less support within the party, these neo-liberals, or *'los beautiful'*, as they were more colloquially known, were prepared to promote unpopular economic policies, safe in the knowledge that they could join the commercial or banking élite should they suffer electoral defeat at the hands of a discontented public.

The PSOE also had close links with the banking sector. In particular, José Angel Sanchez Asiain and Pedro Toledo, presidents of the Banco de Bilbao and the Banco de Vizcaya (which merged in the early 1990s), were personal friends of González, sometimes being referred to as 'socialist bankers' due to these links (Holman 1989: 17).

The regional leaders or 'barons' of PSOE, in particular those who headed party federations and regional governments simultaneously, asserted themselves in the 1980s and 1990s by promoting policy issues that had an independent if not rebellious flavour to them (Gillespie 1994: 59). In Extremadura, the support by PSOE barons for strong centralism as the best way of securing a national redistribution of wealth ran counter to the PSOE government's policy of extending the autonomy process, albeit within limits. It also ran counter to the stance of other regional barons, for example in Catalonia and Andalusia where Miquel Roca and Manuel Chaves, respectively, advocated more regional autonomy.

Within the PP, the influence of Manuel Fraga has already been alluded to. From his 'retirement' role as president of the *Xunta de Galicia* he prepared the ground for the emergence of another regional president from Castilla-León, José María Aznar, who became party leader (see Chapter 3). Under Aznar, PP produced a set of policies which reflected liberal, conservative and Christian democrat influence. Aznar's success was in winning sufficient support for his policy agenda to enter government, but the fact that he failed to get an overall majority meant that residual doubts and fears still remained about the underlying goal of that agenda. Close links with the business élite would mean that PP would pursue an appropriate agenda in government, to provide a return for this support. Privatisation initiatives provided just one method of repaying friends according to the ex-PM and PSOE leader, González, who labelled it 'institutionalised corruption' (*El País*, 18 December 1998: 1).

Conclusion

Agenda-setting in Spain is directed largely by the key Spanish élites. While environmental factors such as the institutional setting and demographic trends are significant, their precise impact is usually difficult to measure. As Lane suggests, 'maybe what matters is how decision-makers take environmental factors into account and how they wish to give differential recognition to various factors in their preferences' (Lane 1993: 72). Party and government élites have an important influence over issue selection by their control of party manifestos, programmes for government and parliamentary agendas. Bureaucratic élites have had some autonomy historically, but the party-patronage system together with administrative reform initiatives have served to undermine this somewhat, and to loosen their impact on agendas. But the élite corps system still prevails and is influential. The institutional environment of the policy process generally continues to have a strong impact. In particular, the emergence of the autonomous regions has given rise to regional 'barons' or élites who have considerably increased their influence over government agendas in the 1990s. Business élites have straddled the public and private sectors because of the structure of Spain's industrial/utility sectors and have, for example, served to reinforce the wider market-friendliness of Spanish policy agendas. In so doing, they have helped to reinforce at national level an international bias in favour of neo-liberal policy initiatives, such as the privatisation and deregulation of Spain's public utilities.

References

Arroyo Llera, F. (1993) *El Reto de Europa: España en la CEE*, Madrid, Editorial Síntesis.

Bachrach, P.S. and M.S. Baratz (1962) 'Two Faces of Power', *American Political Science Review*, 56.

Camiller, P. (1994) 'Spain: The Survival of Socialism', in P.A. Anderson and P. Camiller (eds), *Mapping the West-European Left*, London, Verso.

Castles, F.G. (1983) *The Impact of Parties: Politics and Policies in Democratic Capitalist State*, London, Routledge.

Chari, R.S. (1998) 'Spanish Socialists: Privatising the Right Way?' *West-European Politics*, 21:4, pp. 163–78.

Edelman, N.J. (1988) *Constructing the Political Spectacle*, Chicago, Chicago University Press.

El País (1998) 'La Corrupción del Gobierno', 18 December, p. 1.

Gillespie, R. (1993) 'Programma 2000: The Appearance and Reality of Socialist Renewal in Spain', *West European Politics*, 16:1.

Gillespie, R. (1994) 'The Resurgence of Factionalism in the Spanish Socialist Workers Party', in D.S. Bell and E. Shaw (eds), *Conflict and Cohesion in Western European Social Democratic Parties*, London, Pinter.

Heywood, P. (1991) 'Governing a New Democracy: The Power of the Prime Minister in Spain', *West European Politics*, 14:2.

Heywood, P. (1992) 'The Socialist Party in Power, 1982–92: The Price of Progress', *ACIS: Journal of the Association of Contemporary Iberian Studies*, 5:2.

Heywood, P. (1995) *The Government and Politics of Spain*, London, Macmillan.

Heywood, P. (1998) 'Power Diffusion or Concentration? In Search of the Spanish Policy Process', *West European Politics*, 21:4, pp. 103–23.

Hogwood, B. (1987) *From Crisis to Complacency: Shaping Public Policy in Britain*, Oxford, Oxford University Press.

Holman, D. (1989) 'Felipismo or the Failure of Neo-liberalism in Spain', Political Studies Association Conference Paper, University of Warwick.

Hooper, J. (1987) *The New Spaniards*, London, Blackwell.

Howlett, M. and M. Ramesh (1995) *Studying Public Policy: Policy Cycles and Policy Subsystems*, Oxford, Oxford University Press.

Lane, J.E. (1993) *The Public Sector: Concepts, Models and Approaches*, London, Sage.

Laswell, H.D. (1951) 'The Policy Orientation', in D. Lerner and H.D. Laswell (eds), *The Policy Sciences*, Stanford, Stanford University Press.

Newton, M.T. (with P.J. Donaghy) (1997) *Institutions of Modern Spain: A Political and Economic Guide*, Cambridge, Cambridge University Press.

Norton, P. (1993) *Does Parliament Matter?* Hemel Hempstead, Harvester Wheatsheaf.

Parrado, S. (1996) 'Spain', in D. Farnham (ed.), *New Public Managers in Europe: Public Servants in Transition*, London, Macmillan.

Parsons, W. (1995) *Public Policy: An Introduction to the Theory and Practice of Policy Analysis*, Aldershot, Edward Elgar.

Pridham, G. (1996) 'Tourism Policy in Mediterranean Europe: Towards Substainable Development?', University of Bristol, Centre for Mediterranean Studies, Occasional Paper, 15.

Salmon, K. (1995), *The Modern Spanish Economy: Transformation and Integration into Europe*, 2nd edn, London, Pinter.

Scobie, H.M. (1998) *The Spanish Economy in the 1980s*, London, Routledge.

Segarra, D. (1992) European Parliament Debates, 10 March 1992, p. 52.

Smith, M.J. (1990) *The Politics of Agricultural Support in Britain: The Development of the Agricultural Policy Community*, Aldershot, Dartmouth Press.

Story, J. (1993) *The New Europe*, London, Blackwell.

Weber, M. (1957) *The Theory of Economic and Social Organisation*, Berkeley, Calif., University of California Press.

6

Policy processes

The way a government approaches policy-making and, in particular, its relationship with the other key policy actors and institutions, may, according to Richardson, be depicted as a 'policy style' (Richardson 1982: 13). In his analysis, he identified many possible variations. These were governed by two main variables: first, the structure of the policy subsystem, consisting of relevant policy actors and institutions in policy networks and their inter-relationships and, second, the degree of state autonomy and resources there are, together with the administration's capacity to act on policy initiatives. An examination of policy-making in Spain from the perspective of various 'styles' might allow us to see the considerable diversity of factors influencing Spanish policy-making and implementation. But as Allum has pointed out, there are methodological difficulties in attempting to develop typologies of national policy style (Allum 1995: 402–6). Consequently, we confine ourselves here to exploring the main traits that are evident in the policy process in Spain, across a variety of sectors and issues and over a period of time (mainly post-1975). We identify not so much a single Spanish policy style but a variety of strategies of policy deliberation involving the following key traits and features: consensus and conflict; majority and minority party government; patron–client and group networks.

Consensus and conflict

Consensus

Periodically, policy-making in democratic Spain has been consensus driven, with interest groups, parties (or party factions) and the economic and state élites propelled, either by desire or necessity, into negotiated and bargained policy outcomes: 'concertation' as Richardson describes it (Richardson 1982: 19). However, that has not made it the prevalent style; instead, it intermittently appears on the horizon as just one approach to policy formulation among others, directed at achieving particular ends. It may, in fact, be more accurately depicted as a strategy of conflict avoidance, influenced not a little by European fashions in policy-making such as (neo-)corporatism.

In the Franco era, consensus was a concept noteworthy for its absence in the relations between government, the real (as opposed to official) sectoral interests and the opposition groups. If there was consensus during the dictatorship, it existed among the self-serving 'party' factions in power. It was a form of consensus that held regime élites together on a fairly steady course until after the death of the Caudillo, despite the many challenges they faced, especially in the last years. Most crucially, it worked on the basis of the complete exclusion of those elements that questioned the state's legitimacy in any way. It was not a style of governance based on widespread or societal consensus. For this reason the dictatorship collapsed quickly after the death of Franco (see Chapter 1).

The transition to democracy itself, plus economic and social policy-making in the first years of democracy, were characterized by quite a wide degree of consensus-building and a politics of accommodation. As far as the early days of transition were concerned, too much should not be made of this point. The opposition favoured a *ruptura* or break with the existing system, but Suárez persuaded the Cortes to pass the Law of Political Reform to reform the existing system. As such, the opposition were not directly involved in the initial process of internal regime change. The preparation of the new Constitution was a somewhat different matter.

By the time work on this began, the opposition parties were legalised, elections held and Suárez was prime minister, backed by the parliamentary majority of his party, the UCD. Political and constitutional reform proceeded with widespread support, despite the fact that there had been little time for the opposition parties to prepare for the general elections and the electoral system had been imposed. However, there exists considerable evidence to indicate that the procedure adopted for arriving at a consensus on the draft Constitution was flawed (Heywood 1995: 43). The exclusion of non-parliamentary groups, including trade unions and employers' organisations, is just one aspect of this (although the Constitution did require the establishment of a representative body for the social partners). The prominent role of party élites in drafting the Constitution is another (see Chapter 1). Furthermore, the political consensus arrived at through the referendum was only partial in another very important sense, as it has since transpired. In parliamentary negotiations on the Constitution, the Basque nationalists in the PNV had been marginalised and excluded from the key working party. Their proposed amendments to the Constitution were also largely rejected. The PNV subsequently abstained in the parliamentary vote, and also recommended that the electorate do so in the referendum. More than 50 per cent of Basques chose this path, and many (including ETA) subsequently argued that the Constitution excluded their interests.

Observations on consensus-building in the making of the 1978 Constitution must therefore be made with extreme caution. So, too, must they be regarded as somewhat conditional in the social and economic sphere. That said, what are known as the Pacts of Moncloa represent something of a high-point in these few moments of consensus-style government in Spain. They were the agreements struck in October 1977 on a variety of economic and social measures, chiefly wage controls, for which unions would seek the agreement of their members, and price controls, which manufacturers would implement. The negotiations included face-to-face meetings between the prime minister (Suárez) and the leaders of the PSOE (González) and the PCE (Carrillo) at the Moncloa Palace. The adoption of this strategy was chiefly motivated by Suárez's desire to enhance the legitimacy of the still very new and fragile regime and to underwrite its future with a policy consisting of economic and social agree-ment, in which a wide range of groups would have a vested interest.

Neo-corporatist trends evident in industrialised western European states in the 1970s also had a bearing on state relations with organised interest groups in Spain (Berger 1981). It was not out of place to adopt a policy approach which was fashionable in neighbouring, and more mature, democratic systems. It was also in keeping with the modernising Spanish instinct to seek to converge with the rest of Europe. But the commitment to this approach to policy-making was partial. (The representative body suggested by the 1978 Constitution became the CES (*Consejo Económico y Social*/Economic and Social Council) which was set up, after a long delay, in 1992, with 61 members, and little more than sym-bolic significance.)

Corporatist traits were evident in the approaches adopted by the UCD government in 1980 to the AMI (*Acuerdo Marco Interconfederal*/National Agreement on Employment). In this, the main trade unions and employers fed-erations reached agreement with the government on a variety of issues relat-ing to working conditions, pay, pensions, productivity and dispute arbitration. However, these were negotiations entered into in order to achieve particular short- and medium-term policy goals rather than part of a broad, system-wide, consensus-based policy approved for the long term.

Such sporadic 'events' took place occasionally up to the mid-1980s, the last of which was the AES (*Acuerdo Económico y Social*/Economic and Social Agreement) in which the UGT and the CEOE were invited to participate in the allocation of 10 per cent of the budget. Although the PSOE (having close links with the UGT) was theoretically well disposed to corporatism, with its large majority in the Cortes, in 1982 and 1986, it had little incentive to adopt such an approach. Instead, it could rule with virtually unchallenged executive authority. Moreover, in the years following that election, the UGT, not to mention the other unions, became disenchanted with the PSOE's increasingly neo-liberal agenda. It was in fact, the beginning of a process of detachment between the PSOE and the unions that culminated in the one-day general strike of 1988.

In the 1990s, relations between unions, business and the State displayed ambiguous traits. On the one hand, there were important landmarks in co-operation and consensus-building. National tripartite agreements in 1992 and 1996, involving trades unions, employers and the PSOE and PP governments, provided good examples. The comprehensive labour market reform deal, signed in the spring of 1997 by trades unions and employers with the backing of the PP government, was another. As a result of the latter deal, the employers pledged to promote long-term jobs while the unions agreed to reduce the severance pay for employees under new indefinite contracts established to reduce the proliferation of short-term contracts in the Spanish labour market.

'Consensus' was an important part of the vocabulary of the PP government formed in 1996. Aznar positioned himself in the centre of the ideological spectrum and advocated 'consensus' and 'stability' on such issues as labour market reform (*The Economist* 14 December 1996: 5). On the other hand, public demonstrations and strike action continued to form a frequent and popular form of protest against government policy. In December 1996, for instance, such confrontation tactics brought two million civil servants on to the street in protest against a pay freeze introduced by PP as part of a package of austerity measures. However, unions and employers were represented on a variety of quangos and state agencies, and in regions such as Andalusia corporatist mechanisms evolved giving the social partners a role in the regional sphere of policy-making. These developments suggested that while a consensus-based system of policy-making was unlikely to develop across Spain, policy-makers of all political persuasions were prepared to pursue consensus-type strategies where necessary or appropriate to achieve policy goals (Martínez Lucio 1992: 507).

Conflict

Imposed policies are the flip side of those born of consensus and may give rise to conflict. They may be based on covert or overt forms of conflict. Covert forms include those potentially challenging viewpoints which are concealed and not openly articulated, because the forces of the state – legal, political, military and ideological – tightly regulate them and give rise to 'non decision-making' (Lukes 1974: 18–19). This certainly existed in the Franco era when relative political quiescence should not be mistaken for true consensus or the absence of conflicts of interest.

The conflict of ETA is the most extreme form of conflict faced by policy makers and the public in Spain. It is directed at forming a fundamental change in the relationship between the Basque County and the Spanish state. Policy-makers vacillate between repression and conciliation in response (see Chapter 2). Conflict may, also, be seen in the overt behaviour of disaffected groups engaged in demonstrations, strikes and various forms of pressure politics. In democratic Spain these have emerged onto the political landscape from time to time. Education and labour market policies offer a few good illustrations of the effects of the absence of consensus decision-making in two major sectors.

Education policy

In 1978, state schools were closed for over two weeks as public sector teachers sought pay increases. Ten years later schools were again closed down in a dispute over teachers parity of pay with government officials generally. That particular strike forced the resignation of the Education Minister, José María Maravall, and acquiescence to the teachers demands by the incoming minister, Javier Solana. However, it was the dispute over the LODE (*Ley Orgánica del Derecho a la Educación*/Organic Law on the Right to Education) which provoked most widespread protest. Passed in 1985, it attempted to put private and state schools on a similar footing in terms of finance, admissions, management and teachers salaries. It was the most controversial piece of PSOE legislation in its first term of office, provoking demonstrations by an alliance of middle class parents and the Church. Opposition parties also weighed in with amendment after amendment, consuming much available parliamentary time. Ultimately, it went all the way to the Constitutional Court before finally coming into effect: it was a breakdown of consensus that proved to be expensive. The LOGSE which was passed in 1990 was preceded by two years of consultation and not a little acrimony among some opponents. Supported by the main political parties, it emerged with more widespread backing than previous initiatives in education. Its implementation was threatened by limited finance (Lawlor and Rigby 1998: 209–11).

Labour market policies

In 1987–88 the UGT and CCOO led strikes and demonstrations in protest against high levels of unemployment and in opposition to the govenment's panacea: temporary employment schemes for young people. The one-day general strike of 14 December 1988, which the PSOE government attempted to thwart, was the high-point of this upsurge in public confrontation. It won huge public support and marked a major landmark in poor government–union rela-tions. While the government attempted to engage in some appeasement of the unions, by making minor policy concessions in 1989, Spain's increasing com-mitment to convergence with other EC economies in the Single Market and EMU made further confrontation more likely. One-day general strikes held in 1992 and 1994 confirmed that point. However, these events also reflected the fact that the public mood towards such conflict-based strategies was changing: support for the later strikes was considerably less than for that in 1988.

It seems that in labour market policy, as in education, policy-makers could proceed to formulate policy, despite the absence of consensus among client groups and even in an atmosphere of conflict. One over-riding outcome of the failure to build a consensus in such policy areas has been the breakdown of the historic link between the PSOE and the UGT, formalised in 1990.

Majority and minority party government

Majority government

The influence exercised by the prime minister and his leading ministerial colleagues over policy formulation and decision-making in democratic Spain displays considerable variations, affected by, among other factors, the characteristics of the policy area being looked at, the power and personality of the individual ministers or prime minister involved, and the size of the parliamentary majority of the governing party. Duverger identified 'majority government' as one model of parliamentary government whose most salient feature is that the winner takes all and the loser is completely marginalized until the next election (Allum 1995: 313–14). Lipjhart points out that Spain's political leaders explicitly rejected majoritarianism and (to the extent that we have seen) embraced consensus during the most critical stages of democratic transition (1977–79). It is thus surprising that majoritarianism was so prevalent in the 1980s in Spain (Lipjhart 1988: 12–13).

The absence of free elections and the exclusive hold on power of the dictator and his allies firmly separates government in the dictatorship era from those forms of 'majority government' that have emerged in the democratic era. Extensive state intervention was the trademark of economic policy during the dictatorship. A wide range of prices, wages and trade were, for example, subject to regulations imposed by central government. Under Franco, the executive was composed of highly autonomous ministers who had extensive decision-making powers in what were hierarchically ordered, clearly defined and jealously guarded areas of policy jurisdiction. The position of the Cabinet as a policy-making arena was thereby marginalised. Collective responsibility for public expenditure decisions was almost non-existent. Instead, personal individual ministerial responsibility for policy outcomes was the means by which accountability was achieved in this system.

Bilateral deals worked out between spending departments and the Ministers both of Finance and Development Planning, when put together, led to the creation of the annual state budgets and the four-year Development Plans (Gunther 1996: 163). No overall guidelines were set by the Council of Ministers, which largely rubber-stamped those bilateral decisions. Furthermore, the Caudillo himself took little interest in public expenditure issues. But he did exercise overall power over policy formulation by his influence over the appointment or dismissal of ministers, thereby regulating the strength or weakness of various governing factions. He also directly intervened when there arose important questions of state of interest to him, involving such issues as public order, defence and security, government institutions and Church–State relations. The National Defence Law of 1971, which enhanced defence and security spending, is one such example.

Since the establishment of democracy, as we have already noted, overall priority-setting for government expenditure policy has been undertaken by the executive, in particular by the prime minister of the day and the senior members of government. Moreover, the exigencies of democratic representation and electoral competition have given rise to the need for collective responsibility for government policies. However, that has not stimulated collective cabinet decision-making as a policy style. With Suárez, constitutional policy-making was uppermost in mind. Overall charge for economic and social policy was given over to the vice-president and the Minister for Finance and Economics (*Ministro de Economía y Hacienda*). Co-ordination of policy proposals was provided through the (Cabinet) Committee on Economic Affairs, chaired by the vice-president, on which departments with important economic policy roles were represented by their ministers (Gunther 1996: 186). This Economic Affairs Committee also had some actual decision-making powers in economic matters.

New proposals for legislation in parliament or for passage as decree laws of government have been examined by the General Committee of Undersecretaries (see Chapter 5). It has served as a filter for those issues requiring decisions. As we have already noted failure, to reach agreement at this level (i.e. so-called 'green list' status and rubber-stamping by the Council of Ministers) has meant that items get 'red list' status, requiring the close attention of Cabinet. Disputes between spending ministers have been resolved, not by the Cabinet, but rather by the intervention of the prime minister, while the key overall influence on spending decisions remains in the hands of the finance ministry.

Under González's first three governments, the finance ministers were given sole charge over bilateral negotiations with various spending ministers, leaving the vice-president to monitor the overall passage of budgetary and public expenditure policy through the policy process. The prime minister himself was more actively involved in the broad agenda and priority-setting aspects of policy, but would play the role of final arbitrator in unresolved spending disputes after the relevant issues had been aired at Cabinet level. The collective role of the Cabinet as a decision-maker continued to be weak under González.

The authority of the executive in its policy-making role has been underpinned by the rules of parliament which have reinforced party discipline through the parliamentary party group system. Rebellion against the party whip by MPs and senators has carried the threat of exclusion from parliamentary posts (e.g. membership of committees) and a marginal role in the legislative business of parliament. This is due to the strong grip of the chairmen and spokespersons of the parliamentary party groups in these matters. During González's first two governments, the existence of a parliamentary majority for the PSOE also enabled the party to adopt a predominantly majoritarian top-down, or executive-led, style of policy-making. One product of this era, the Medium Term Economic Programme, which was devised for the period 1984–87, attempted to give overall shape to economic policy. Potentially unpopular criteria, such as the control of inflation, public expenditure controls and labour market reforms, were prioritised (Lawlor and Rigby 1998: 103). The absence of such a decisive majority for the government party, between 1979 and 1982 and after the 1993 and 1996 elections, encouraged a shift to coalition-building approaches to decision-making.

The process engaged in during the 1990s by nationalist and regionalist parties, of drawing up detailed annual legislative agreements with the PSOE and the PP, has most certainly undermined the degree of autonomy and power which was experienced by the executive in the period between 1982 and 1989. Moreover, it has weakened the explanatory value of the concept of 'majority party government', in analysing Spanish policy-making. Parallel with the declining parliamentary influence of the PSOE in the 1990s, and the replacement of Alfonso Guerra with Narcís Serra, González displayed growing signs of tiredness, or even boredom, and somewhat disengaged himself from direct involvement in domestic politics and policy.

Aznar has not been able to afford such a political luxury, is more directly involved in domestic affairs and keeps a tight rein on policy agendas.

Coalition-building and minority government

Paul Sabatier suggests that the policy process can be characterised as involving what he calls 'advocacy coalitions', consisting of actors from various public and private organisations who share a set of beliefs and who seek to realize their common goals over time (Lane 1993: 100). The institutional framework of the Spanish policy process as designed by its Constitution writers (e.g. the provisions for autonomous communities) is compatible with a process of 'coalition-building' or 'pact-making' more than to 'consensus-seeking' or 'majority government'. Coalition-building of the sort we see in Spain, however, involves a selective or limited type of pact rather than one based on a wide political consensus, and occurs between policy actors who have a common interest in combining forces to make and implement a joint set of policies. In the process, they may be inclined to make short-term concessions to each other for the purpose of achieving longer-term objectives. Such a relationship, as we see below, is chiefly pragmatic and it is not implied that the policy actors involved necessarily have a shared political identity. In fact, in areas outside of those agreed, policy actors may politically be diametrically opposed. It is more likely to be a relationship brought about by the political potential of their combined voting strengths or support bases, than through policy actors having an ideological affinity towards each other. In this sense, it is a type of coalition-building that is not characterised by common beliefs and shared values inherent in Sabatier's 'advocacy coalitions'. Instead, it is mainly driven by the desire for public office and policy spoils, that are the anticipated outcome of the exercise of coalition-building and the politics of government formation conducted by political parties (Laver and Schofield 1990).

In the Franco era, the lack of either elections or the free organisation of interests in what was a weak civil society meant that there was no incentive or opportunity for the interest-aggregating process that lies at the heart of coalition-building. (Unlike in most democracies, Franco's policy members were not under pressure from organised interests, if we exclude the special cases of the regime factions.) The concentration of the political system on one individual meant that coalition-building between ministers who wished to bring about significant policy change was of little importance, especially in policy areas such as the economy, in which the Caudillo had faint interest anyway. Bilateral negotiations brought greater results.

The Constitution of 1978 seems to envisage a policy process characterised by pact-making and coalition-building and involving policy actors from all levels of government and society. That this was indeed the intention of its authors may be seen, for instance, by looking at the provisions for the construction of a state of autonomous communities (see Chapter 2). The creation of a variety of routes to autonomy, with different powers attached to them, prompted the development of a culture of negotiation and bargaining amongst the upsurgent regional political and administrative classes and the central state in Spain. The impact of this may be seen, for example, in many aspects of tourism policy which has been devolved to the regions and local authorities. A variety of ministries are also involved in dealing with this policy area. The difficulties arising from such fragmentation led to the publication of a strategic plan in 1995 which proposed, among other initiatives, strengthening the co-ordinating committee for tourism development, by including regional and central government representatives. Such institutional changes favour the development of a coalition-building approach to policy-making among the various policy actors participating in the process (Salmon 1995: 257–8).

The electoral system, too, by being centred on the 52 provincial constituencies rather than a single national constituency, prompted the growth of regional parties as a parliamentary force, with whom, in the statistically likely event of a 'hung parliament' or Congress, deals would have to be struck during the process of government formation. The minimum size of 15 MPs required for parliamentary groups was also likely to encourage pact-making among well-balanced blocks of MPs. It is perhaps all the more surprising in the light of these observations that it took until 1993 before it came to be a prominent characteristic of the Spanish policy process. True, there were some instances of interparty negotiations between 1979 and 1982 when Suárez's UCD government, lacking a stable parliamentary majority, relied, from time to time, on the votes of other parties to get legislation through. These arrangements were, however, *ad hoc* and temporary and did not amount to any sort of ongoing agreement. If there was any sustained coalition-building during this period it was among the factions within the UCD, who sought and were awarded control of ministries which gave them the greatest opportunity of pursuing their particular agendas (e.g. Christian democrats and education, social democrats and the economy). Even during the 1980s, when the PSOE had a strong majority in the Cortes, there were still occasions of low-key coalition-building. Inter-party agreements between the PSOE and CiU or PNV were quite common, as Gunther has noted (Gunther 1996: 191). Even some legislative concessions were privately negotiated with AP/PP from time to time. The purpose of the agreements with CiU and PNV was to provide security for a future parliament in which the PSOE would only be able to form a majority with the support of other parties. The concessions to AP/PP seem to have been motivated by the calculation that by allowing some leeway to AP/PP, the PSOE made it less likely that future AP/PP governments would completely overturn its legislation. However, the PSOE was not usually so magnanimous towards its political opponents.

One of the centrepieces of the PSOE's first government was the LGS (*Ley General de Sanidad*/General Health Law), which set out the framework for the health service in Spain. Its slow progress into legislation is evident from the fact that it was approved only just before the 1986 elections. The explanation for the difficult progress of such a key piece of legislation lies in the failure of the government to engage in appropriate consultation and coalition-building with the relevant organised interests and political parties. It came under fire from both the left and right of the political spectrum. From the left, the Federation of Associations for the Defence of Public Health declared the law to be ambiguous and contradictory. The UGT regarded provisions for private health care as additional ammunition for its view that the PSOE government was shifting away from its socialist principles. From the right of the political spectrum, the confederation of medical unions depicted the proposed law as bureaucratic and socialistic, while the AP suggested that the Act amounted to a lost opportunity for more ambitious reform. And, if those criticisms did not suggest a complete rejection for the government in its navigation of the policy into law, the regions too, were heavily critical: after all, the concept of a national, central health service, which the law embodied, was contrary to the aspirations of some regions and nationalities, i.e. to take control of their own health policies and services.

After 1989, when the PSOE had a wafer-thin hold on Congress, and especially following the 1993 election, when it was in a minority, the formation of coalitions of support in parliament was essential to survival. González struck agreements annually with Jordi Pujol of CiU, in return for parliamentary support. These agreements included considerable concessions to the autonomous communities, especially Catalonia, but also commitments to greater overall budgetary stringency (Pujol was involved in direct negotiations on the Budget) and labour market flexibility, in keeping with CiU's economic liberalism. One small example of the concession of responsibilities and functions to the regions, which arose from this coalition-building process, was the transfer in 1994 of sole regional government responsibility for anti-fraud and quality assurance measures in the food and farm sectors of Catalonia, the Basque Country and Galicia (Real Decreto 8 July 1994).

In October 1995, against a background of mounting allegations of corruption, the CiU withdrew its parliamentary support for the PSOE government and denied backing for the proposed 1996 budget. The PSOE still limped on in government for some more months extending the 1995 budget by decree, but in March 1996 González went to the country again. The mathematics of the election outcome also imposed on the PP the need to quickly become acquainted with the culture of coalition-building, following its emergence as the largest party in Congress, but without an overall majority (see Chapter 4). The long drawn-out process of negotiations, and the insistence on written commitments by the regional and nationalist parties, were part-and-parcel of their fear and suspicion that PP was not genuinely committed to coalition-building, and would more readily renege on any agreement that was not in writing. As for Aznar, he was surprisingly comfortable with the process of negotiation and bargaining in coalition-building, considering the disappointment of his party that it did not receive the overall majority that was widely predicted in the polls. In fact, he had little choice but to bargain. He rationalised his conversion to the coalition-building strategy by arguing that the electorate had charged him with this task and that, therefore, he had no choice but to complete it. And having concluded negotiations with the nationalists and formed a government, Aznar showed that he would adopt this strategy in other policy negotiations, when he set about enticing the unions and employers into another pact to limit wage increases and stimulate job creation.

It might be said that the Constitution writers intended the exercise of coalition-building to be part of the job description of aspirant prime ministers, a practice which has only belatedly come into its own. Ironically though, the outcome of these exercises in coalition-building has been the formation of a series of minority governments, which underlines the distance that still exists between the parties who have negotiated these deals.

Paul Sabatier's notion of 'advocacy coalitions', involving agreements forged between state and societal actors who come together on a basis of common beliefs and values, has limited explanatory value in the context of the big policy issues dominating contemporary Spain. The sort of coalition-building that does take place is mainly between and within political parties and is facilitated and encouraged by the constitutional rules in Spain (Lane 1993: 234). However, weaknesses in Spanish civil society have impeded the process of widespread coalition-building between interest groups and other policy actors. The breakdown in relations between the UGT and the PSOE in the late 1980s in fact reveals a tendency in the opposite direction to coalition-building. But there are signs of change, evident from the relations between the PP government and the social partners in the 1990s.

Client and group networks

Clientelism

The existence of complex networks of 'patrons' and 'clients' at all levels of Spanish society and in its polity has been widely observed. Labelled 'clientelism', it has been presented as a way of conceptualising relations between policy actors and the general public in Spain. Writing in the 1960s, Kenny characterised the Spanish tradition of bureaucratic absolutism since the sixteenth century as involving those seeking bureaucratic posts in direct nepotism or via the conscious use of a patronage group. They (i.e. bureaucratic appointees by this method) subsequently tended 'to perpetuate a procedure which they originally resisted and to which they are committed and indebted' (Kenny 1977: 357). Thus each official, major or minor, 'weaves himself a web of influence and support with the object of absorbing the maximum possible power into his own hands' (Kenny 1977: 357). The widespread nature of this phenomenon during the Franco era may be illustrated by the fact that even at the village level the mayor and *cacique* (the political 'boss') consciously traded patronage for political and material support. The securing of certificates for social benefits, trading and even migration involved the need for an *amigo* (friend) to put in an *enchufe* (a plug) with the right people, at the right time. The success of the client led to a duty of reciprocity, to offer loyalty and support in return to the patron and 'thus to assist in the expansion of the patron's reputation and his emergence as a 'strong' man'. Public policy-making during the dictatorship was also characterised by the articulation of particularistic concerns via such clientelism and, as we have noted, the absence of real interest aggregation. High-level decision-making was open to influence only by those individuals of high socio-economic status who had close enough links with senior regime figures, or local government and quango leaders, to be able to engage in *enchufismo*.

The clientelistic system has continued to thrive in the democratic era, especially during the 1980s and 1990s when the long timespan of the socialists in government allowed the possibility of continuity and regularity in the relationships between patrons and clients, which is, as Clapham notes, an essential ingredient for clientelism (Clapham 1982: 7). At the heart of the biggest network of all was Alfonso Guerra, vice-president (until 1991) and PSOE deputy secretary general. The source of his extensive power lay in the communications and reports coming to him as deputy secretary general from the provincial and local branch leaders about the activities of his supporters and opponents. The rapid expansion of the public sector during the 1980s, particularly due to the establishment of the system of *autonomías*, gave the party élite, including Guerra, substantial resources with which to award its supporters. It reinforced the image of a policy process characterised by clientelism. The electoral system also reinforced the power of the party leadership to control the political future of supporters and opponents: the latter could be demoted on the list, while the former could be promoted, to the extent that their respective political 'debt' or 'credit' implied. It is hardly surprising then that at its peak, Guerra's empire included:

> the party executive and apparatus, the socialist parliamentary group, some key positions in the Moncloa, seven ministries, three regional governments, two universities and growing influence in the judiciary while in its principal regional fief of Andalucia the empire extended to the regional government, seven of the eight provincial councils *(diputaciones)*, 80 per cent of the municipal councils, the regional television channel, cultural and sporting associations and several state savings banks (Gillespie 1994: 56).

The extent of clientelism in public policy-making is, despite such observations, impossible to measure precisely. But its presence in one form or another in the various policy sectors is widely confirmed. Even the *oposiciones*, the system of competitive examinations for most public posts, is widely thought to be rife with abuse.

In rural policy, the REA (*Régimen Especial Agrario*/Special Agricultural Regime) is cited as one particular policy which provided substantial opportunities for clientelistic decision-making by members of the PSOE regime. The policy provided subsidies for rural labourers in Andalusia and Extremadura experiencing temporary unemployment. The main requirement was that they had to have worked for 60 days per annum to secure entitlement to the nine months' subsidy of the REA. Conveniently, one way of doing this was through another scheme, the PER (*Plan de Empleo Rural*/Rural Employment Plan) which was changed in name but little else by the PP in 1996–97 to the Agricultural Employment Scheme, which enabled them to build up the 60 days, if necessary, by undertaking small-scale public works in the villages across these regions. In some cases, PSOE mayors signed the appropriate papers to say they had completed such work, when there was little evidence of it on the ground.

Free holidays for the elderly was another policy open to clientelistic malpractices aimed, in this case, at the 'grey' vote. It is perhaps unsurprising therefore that the PSOE rural and elderly vote rose when its overall vote was in decline. The proliferation of corruption scandals (see Chapter 4), some of them involving relationships between policy-makers and members of the public which directly or indirectly conflict with the law, give some indication of other types of clientelistic decisions. Public contracts for building projects, as emerged in the Naseiro case are a good example of this, not least because that case shows how a political party (PP, in this case) with only (until 1996) a regional power-base could build clientelistic networks in the new Spain. The existence of a thin line between the legal and the illegal in clientelistic exchanges is described by Clapham in the following observation:

though the patron-client bond is a moral one, it is based on a personal or private morality of obligations between individuals, which is reasonably at variance with a public morality based on the goals which an organisation is intended to achieve or the internal virtues which it is intended to exhibit. It is because of this that clientelism acquires its characteristic aura of illegitimacy or corruption (Clapham 1982: 5).

Clientelism also is a particularistic policy strategy that may best be understood within the wider contexts of the development of the Spanish state and the Spanish economy, and the opportunities for abuses of power that such developments have offered individual policy actors.

Policy networks

Policy networks are a way of categorising the many relationships which occur between interest groups, government departments, quangos and the variety of policy actors that play a part in the policy process. Smith defines policy networks as a meso-level concept which is concerned with explaining behaviour within particular sections of the State or particular policy areas (Smith 1993: 7). Rhodes and Marsh distinguish between two main types of policy network: first, a 'policy community' in which the number of participants is limited and share similar economic interests and basic values, possess resources and have a fairly even balance of power between them; second, an 'issue network' in which the number of participants is large, with wide-ranging interests, fluctuating contacts, and viewpoints and values in conflict as well as shared (Rhodes and Marsh 1992). These terms embody two extremes – one highly integrated, the other highly fragmented – in the way that groups and state institutions conduct their relations. Do they offer a useful framework for analysing policy-making in Spain? One way of addressing the question is by looking at the actual range of organised interests in Spanish political life. The weakness of Spanish civil society has already been alluded to (Chapter 1) and the limited degree of integration facilitated by interest-group organisations makes rather unlikely the widespread applicability of a theoretical framework which hinges on horizontal linkages between groups in society. Moreover, the persuasiveness of the party grip over state institutional structures is reflected, to at least some extent, in civil society. (Even the Red Cross and the Spanish Organisation for the Blind are government controlled.) This suggests a set of circumstances which are less than congenial for the growth of policy networks in Spain.

The organisation of interests in Spain

Military interests and Catholic Church interests were closely linked to the Francoist state by means of interlocking networks. The élitist Catholic lay organisation, the Opus Dei, was at the heart of some influential networks, particularly in the 1950s and 1960s when members played a key role in developing Spain's economic policy (see Chapter 1). Opus Dei continues to have a presence among the conservative and business élite that support the PP government, and some members of that government are said to be members (Ross 1997: 113). The mobilisation of independent, economic and social interests was banned for the period of the dictatorship, and existed only in clandestine form. With democracy came a resurgence of interest group activity.

Trade unions

Despite the establishment of what were called 'vertical syndicates' (*sindicatos verticales*) in the OSE, under the direction of the Franco government which jointly represented the official interests both of labour and management, the real demands of labour stimulated the growth of unofficial union activity. This was most notable from the development of the *comisiones obreras* in the 1960s, whose activities included negotiations with employers. The legalisation of the trade unions after the restoration of democracy led to the emergence of two main forces: the UGT and CCOO, led by Nicolás Redondo and Marcelino Camacho respectively.

The UGT was founded by the PSOE in 1888 and maintained close links with it in the early years of post-Franco democracy, until the mid-1980s. Disillusionment with neo-liberal aspects of the labour market policy shift of the PSOE led to the break-up of this relationship in 1990. The objective of the UGT, to depoliticise industrial relations and to establish a neo-corporatist machinery for labour market policy-making and delivery, was only half-heartedly supported by the PSOE in the early 1980s and hardly at all as the decade wore on. Membership of the UGT, as with all Spanish trade unions, was also contracting (it declined from about 50 per cent to 10 per cent of the workforce between 1975 and 1995) despite the fact that it was the largest trade union. This was just as important a reason for its decreasing significance to the PSOE government. The CCOO emerged out of the semi-clandestine factory floor *comisiones obreras* and was closely linked to the PCE – itself, since 1986, a part of the IU coalition – after the re-establishment of democracy (see Chapter 3). The increased disillusionment of the UGT with the PSOE government gave rise to greater co-ordination and joint action in industrial disputes (e.g. the one-day general strikes of December 1988, May 1992 and January 1994), but this signified weakness in both organisations more than strength. The changing role of trade unionism in the economic landscape of 1990s Spain led to more moderation and less militancy in trade union tactics. New leaders of UGT (Cándido Méndez) and CCOO (Antonio Gutiérrez) reflected this change of emphasis. Smaller union organisations also emerged with varying bases of support: the USO (*Unión Sindical Obrera*/Syndicalist Workers Union), influenced by progressive Catholic ideas, was closely associated with the UCD; the ELA–STV (*Eusko Langileen Alkartasuna–Solidaridad de Trabajadores Vascos*/Basque Workers

Solidarity) and the CIG (*Converxencia Intersindical Gallega*/Galician Trade Union) were regional unions while the CNT (*Confederación Nacional de Trabajadores*/ National Workers Confederation) and its offshoot the CGT (*Confederación General del Trabajo*/General Labour Confederation) were anarcho-syndicalist organisations. Also, independent unions grew from the higher skilled and better paid occupational groups. Even the establishment in 1992 of the CES, while paying lip-service to the 'neo-corporatist' approach, did little to alter the predominant image of trade union weakness and detachment from key policy-making in Spain. Nor did it suggest the prevalence of a policy style based upon firmly entrenched 'policy networks'. However, ministers have continued to be sensitive to trades union concerns, such as any threats to labour market regulations, and have treaded carefully in trying to make the labour market more flexible.

Employers organisations

The CEOE, while more representative of interests (about 90 per cent of employers) than trades unions, has not been formally incorporated into policy-making in Spain. It is the co-ordinating body of a multitude of employers confederations operating at regional, provincial and sectoral levels and represents their concerns at all levels of government and the EU, tending to avoid conflict and controversy on issues that divide its members. (For example, it represents employers interests on the CES.) In combination with its partner organisation, the CEPYME (*Confederación Española de Pequeñas y Medianas Empresas*/Spanish Confederation of Small and Medium-Sized Firms), it has tended to eclipse all other rival employers groups. It played a supportive role with the trades unions in forging the tripartite agreements of the late 1970s and early 1980s, but like them has been denied a central role in policy-making.

After the election of José María Cuevas to its leadership in 1984, the CEOE worked to forge a right-of-centre opposition to the PSOE. It provided a means of articulating an anti-statist vision of Spanish society (Martínez Lucio 1991: 54). After establishment of PP, the CEOE gave it considerable support. However Aznar was careful not to be seen to be the employers party and distanced himself from CEOE's post election demands issued in 1996.

Farming and food policy: the EU and the growth of policy networks

After the transition period and the restoration of freedom of association to various groups in Spanish society, there followed some interest aggregation in rural Spain reflecting the heterogenous structure of its agrarian society. From the 1970s, a process of consolidation took place which led to the emergence of some major groups in the sector. The impact of the EC-EU has been one factor that has led to the emergence of some policy networks in this sector.

Representing mainly the large landowners, CNAG (*Confederacíon Nacional de Agricultores y Ganaderos*/National Agricultural and Livestock Farmers

Federation) has regarded itself as a business organisation mainly concerned with negotiating good farm product price levels. It is a member of the CEOE. It inherits a tradition of large farmer organisation, albeit interrupted by the Franco era, stretching back to the nineteenth century. Closely linked to CNAG is CNJA (*Centro Nacional de Jóvenes Agricultores*/National Centre of Young Farmers. Another group, COAG, has emerged to represent the interest of small farmers, in what is a more locally and regionally autonomous interest group. Its policies reflect a more global view of the problems affecting its members, with an emphasis on farm structures. The COAG has also been more ready to confront the government and food industries than CNAG. More significantly, both these organisations are very widely stretched in the range of interests they represent, covering many regions and products, a factor which gives rise to some conflict in the sector (García Delgado 1988). At the end of the 1980s other farm groups emerged. Spain's membership of the EC was an important stimulus to the reorganisation of representation in the farm sector. Among the new groups the most important was ASAJA (*Asociación Agraria Jóvenes Agricultores*/Agricultural Association of Young Farmers) (Molins and Casademunt 1998: 139).

Besides these organisations there are weaker groups, such as the UPA (*Unión de Pequeños Agricultores*/Small Farmers Union). Farm workers are mainly affiliated to the Farm Workers Commission, which is linked to the CCOO. To a lesser extent, farm workers are members of the UGT via its landworkers federation, and, historically at least, closer to the PSOE.

Since Spain entered the EC, relations between the farm organisations and the government have been fraught with difficult circumstances, not helped by the reluctance of the government to grant them any significant negotiation or consultation rights. The fragmented structure of representation which we have described means that 'issue networks' rather than 'policy community' would appear to serve as a more appropriate metaphor to describe the relationships between policy actors in the Spanish farming sector. Particularly difficult have been relations between these groups and Carlos Romero, when he was agriculture minister, making the creation of a close-knit policy community doubly unlikely. In 1987, the denial of consultation rights became a contentious enough issue for COAG, CNAG, CNJA and other groups to hold a series of demonstrations and road blocks across Spain. At various meetings, Romero was attacked for not consulting with them. Eventually in 1988, a meeting took place between representatives of the agriculture ministry, MAPA, led by Romero and the farms organisations, in addition to the two Spanish agricultural co-operative organisations, the UCAE (*Unión de Co-operativas Agrarias de España*/Spanish Farmers Co-operatives Union) and the AECA (*Associación Española de Co-operativas Agrarias*/Association of Spanish Farm Co-operatives). The Spanish food and drinks industry federation FIAB (*Federación Española de Industrias de Alimentación y Bebida*/Food and Drinks Federation) was also represented. According to Romero, the meeting was intended to eval-

uate developments in the agricultural sector after two years of EC membership. More importantly, as Spain held the Presidency of the EC for the first time
in 1989, a quiescent farm lobby was desirable, to save the minister embarrassing domestic disturbances while he chaired Council of Ministers' meetings. In
any event, controversial issues were skirted and the meeting was mainly taken
up with a rather harmless (and irrelevant for most of those present) analysis
of departmental statistics for the agricultural sector. Working groups met subsequently to discuss alternatives to the government–EC policies in each sector.
Farm organisations remained sceptical and suspicious of Romero's motives
although they welcomed the meeting generally as a shift towards dialogue in
the policy process. Nevertheless demonstrations continued into 1989 including, embarrassingly for Romero, at Salamanca, where he hosted an EC
Council of Agriculture Ministers meeting, within earshot of Spanish farm
demonstrators.

Romero's successor, Pedro Solbes, tried to change this atmosphere of suspicion by promising open dialogue with all areas of Spanish agriculture, from the
unions to the farm and food industry organisations (*El Agraa* 12 April 1991:
N4). Significantly, it was pressure arising from preparations for the SEM (Single
European Market), as well as the completion of Spain's EC transition period and
CAP reforms that led to at least a partial shift and improvement in relations
between agricultural and food organisations and the state. Organisations with
an interest in food exports, in particular, participated in policy networks on a
limited scale. The SEM prompted initiatives to co-ordinate and enhance agricultural marketing, in which MAPA was to be a key policy actor, such as a special
export promotions department. It also prompted the formation of consortia of
Spain's many small food industry firms, to encourage joint sales and advertising strategies. Examples of such consortia included such diverse sectors as
those of Spanish cheese-makers, citrus fruit and serrano ham producers, the
latter comprising 32 members, who reached agreement on rigorous quality
standards and the conduct of joint advertising campaigns. The availability of
EC funds to encourage such co-operation as well as the restructuring of the
farm and food sectors served as an important incentive to the construction of
policy networks, not least to those sectors fearing the worst form of competition
after full integration in the EC. For instance, the ANNP (*Asociación Nacional de
Productores Pollo*/National Association of Broiler Producers) submitted a
restructuring plan to MAPA in 1991 seeking government and EC funds to
enable their members to survive competition in the EU after the Single Market
came into effect. The establishment of producer associations in line with EC
directives were also encouraged. Abel Matutes noted, in response to a European
parliamentary question in 1992, that there were 51 recognised producer associations in Spain with 57,000 members which compared favourably with other
member states (European Parliamentary Debates 10 April 1992: 323). At the
local level, the development of farmer co-operatives were also encouraged,
under the direction of the Ministry of Labour and the regional governments.

These bodies and groups provided the participants for some policy networks in the food and farming sectors.

One of the most comprehensive and integrated consultation and planning exercises, involving the government and the food and agriculture sector, resulted in the preparation in 1992 of a Fresh Fruit and Vegetables Harmonisation Promotion Plan. A wide range and large number of organisations participated. The plan which emerged from these consultations contained a clear set of objectives on matters such as quality control. It listed various measures and actions to be taken to achieve the objectives, like the creation of an inter-ministerial team to co-ordinate policy. It also identified various instruments to make its actions effective, including legal rules (MAPA 1992: 272–6).

It is not so surprising that the fresh fruit and vegetable sector should have been brought into close co-operation with state institutions in 1992 in a policy network concerned with planning for the sector. However, a number of points need to be made about this development: first, this sector was one of the newest and most rapidly expanding in Spain and it was unencumbered by the more deeply embedded political suspicions present in the more traditional farm sectors; second, this policy network was prompted by the State, as much to fulfil its own obligations in the EC under the SEA, as to mollify the demands of sectoral organisations; and third, the negotiation by Spain for early full integration for most of its agricultural products into the common market organisation created an added impetus to engage in this way with producers and other groups.

This co-operation between policy actors has been an increasing reality in Spain 's agricultural food sector in the 1990s and it is likely to continue as state and sectoral organisations fight parallel battles for Spanish agriculture in EU and international policy arenas. But conflict between the policy actors involved in these networks on national policy issues (e.g. taxation) is likely to continue too. Central government control over policy resources emanating from the EU is still firm in Spain. Moreover, the fragmented pattern of policy networks there indicates that MAPA encourages, as it deems necessary, the development of appropriate policy networks to meet its own and EU needs for decision-making and policy implementation.

Implementation

The complexity of the many policy-making strategies described above does not give way to a straightforward implementation process. The labyrinthine administrative and agenda-setting process described in Chapter 5 reveals an extensive machinery for policy delivery at all levels of the Spanish state and its subsidiary parts. This machinery incorporates, too, a variety of organisational and political environments which, in some cases, serve to constrain and in all cases to shape the manner and timing of the delivery of public policies, thereby affecting their outcome. As Pressman and Wildavsky discovered in the 1960s about policy implementation generally: problems can arise at the implementation stage which frustrate the objectives of decision-makers.

Difficulties in implementation may be analysed from two main perspectives. One would lead us to explore the failure of policies to fulfil their objectives or to achieve the outputs anticipated by the policy-makers, essentially an exercise in evaluation. The other difficulty is more complex and involves observing the failures and obstructions that occur in the processes of implementation in Spain. It is this latter concept with which we are concerned here, when we ask the question: why is it that some policies fail to get implemented in the Spanish policy process? (Gunn 1978: 169–76).

One reason for this can be the **absence of sufficient political will** among those undertaking the making of policy, a factor which points strongly to the sort of policies designed for what Edelman terms 'symbolic' more than real implementation (Edelman 1964). This reluctant approach to implementation can be explained by such reasons as the fear of an electoral backlash or an unwillingness to alienate party supporters or regime clients. The non-enforcement of the rules covering those many thousands who undertook construction activities, such as building holiday homes, without planning permission along the Spanish coastline is a small but instructive environmental policy case in point (Hooper 1995: 223–4). The existence of only small penalties for breaches to these same rules, which are imposed after a lengthy process of investigation, suggests that the relevant policy regulations have largely had symbolic significance from the outset and were never actually intended to be fully applied. Another case is industrial policy, which has been affected by a reluctance of policy-makers to tackle key implementation issues. Substantive reform to labour legislation, which would have made the declared goal of a flexible labour market achievable, was delayed until 1993 because the PSOE government was reluctant to confront the trade unions.

Weak control mechanisms explain why many EC/EU directives, for instance, are only slowly implemented, indicating a considerable degree of ground-level discretion for policy actors engaged in implementation in the relevant policy areas. By accommodating a flexible approach to implementation there is greater opportunity for caution and tardiness if not downright obstruction, than if a centrally controlled top-down approach applied. Abattoir compliance with health and safety regulations and sugar factory rationalisation programmes are some small examples. By June 1992, only 4.2 per cent of abattoirs in Spain were said to have conformed to EC requirements enabling them to trade in the SEA, compared to a 15 per cent EC average. However, in the case of the sugar manufacturing sector, the government was much more forceful in implementing a 'rationalisation' plan that made the closure of many sugar factories inevitable, with knock-on effects for sugar beet growers. Regional policy also reveals the weaknesses sometimes inherent in policy implementation.

Despite the concentration of state subsidies in old industrial regions such as Asturias, there is no guarantee that the much coveted high-technology industries will locate there. Multinationals, particularly, will have a variety of options to choose from and not necessarily within Spain.

Lack of finance is a common problem lying behind policy implementation failure which, especially in 'neo-liberal' political environments, tends to be spoken of in the same breath as management inefficiency:

- Back in the Franco era, the paucity of tax inspectors made tax collection only partial, thus creating a cycle of revenue shortage. So widespread was the problem that the government adopted a system for calculating corporation tax, not based, as one might expect, on the profits of individual firms, but by estimating the profits of a particular industrial sector in each region and dividing the profit total by the number of firms in the same regions. Thus the tax liability of a firm was calculated by reference to the profitability of its competitor as well as itself: hardly a fair or efficient method of taxation. With democracy, the government introduced tax law reforms and allocated more funds for the recruitment and training of extra tax officials, with considerably improved results in the area of tax collection. This led to an increase in funds available for other public expenditure projects.
- Health policy implementation, in Spain as elsewhere, has been constantly affected by funding shortfalls. As the health services were reformed through the Health Act passed in 1986, funding needs also increased, caused by wider public eligibility for services, together with the availability of more expensive treatments. Attempts by Health Minister Abril Martorell to introduce reforms using stricter management guidelines for hospital expenditure, following their transformation into separate trusts or companies, were blocked by health workers who threatened strike action.
- In education policy, the lack of sufficient finance has been linked to the high drop-out rate in pre-university education. The availability of limited choices of courses for students was just one of the factors identified for the high wastage.
- In transport policy, the practice of granting private concessions for the construction of motorways was changed in the late 1980s to direct construction by the State. Private builders were borrowing funds on the international money markets for these projects and the government was obliged to underwrite the many foreign exchange risks involved (*Euromoney Supplement* March 1989: 159).

Technical difficulties, unforseen by those who draft legislation or policy, are another and not uncommon occurrence generally in the policy process and **link implementation failure to policy ambiguity.** The 1985 Tax Act of Miguel Boyer contained a loop-hole which enabled savers to avoid tax on their savings interest by investing in single premium insurance policies, including those of bank-controlled insurance companies (Hooper 1995: 239). Bank officials consequently advised their clients to move savings out of all tax-attracting accounts into such policies. This was a form of legal tax evasion facilitated by technical weaknesses in the law, which was exploited by both the banks and their customers at the expense of the state. The elimination of this ambiguity in the law thereafter improved the level of tax collection on savings.

Legal disputes have dogged the relationships between the nationalities and regions and the state, particularly during the 1980s, when the large PSOE majority in the Cortes made political disputes a rather less effective way for the regions to achieve results. Part of the problem has been the competition between regions, caused by the existence of various routes by which they could attain autonomy, and the different powers attached to each statute of autonomy (see Chapter 2). Interestingly, as coalition-building increased between the regions and the centre in the 1990s (when the PSOE and PP did not have an effective parliamentary majority), the amount of legal challenges dropped sharply (see Chapter 2).

- Legal disputes have also involved the EU. The Galician regional government was accused of offering payments to milk-processing companies to cover the complete cost of transplanting their operations from other regions of Spain. The European Commission felt it necessary to investigate whether such incentives served as a flaunting of its competition rules.
- The weakness of the law in ensuring that policies are fully implemented is a problem also illustrated forcefully by the failure to prosecute environmental offenders in Spain, despite the existence of the concept of an environmental offence in the country's criminal code since 1983.

The absence of adequate coalition-building at the implementation stage may be linked to the existence of **poor co-ordination** in policy delivery. It is not difficult to find examples of this in Spain, where the machinery of policy implementation is so complex:

- Policing Spain, for instance, involves many overlapping bodies: the *Guardia Civil* (Civil Guard), the *Cuerpo Nacional de Policía* (CNP – National Police Force), the Basque *Ertzaintza*, the Catalan *Mossos d'Esquadra* and the municipal police forces in various towns. It creates many opportunities for poor co-ordination in police activities.
- Duplication and overlapping responsibilities between regional and central government in many policy areas is a particular and expensive by-product of the growth of the autonomous system. One proposed solution to this has been the suggestion by Manuel Fraga (President of the *Xunta de Galicia*) for an *administración única* (a single administration) which would apply the principle of 'subsidiarity', or minimum interference from the centre, to regional government.
- The consequences of poor co-ordination can be very serious if not fatal. One small example illustrates the point. The discovery of illegal traces of

Clenbuterol in livestock products in Catalonia in 1992 pointed to a break-down in the administrative procedures for regulating this aspect of public health and blocking such illegal practices. The failure required an urgent response in the form of clearly designated and demarcated responsibilities for public health policy implementation.

- In tourism policy, co-ordination problems may also be identified (Pridham 1996: 22). In theory, regions have 'exclusive' responsibility for this sector. In practice, the role of the central administration can be crucial in delivering policies such as the awarding of preferential loans for tourism development.
- In some cases, such as in environmental policy, the lack of co-ordination was due to the wide dispersal of responsibility for this policy area across many ministries (Ross 1997: 174). This, in turn, reflected the absolute priority given for many years to economic growth, which was built into the structure of the government administration. It only altered, in 1996, when an Environment Ministry was established by Aznar.

Competition policy and implementation

The case of competition policy illustrates how policy implementation in Spain may be affected by a number of factors simultaneously (Cases 1996: 180–200). The protection of market competition in Spain was first given legal status by the Law for the Prohibition of Anti-competitive Practices (*Ley de Represión de Prácticas Restrictivas de la Competencia*) passed in 1963. It was a response to the pressures, mainly external, on the Francoist regime for the liberalisation of the Spanish economy.

The Competition Tribunal established under the Act was the main implementing body with responsibility for identifying the existence of anti-competitive practices. The failure of the Tribunal to implement the 1963 law has been attributed to a number of factors. These included the low level of commitment of the public authorities to having an effective competition law, weaknesses in the organisational framework responsible for the co-ordination of competition policy (e.g. the Competition Tribunal would not impose sanctions for breaches of policy and none were imposed until 1988), and insufficient resources available to monitor competition. As a result of those implementation failures, the 1963 Act had little or no deterrent effect to businesses intent on breaching market competition.

Competition law was revised through the Competition Law (*Ley de Defensa de la Competencia*) enacted in 1989. It was prompted, first, by the 1978 Constitution which gave the public authorities a responsibility for protecting the free operations of the market economy (article 38). Second, Spain's accession to the EC required a complete revision of its competition law to bring it into line with EC norms. Although the 1989 law gave the Tribunal greater powers in some key areas, such as the control of mergers of enterprises, it is the government (notably the Ministry of Economy and Finance) and not the Tribunal which has been given the power to control them. The Tribunal role in this respect is reduced to that of giving an opinion. Problems of policy implementation still persist. Duplication and delays persist. Thus EU commitments may have revised the status of competition policy and ensured that Spanish law is by and large consistent with the EU, but it does not guarantee that the quality of policy implementation is enhanced.

Policy implementation in Spain

The prevailing **environment of implementation** is, arguably, the most significant factor in determining how particular policies are implemented. As Lane notes, **'trust and responsibility'** are basic requirements in the implementation process: 'An implementation process is a combination of responsibility and trust, both in the relation between citizens and the public sector in general and in the relation between politicians and officials' (Lane 1993: 103–4).

The historic reluctance of policy-makers in Spain to incorporate collective policy actors such as pressure groups into the policy process other than in a temporary, rather expedient, way has led, as we have seen, to a top-down policy implementation style, with élitist tendencies. The related absence of mutual trust between policy actors has been symbolised by strikes and demonstrations. Decentralising tendencies in government, through the autonomous communities system, has generated another tendency with greater room for manoeuvre and discretion in policy implementation as well as opportunities for rule-challenging, disruption and defiance of central government.

Policy delivery within clientelistic networks mediated through political and party 'brokers' is widespread throughout the system. It has emanated from a fundamental public distrust of the capacity of bureaucratic structures to implement policy and allocate public goods in a rational and fair way. Rather than generating widespread trust in public organisations leading to the decline of this phenomenon, the emergence of democratic structures and the autonomous state appears to have led to its renewal and refinement to fit the new circumstances. Moreover, privatisation and commercial opportunism have apparently reinvigorated the trend by providing new resources for 'patrons' to distribute: the many cases of 'sleaze' and corruption already discussed (Chapter 4) illustrate only some of its ugly public manifestations.

More positive images of policy implementation may also be observed. The outcome of some indeterminate regional elections and the general elections of 1993 and 1996 have stimulated a multitude of coalition-building measures among regions and nationalities, and between them and the centre, in making as well as implementing policies. Unlike Sabatier's concept of 'advocacy coalitions', the resulting relationships are, so far, quite fluid, opportunistic and the result of electoral 'accidents' or institutional requirements such as EU regional programme rules, rather than based on a shared ideology and belief-system. The emergence of two unstable 'minority' governments in the 1990s provide proof of this. It may be surmised that the persistence of many of these relationships and informal coalitions will eventually generate the requisite levels of trust and responsibility, to achieve objectives which Lane holds to be at the core of good implementation (Lane 1993: 105). This could be helped by the development of more 'ideologically compact' alignments in government formation: the PSOE and IU on the left and PP, PNV and CiU on the centre right for example.

Conclusion

Consensus based, policy-making strategies were evident in the early years of democratic transition but were reserved mainly for constitutional issues. Social and economic policy occasionally wore some of the trappings of 'corporatist' interaction but more frequently was riven by overt forms of conflict, and public clashes between policy actors, e.g. in street demonstrations. An executive-dominated style of policy-making was evident, particularly in the 1980s, when the absence of effective parliamentary opposition gave the government a virtual *carte blanche* on policy. Coalition-building and negotiated strategies were signalled as the preferred approach by the authors of the Constitution, e.g. through their provision for various layers of government. It is only in the 1990s, however, that this has become the predominant *modus operandi*, mainly with the key nationalist parties, but to some extent too with unions and management on policy issues such as the conditions of employment contracts. Clientelism presents itself at all levels of the policy machinery in Spain as a persistent phenomenon in the routine delivery of policy resources, in exchange for such 'commodities' as political support or, in some cases, individual material gain for the policy actors with access to such policy resources. There is no clear evidence to suggest that clientelism in Spain is just a vestigial hangover in the process of transformation from a traditional to a modern society. Instead, it appears to be an intrinsic part of the structure of Spain's policy process. Policy networks provide a way of depicting a style of interaction between policy actors at the middle (or meso) levels of policy-making in some sectors. The absence of widespread interest group organisation in Spain makes the pertinence of this approach rather limited, especially as whatever interest group penetration there is tends to be rather weak in the Spanish polity. But EU membership has prompted some policy network development in Spain.

Policy implementation approaches tend to reflect those of policy-making. Successful policy implementation in late 1990s Spain, therefore, tends to depend mainly on coalition-building exercises, especially between the regions and the centre there. The continued enhancement of the role of the regions in policy delivery is likely to require continued co-operation and negotiations between regional and central government policy actors.

References

Allum, P. (1995) *State and Society in Western Europe*, Cambridge, Polity Press.

Berger, S. (1981) *Organising Interests in Western Europe: Pluralism, Corporatism and the Transformation of Politics*, Cambridge, Cambridge University Press

Cases, L. (1996) 'Competition Law and Policy in Spain: Implementation in an Interventionist Tradition', in G. Majone (ed.), *Regulating Europe*, London, Macmillan.

Clapham, C. (1982) *Private Patronage and Public Power*, London, Frances Pinter.

The Economist (14 December 1996) 'Spain: A Survey'.

Edelman, M. (1964) *The Symbolic Uses of Politics*, Urbana, University of Illinois Press.

El Agraa (12 April 1991) N4.

Euromoney Supplement (March 1989) 'Spain Banks on its Bootstraps', pp. 146–66.

European Parliamentary Debates (1992) 10 April, p. 323.

Garcia Delgado, J.L. (ed.) (1988) *España: Economía*, Madrid, Espara Calpe.

Gillespie, R. (1994) 'The Resurgence of Factionalism in the Spanish Socialist Workers' Party', in D.S. Bell and E. Shaw (eds), *Conflict and Cohesion in Western European Social Democratic Parties*, London, Pinter.

Gunn, L. (1978) 'Why is implementation so difficult?', *Management Services in Government*, 38, pp. 169–76.

Gunther, R. (1996) 'The Impact of Regime Change on Public Policy: The Case of Spain', *Journal of Public Policy*, 16:2.

Heywood, P. (1995) *The Government and Politics of Spain*, London, Macmillan.

Hooper, J. (1995) *The New Spaniards*, London, Penguin.

Kenny, M. (1977) 'Patterns of Patronage in Spain', in S.W. Schmidt, J.C. Scott, J.C. Landé, and L. Guasti (eds), *Friends, Followers and Factions: A Reader in Political Clientelism*, Berkeley, Calif., University of California Press.

Lane, J.E. (1993) *The Public Sector: Concepts, Models and Approaches*, London, Sage.

Laver, M. and N. Schofield (1990) *The Politics of Coalition in Europe*, Oxford, Oxford University Press.

Lawlor, T. and M. Rigby (eds) (1998) *Contemporary Spain*, London, Longman.

Lipjhart, A. (1998) 'A Mediterranean Model of Democracy? The Southern European Democracies in Comparative Perspective', *West European Politics*, 11:7.

Lukes, S. (1974) *Power: A Radical View*, London, Macmillan.

MAPA (*Ministerio de Agricultura Pesca y Alimentación*) (1992) *La Agricultura, La Pesca y La Alimentación*, Madrid, Centro de Publicaciones.

Martínez Lucio, M. (1991) 'Employer Identity and the Politics of the Labour Market in Spain', *West European Politics*, 14:1.

Martínez Lucio, M. (1992) 'Spain: Constructing Institutions and Actors in a Context of Change', in A. Ferner and R. Hyman (eds), *Industrial Relations in the New Europe*, London, Blackwell.

Molins, J.M. and A. Casademunt (1998) 'Pressure Groups and the Articulation of Interests', *West European Politics*, 21:4, pp. 124–46.

Pridham, G. (1996) 'Tourism Policy in Mediterranean Europe: Towards Sustainable Development?', University of Bristol, Centre for Mediterranean Studies, Occasional Paper 15, pp. 5–27.

Real Decreto 8 July 1994 Num. 1552/1994, 2165/1994.

Rhodes, R. and D. Marsh (1992) *Policy Networks in British Government*, Oxford, Oxford University Press.

Richardson, J.J. (ed.) (1982) *Policy Styles in Western Europe*, London, George Allen and Unwin.

Ross, C. (1997) *Contemporary Spain: A Handbook*, London, Arnold.

Salmon, K. (1995) *The Modern Spanish Economy*, 2nd edn, London, Pinter.

Smith, M.J. (1993) *Pressure, Power and Politics*, Hemel Hempstead, Harvester Wheatsheaf.

7

Spain in the European Union

The story of Spain's post-war journey from European pariah to EC presidency in the years between the 1950s and the 1990s is, on the face of it, quite remarkable. The first tentative efforts of the 'technocrats' of Franco's government to gain entry to the EC in 1962 and 1964 were rejected, not least because of the member-states' opposition to the Franco dictatorship. By the end of 1989 Spain had already assumed the EC Presidency for the first time and, on that occasion and in 1995, proved itself to be a strong advocate of further European integration. Of course, Spain was not the only country to have had its initial application to the EC rejected. The UK was also rebuffed. However, the case of Spain was extraordinary in that, during this time, it not only succeeded in becoming a key player in the EC/EU, but also entirely reshaped its external relations policies. This it did by moving away from isolationism and neutrality, to economic and political integration in Europe, and by joining and playing an active role in the major western alliances and international organisations. This occurred against the backdrop of democratic transition and consolidation in the late 1970s and early 1980s. The choice of Spain's Foreign Minister, Javier Solana, to succeed Willy Claes as Secretary General of NATO at the end of 1995, neatly symbolised the restoration of Spain as a leading player among the western family of states, a status it had lost as long ago as 1815, at the Congress of Vienna. Qualification for membership of the first wave of EU states joining EMU from January 1999 reinforced Spain's European credentials.

The road to European Community Membership

Spain's policy towards Europe is partly shaped by history. Important landmarks include the following:

- The fact that since the Napoleonic wars Spain did not have the status of a

great European power, a steep fall from the illustrious position it had occu-
pied in earlier centuries.
- Despite official neutrality during the Second World War, Franco's Spain was
still identified with the Axis powers. In 1946, the United Nations encouraged
its member-states to break diplomatic relations with Spain (it reversed its
policy in 1950). Spain did not receive any Marshall Aid money.
- In 1953, Spain's isolation was broken by military-base agreements reached
with the USA and a concordat with the Vatican.
- A legacy of the Franco regime was that 'Europe' became synonymous with
the EC and democracy, and the USA and NATO with the dictatorship.

Despite the rejection of its initial applications to the EC, later negotiations produced a limited preferential trade agreement in 1970. This gave Spanish goods
(mostly industrial) some access to the EEC markets of the then six member-
states,[1] without eroding Spain's own protective barriers. Although beneficial to
Spanish exports, this foothold was precarious. Efforts to extend the agreement
in 1975, to include the three new members who had joined in 1973 (UK,
Ireland and Denmark), were abandoned by the EEC, in protest against controversial executions of ETA and FRAP (*Frente Revolutionario Anti-fascista y
Patriota*/Revolutionary Anti-Fascist Patriotic Front) members by the Franco
regime during that year. Not until after the death of Franco was further
progress made, and in July 1977 a formal bid for membership of the EEC was
lodged, coinciding with the long sought-after extension of the 1970 preferential trade agreement.

The North Atlantic Treaty Organisation membership debate

The circumstances leading up to Spain's membership of the EC cannot be
viewed in isolation from the events which punctuated the evolution of its external relations policies generally after the end of Franco's rule in 1975. A controversial issue was the renewal of the US military-base accords (first signed at the
Pact of Madrid in 1953), negotiations on which were postponed in 1978, with
the promise of a 'national debate' on NATO membership generally sometime in
the future. In 1981, that debate commenced. It was dominated by the figure of
Leopoldo Calvo-Sotelo, the UCD minister in charge of negotiations with the EEC
who, in January 1981, became prime minister, succeeding Adolfo Suárez.
Despite a weak parliamentary position, he declared in his opening speech to
parliament, in February 1981, the intention of integrating Spain into NATO.
His efforts were almost rendered obsolete by the *coup* attempt of 23 February
1981 but its suppression meant that Calvo-Sotelo was able to press on with his
plans which were informed by a pro-American, internationalist outlook. In
spring 1981, during a visit to West Germany, he declared that the desire for
Spanish membership of NATO was a product of Spain's European policy,

---

[1] France, Germany, Belgium, Netherlands, Luxembourg, Italy

linking the NATO accession plan firmly to its EEC ambitions. The UCD government pushed the process forward so as to reach agreement with the USA as quickly as possible before the general election in Spain. Calvo-Sotelo first won parliamentary support for adhesion to NATO in October 1981, and in December, the protocol of adhesion was signed by the foreign ministers of the Atlantic Alliance (Rodrigo 1995: 58).

The election, which took place in October 1982, put the PSOE – which was formally committed in its election manifesto to a policy of revoking the UCD's NATO agreements – into government. Despite its manifesto commitment, the new PSOE government was, in reality, divided. On the one side were those, led by the prime minister, Felipe González (and including the then Secretary of State for EEC Affairs (Manuel Marín), the Economy Minister (Miguel Boyer) and the Defence Minister (Narcís Serra) who were concerned that withdrawal from NATO might jeopardise Spain's chances of gaining EEC membership. On the other side were those, led by the deputy prime minister, Alfonso Guerra (and including the Minister for Foreign Affairs (Fernando Morán) and (ironically, in retrospect) the Interior Minister and future NATO Secretary General (Javier Solana), who refused to see any important connection between membership of the two organisations that could over-ride the PSOE's principled objection to NATO membership. How was this conundrum resolved? Initially under the Socialists, the base accords were ratified, while membership of NATO was suspended, until the outcome of a proposed referendum on the matter was known. The events leading up to that referendum in March 1986, which González won, were also closely linked to the circumstances of Spain's accession to the EEC.

The so-called 'Decalogue of Peace and Security', presented by González to parliament in October 1984, broadly supported membership of the NATO Alliance and promised talks on the issue with those opposition parties who had been in favour of NATO membership in 1981. Then, at the thirtieth party congress of the PSOE in December 1984 he won votes of support both for his policy and for the proposed referendum, although some socialists continued to be opposed to NATO membership (Rodrigo 1995: 61–3). Military acquiescence towards the policies of a socialist government in Spain was strengthened by the ongoing process of army modernisation and the appointment of new chiefs-of-staff in 1984. The appetite of the military-industrial élite, mainly vested in INI, was whetted by the PSOE government's preference for joint-European and US defence industry projects. Public opinion, however, was the major unknown. Polls in March 1983 revealed that while 49 per cent of the public were against NATO membership, only 13 per cent were in favour. For a decision that would be taken by a referendum, the situation did not augur well for González, but he also had some leverage to employ in countering the prevailing trend.

While public opinion was opposed to NATO membership, it was favourably disposed to EEC membership and González used the knowledge of this to good effect. To the recalcitrants in his party and in the public debate he suggested that the support for Spain's membership of the EEC in some member-states, such as Germany and Britain (in the face of opposition from France, for example), would not be as vigorous if it removed itself from NATO. To the EEC member-states, it was made clear that generosity in their terms of agreement to Spain's accession would make the task of overcoming public opposition to NATO easier (Gillespie, Rodrigo and Story 1995: 39). Ultimately, the timing of the NATO referendum was in González's hands. He refrained from holding it until he was satisfied that the degree of generosity being offered in the negotiations for Spain's membership of the EEC had maximised his chances of winning a majority in the referendum vote on NATO. When he did hold that referendum vote, he won it with the support of 52.5 per cent of the voters. Between 1986 and 1989 the precise form that Spain's integration into NATO would take was negotiated. Agreements were subsequently signed in 1989 and in later years (Rodrigo 1995: 62–5).

Other obstacles to European Community membership

France provided the main source of objection to Spanish, and indeed Portuguese, EC entry. There were a number of difficulties in the relationships between them:

1 Spain, like Britain in the 1960s, was reluctant to bow deferentially to French leadership in the EC. It was difficult to ignore its own historic status as a leading European state;
2 France was reluctant to open the doors to the waves of immigrants, which it feared were poised to cross its frontiers from the Iberian peninsula, brandishing newly acquired EC citizenship;
3 Spain was intermittently in rancorous dispute with France over the issue of alleged French foot-dragging in extraditing suspected Basque terrorists;
4 the large size of Spain's agricultural industry presented economic threats, especially to small, southern (and socialist-voting) French farmers;
5 fisheries disputes occasionally arose between the two countries, further fraying diplomatic tempers;
6 democratic transition was a condition of membership of the EC and France did not consider democratic transition to have taken place in Spain until 1982, when a change of government occurred (Breckinbridge 1996: 17).

Relations with other member-states also coloured the way in which the Spanish case for EEC membership was viewed among the ten. The British position was complicated by the persistence of the blockade by Spain of Gibraltar, until after an accord was signed in 1984, and by public support in Spain for Argentina in the Falklands/Las Malvinas War of 1982. Germany, especially under Chancellor Kohl's government, was a strong supporter of Spanish entry and, in 1983, offered increased resources to the EEC budget on condition that the accession treaties for Spain and Portugal were ratified by the ten existing member states.

Spain's relations with 'third countries' (states outside the EEC) also required review, to iron out the more anomalous or serious differences of opinion that existed between it and other member-states on foreign policy issues. So, for The Netherlands, Spanish entry to the EEC could only be acceptable if an exchange of ambassadors and full diplomatic relations with Israel was forthcoming, thereby eroding Spain's pro-Arab policies (in place since the Franco era), and its long-standing failure to recognise the state of Israel. Even-handedness became the new position in Spanish foreign policy on the Arab–Israeli situation, and the recognition of the PLO office in Madrid followed in the wake of opening full diplomatic relations with Israel (Gillespie, Rodrigo and Story 1995: 39–40).

A considerable amount of lobbying, both inside and outside Spain, was required to negotiate Spanish entry into the EEC. It was conducted by a small political and economic élite, first during the UCD governments and then, after 1982, under the Socialists (Middlemas 1995: 132–3). Apart from Suaréz and González, this élite included such figures as Fernando Morán, Pedro Solbes (the Agriculture minister after 1982) Leopoldo Calvo Sotelo, some leading bankers and business leaders (e.g. José Angel Sanchez Asiain, the head of the Banco de Bilbao). Negotiations for full membership, slow at first, were quickly drawn to a conclusion in March 1985, during the Italian presidency. Pressure was applied on other member-states, especially by the Spanish Foreign Minister, Fernando Morán, who leant heavily on fellow socialist administrations across the Community. Serious difficulties were encountered along the way, especially on the issue of agriculture, but the setting of prolonged transition periods for various products and the emergence of plans for an Integrated Mediterranean Programme from the negotiations satisfied many of the objectors, especially France, Italy and Greece.

Germany and the UK had high expectations from links being forged between the enlargement negotiations and the development of an EC internal market (eventually formulated in the SEA), which was also a factor intertwined in the negotiations. Problems involving the huge size of the Spanish fishing industry, affecting France, Britain and Ireland, were met (but only temporarily) by restrictions on fleet size, while the matter of the free movement of Spanish labour in the Community, worrying France especially, was resolved by agreement on an interim transition period. French opposition was also eased by the shift during the Mitterand presidency, after 1983, to a more outward-looking agenda of strengthening free trade and monetary union in the EC and by the moves towards the SEM. A strengthened Franco-German alliance began to eye up the investment opportunities in Spain and Portugal. In the final analysis, it must be said that it helped that Mitterand had much in common with fellow-Socialist, González. After all, they were both engaged in the task of steering their reluctant socialist parties to the centre-left of the political spectrum. It was during Mitterand's presidency of the European Council, at Fontainbleau in June 1984, that the target date of January 1986 was chosen for Spanish (and Portuguese) accession to the EU (Featherstone 1988: 292).

Inside Spain there was little opposition to the move towards a treaty of accession with the EC. A unanimous vote of the Cortes approved it and only the PCE abstained. In retrospect, it might be said that the absence of internal debate took the edge off Spain's negotiations and led to a set of pre-conditions for Spain's entry which were harsh, especially in agriculture and fisheries, leaving many issues subject to later renegotiation and acrimony (Harrison 1993: 205). However, the Treaty of Accession was signed in June 1985, leading to membership from 1 January 1986. The SEA was endorsed at the European Summit held in February 1986, aiming for a Single European Market by 1992, and González and the PSOE government persuaded the Spanish public to remain in NATO in the referendum held in the following month.

There has been a broad degree of unanimity on the desirability of EC membership among Spain's political parties, though public enthusiasm has waned in the 1990s as economic and social costs have mounted. Further steps towards integration since 1986 have provoked little political controversy. In 1989, Spain joined the wide band of the ERM (European Exchange Rate Mechanism) and stayed within it (unlike Britain) despite some adverse currency speculation. In 1991, it became a signatory to the Maastricht Treaty, ratified in 1993, and in the following year agreed a four-year economic convergence programme to qualify for membership of the Single Currency Zone. Salmon has pointed out how much Spain had to do to qualify. The criteria were:

1 a public sector deficit of not more than 3 per cent of GDP (in 1991, it was 4.4 per cent and rising in Spain);
2 public debt no more than 60 per cent of GDP (in May 1992, it was 45.6 per cent);
3 interest rates no more than 2 per cent above the average of the three lowest rates in the EC (Spain had the highest interest rates in the EC in July 1992);
4 inflation no more than 1.5 per cent above the three lowest in the EC (in May 1992, it was 4.1 per cent adrift);
5 remain in the narrow band of the ERM for two years (Spain was in the wide band) (Salmon 1995: 13–14).

Despite meeting only one of these objectives to begin with, in 1997 Spain qualified for participation in the single currency programme, its economy having been judged by then to have met the criteria laid down for qualification to join the euro-zone, from January 1999. This development was not without considerable social costs in areas and sections of society affected by public sector cutbacks. But enthusiasm among Spain's political élite for the European project had not waned. It was a signatory to the Amsterdam Treaty, and further 'deepening' of the EU, in 1997.

Spain and the European Union policy process

European Union membership has enhanced state autonomy by giving Spain's political and bureaucratic élites a privileged role in the process of European decision-making with other member-states' élites, the public accountability of whose activities has been increasingly debated in the 1990s. What are the institutional dimensions of this role?

Spain's relations with the Community have been co-ordinated through a highly centralised, bureaucratic and political machinery at the heart of which lies the **Secretariat of State for the** EU at the Foreign Ministry. Fortnightly meetings of the CIAC (*Conferencia Interministerial para Asuntos Comunitarios/* Interministerial Committee for Community Affairs) there include representatives of each ministry and are chaired by the Secretary of State for the EU. The Cabinet Committee for Economic Affairs (*Comisión de Asuntos Económicos*) deals with any ensuing disputes from the CIAC. The influence of the Secretariat depends to a considerable extent on the individual who heads it. For instance, until he replaced Javier Solana as PSOE Foreign Minister at the end of 1995, Carlos Westendorp held this position, having previously had a career in Spanish-EC/EU relations, stretching over a period as permanent representative in COREPER (Committee of Permanent Representatives), back to the preferential trade negotiations of 1970. His skill as a negotiator while Chairman of the Council's Schengen Committee talks on bringing down EC/EU borders won Spain a second six-month presidency of this group, after which he was appointed Chairman of the very important Reflection Group, set up by the Council of Ministers to prepare the agenda for the 1996 IGC (Inter-Governmental Conference).

The system of a rotating **Presidency** of the EU also enhances member-states' capacity to exercise an extra degree of influence over the policy agendas of the various sectors. Spain held the Presidency during the first half of 1989 and the second half of 1995. On both occasions, Felipe González launched initiatives to promote closer links between the Mediterranean states to counter a Community bias towards northern and central/eastern Europe and to promote political stability in the region, for example, through the Euro-Mediterranean conference held in Barcelona in November 1995.

European Council Summits of Heads of Governments and States, usually held twice during each Presidency, have provided an opportunity to debate and sometimes agree on major issues of substance and principle for the EU. It was in Spain, in 1989, that the single currency idea was given a hearing, and at the Madrid Summit in 1995, the currency was officially dubbed the 'euro'. (Samples of the proposed currency were not produced until the Dublin Summit in late-1996.) The Madrid Summit of 1989 also took steps to develop a common foreign policy, by recognising the right of Palestinians to participate in peace negotiations in an international conference organised by the UN. In the Edinburgh Summit, too, the Spanish government was active, negotiating more favourable budget concessions, knowing that a successful UK Presidency hinged on agreement.

Council of Ministers meetings, held, in the case of ECOFIN (Economics and Finance Council of Ministers), Agriculture and the General Council (foreign affairs), as frequently as once a month and in other policy sectors less so, are presided over by the member states which hold the EU presidency. At all times, they give ministers from the member-states a role in the major decision-making arena for EU policy-making, but some member states have greater influence than others: Spain more than Luxembourg in fisheries policy, is an obvious example. Voting strength also counts: Spain has 10 votes at hand for voting under the 'qualified majority' rule.

The success or failure of Spanish ministers in forging alliances with other member-states' ministers on various issues have affected the extent to which Spanish interests have been advanced in the Council, a point not lost on domestic critics who accused Carlos Romero, when Agriculture Minister, of jeopardising Spanish agriculture by falling out with the Greeks and the British in 1989 (in the case of Britain, he failed to turn up to the Royal Agricultural Show after accepting an invitation from his ministerial counterpart there, John Gummer). Romero was credited with having persuaded other agriculture ministers in 1992 to shorten the transition period for Spain to full participation in the CAP, for the outstanding farm products. In the same year the agriculture ministry, MAPA, boasted of 20 main agreements approved by the Council of Ministers which were proposed by its Minister and were of specific concern to Spain.

Spanish Permanent Representation, the ambassadorial team which is located in Brussels, is a key group and works through COREPER to present and co-ordinate Spanish policy positions with the EU Council of Ministers. Consisting of about 60 diplomats, the majority emanate from the Foreign Ministry (which is the main point of contact in Madrid for the Spanish permanent representation), while others are seconded from various ministries with a specific expertise to offer the diplomatic team handling the negotiations of Spanish ministers.

Council of Ministers accountability to the member-states' cabinets has been maintained by a variety of co-ordinating mechanisms. In the case of Spain the need for approval by the Cabinet on the main EU-inspired proposals ensures that ministers do not have too much autonomy. For example, in the case of the important land set-aside programme it was proposed by the SCA (Special Committee on Agriculture), as a way of reducing agricultural output and thus EU subsidy costs, that land should be taken out of production. Romero asked the Agriculture Council for a 50 per cent territorial exclusion zone for Spain, to counter the danger of desertification in parts of the country. After negotiations, he was awarded a 30 per cent exclusion zone from the land set-aside policy, to which compromise the Spanish Cabinet gave its approval.

The Irish Box: summary of a decision

With the largest fishing industry in the EU, Spain faced a variety of restrictions to this sector during the negotiations for entry to the Community. This was a source of conflict that festered in the 1980s and 1990s, with Spain seeking to negotiate improved conditions whenever the opportunity arose. The agreement by the heads of state to allow Norway to enter the EU was supported by Spain, but only after it was given a reduction in the transition period for its fishing industry, and access for Spanish fishing vessels to the so-called 'Irish Box'. Ironically, Norway turned its back on the idea of EU membership in a referendum.

In December 1994, the Council of Fisheries Ministers decided, after various compromises, that 150 Spanish fishing boats (40 at any one time) should have full access to what were known as the Western Waters from 1 January 1996, including that fishing area of controversy around Ireland and close to the British coastline, known as the Irish Box (Portugal won a similar agreement). The need for some sort of control system to ensure compliance by member-states with the various components of the decision was also agreed at that meeting. There follows a summary of how that decision emerged.

During 1995, to fulfil the goal of setting up a control system, the Fisheries Commissioner, Emma Bonino, proposed a tight top-down control system, which involved obliging all fishing vehicles crossing member-states' fishing zones to regularly report by radio to the relevant authorities. The Spanish Minister, Luis Atienza, preferred a loose control system and as Chairman of the Council of Ministers succeeded in the very difficult task of achieving the unanimity required in the Council to get the member-states to overthrow the Commissioner's proposal and to support instead a compromise and looser arrangement. To do this before the Council Meeting of October 1995, he first hammered out a deal and formed a strategic alliance with the UK Minister who, like Atienza, opposed the idea of imposing what he saw as unnecessary bureaucracy on the fishermen. At the meeting, he satisfied the particular concerns of Portugal and France by slightly amending the loose control system he envisaged.[2] Then he turned the floor open to the Commissioner who, faced with the prospect of a unanimous rejection of her plans, grudgingly gave approval to the amended loose control system, citing the principle of 'subsidiarity' to justify it, while retaining her worries about the possibility of abuses of that system.

---

[2] The system agreed was as follows:

Re: Ships over 15 mtrs

1 Vessels in their own country's waters would have only to comply with repective requirements e.g. UK – to keep a logbook of activities.

2 Vessels crossing a zone in western waters would have to report by radio/telex before leaving port if going out for 72 hours and keep logbooks to record catches and movements.

3 Vehicles out for more than 72 hours would have to report regularly to the authorities on entry and exit from the port and fishing zones in accordance with the commissioner's initial demands.

Official links between the member-states and the **Commission** take place at all levels. There are in or around a thousand Spanish postholders in the Commission spread across all DGs (Directorate Generals) but with a strong presence in some, notably, the Latin America directorate in DG1 (External Economic Relations). At the highest level, the Commissioners are appointed to the College of Commissioners by the member-states and, while they are formally committed to European interests above national interests, they have continued to maintain close, albeit ambiguous, contacts with the national political scenes. Marcelino Oreja Aguirre was a former UCD minister and later a leading member of PP, who from 1993 had responsibility as Commissioner for Commission Relations with the European Parliament (EP) and the member-states. He also had responsibilities in the culture portfolio and institutional affairs, preparing for the IGCs. Abel Matutes, who preceded Oreja, was a Spanish Commissioner from 1989 until 1993. He resigned to head the PP list to the European Parliament in the European election campaign of June 1994 and in 1996 became PP's first foreign minister. Manuel Marín of the PSOE was Commissioner from 1986. His major achievement as an external relations Commissioner was to focus an EU, increasingly obsessed with Eastern and Central Europe in the early 1990s, on creating an aid package for the North African 'Maghreb' states, a policy strongly favoured by Madrid. Cynics suggested that González had deliberately kept Marín away from the national political scene in case he posed a political challenge to him. (As Leon Brittan found out after his forced resignation from the British Cabinet during the 'Westland Affair' in 1986, the call of Europe can be a mixed blessing for a politician's career.) In early 1999, as Commissioner in charge of EU–Mediterranean relations Marín became the focus of criticism due to allegations of maladministration and fraud in the Echo (humanitarian aid) and Med (Mediterranean) programmes based in his DG. He was under pressure, particularly from the European parliament, to resign.

Policy planning in preparation for the Single Market, in particular, brought about a multiplication of official links between member state ministries and the Commission. In food industry matters, for instance, the implementation by Spain of new EU directives were dealt with by a MAPA sub-directorate general (for Food Industry Planning and Relations with the EC). It held meetings with other departments and bodies nationally, such as the Directorate General for Public Health (in the Ministry for Health and Consumer Affairs), food industry federations and associations under the overall co-ordination of the Secretary of State for the EC, and a cabinet committee, the Committee for Food Product Regulations (MAPA 1992: 230–1).

Mechanisms for member state parliamentary accountability operate in both the national and EU arenas. The **Joint Committee for the European Union** (*Comisión Mixta para la Unión Europa*) established in the Cortes in December 1985, is composed of equal numbers of representatives of both its deputies and senators derived from the various parliamentary parties. Voting in this committee is carried out by a system of weighted voting, unlike other standing committees in the Cortes which operate by single votes. Moreover, within the committee, members from each Chamber have equal powers, despite the wider differences that exist between the chambers.

Although the Joint Committee has certain rights and powers, for example the government must inform it of all EU policy proposals as well as draft legislation and preparations for policy implementation, its influence has been slow in evolving. To begin with, it served mainly as a conduit from the government to the other parliamentary committees on EU matters. It was, for example, regularly addressed by the Secretary of State for the EU. It was not regarded as having much weight initially and was in competition with the other committees, especially that of External Relations. However, the scope of its activities across all policy sectors has meant that it has evolved to greater significance. Reforms to its powers and activities, introduced in 1988 and 1994, have helped this as has the 1989 Seeler Report on closer institutional relations between parliaments (Sánchez de Dios 1993: 222).

The transfer of sovereignty to the EC/EU, arising from the treaties of accession (permitted in Spain by Article 93 of the 1978 Constitution on the transfer of competences to an international body), has inevitably changed and weakened the policy-making role of parliament in some policy areas. The role of the Cortes has tended to veer towards exercising a review of existing policy, rather than influencing actual government policy negotiations. The level of accountability achieved is dependant to a considerable degree upon the category of legislation. It is clear, however, that legal instruments such as royal decrees (*reales decretos*), orders (*órdenes*) of cabinet committees and the lower category of ministerial orders (*órdenes ministeriales*) cover much of the details in applying EU directives to national law and escape high profile scrutiny in parliament. The technical jargon in which some policy detail is couched, not to mention the sheer range of policies, make it difficult for deputies, apart from those with highly specialised policy interests, to carefully scrutinise the EU policies which come before it.

Through the activities of **European Parliament** (EP) committees and the use of the EP questions procedures, Spain's 64 MEPs, usually in line with their parliamentary groups, express views on proposed policies and the effectiveness or otherwise of measures to implement them. Following the 1994 Euro-elections, the PSE (Party of European Socialists), which includes the PSOE, became the largest group in the EP (Gibbons 1996: 170). The EPP (European People's Party), which has PP MEPs in its ranks, was the next biggest grouping and the President of the EP appointed in 1997 was José María Gil-Robles Gil-Delgado of the PP. Some parties, such as CiU, have had MEPs in more than one group. In June 1999, the EPP gained a majority.

Membership of the 20 or so European parliamentary committees reflects party strength in the Chamber. Four committee chairmanships for Spain in 1995 included foreign affairs, fishing and institutional affairs. However, the legitimacy of the EP and indeed the European Union is somewhat undermined by the low level of public interest in its proceedings. This is evident from analysis of European election campaigns. It is also evident from the willingness of some MEPs to give higher priority to the concerns of their own member-states than to those of their political groups in the European Parliament. For instance, when the Spanish Socialists voted in favour of the Moroccan Agreement on Trade and Fisheries in the early 1990s and against the Socialist group in the European Parliament, they did so because of the commercial and diplomatic gains for Spain which the González government argued would emanate from this agreement (Middlemas 1995: 357).

The EJC **(European Court of Justice)**, which includes one Spanish judge nominated by the Government among its 15 members, has been used by Spain to seek adjudication, in particular, on issues affecting its commercial interests. The results have been mixed: for example, it lost a case involving alleged infringements in the regulations covering the identification of apricot and cherry brandy but won that involving changes to the tax rates on British sherry, distinguishing it from Spanish sherry or *jerez*. On some occasions, Spain has borne the brunt of others allegations against it: in 1993, the Court of First Instance (set up under the SEA) over-ruled the recruitment of Spanish (and Italian) civil servants by the DG for Fisheries on the grounds that they had been primarily recruited because of their nationality rather than their qualifications.

The representation of organised interests and the regions in the EU is formally conducted through the ESC **(Economic and Social Committee)** and the **Committee of the Regions**, respectively. While Spain has 21 representatives in both the ESC and the Committee of the Regions, covering the main European policy sectors and regions (or local authorities), their impact is evident less through these 'advisory' bodies than in the direct and informal negotiations and networking with Commission officials in the various DGs, for which activities attendance at the meetings of these committees create opportunities. The ESC has a balanced representation from Spain, reflecting sectoral, territorial and business-size interests (Molins and Morata 1994: 122). Unlike the ESC, which was established by the Treaty of Rome, the Committee of the Regions is a relatively new institution (established in 1994). Seventeen of Spain's regional presidents are amongst the contingent represented. They have played a leading role in advocating the establishment of such a chamber, and also in its operations. However, neither institution has had a defining influence over Spain's (or any member-state's) role in the EU.

Spain's approach to policy-making in the European Union

What have been the defining characteristics of Spain's role in the EU policy process? The pursuit of national interests is, arguably, the prevalent ethos in the EU policy process. Spain has tended to follow this ethos in a tough and

relentless fashion since it joined the EU. However, it has also shown a capacity to compromise for the sake of wider EU objectives. This was apparent at the 1992 Edinburgh Summit, when Spanish brinkmanship won what were called cohesion funds (additional to structural funds) for the southern European states (and Ireland), but by doing so paved the way for the agreement on the applications for EU membership by Sweden, Finland, Austria (and Norway, whose voters eventually decided to remain outside). Spain feared that the planned EU expansion would shift the centre of gravity north-eastwards. Caution towards EU expansion, therefore, has strongly marked its policy orientation during the 1990s. Spain has also sought to strengthen its credentials as a major EU player by identifying with France and Germany in some major policy initiatives (e.g. a fast-track timetable for privatising state industries). In doing so, it distances itself from poorer member states, such as Portugal and Greece (Scobie 1998: 102).

What is in the 'national interest' of a member-state is not always clear cut. Countervailing forces within Spain have revealed the existence of **conflicting national agendas**. French and German finance ministers encouraged the Spanish government to depreciate the peseta in advance of entering the ERM in 1989. But the government faced a dilemma. While the Bank of Spain opposed the proposal on the economic grounds that it maintained that governments should not manipulate the currency markets but focus their energies on public expenditure matters, the Spanish government was concerned that contrary action might antagonise Germany, its main inward investor. Also, the government had to consider that Germany might later look less than favourably upon Spain's campaign for cohesion funds, if it showed itself to be belligerent to the major EU paymaster on the currency question (Middlemas 1995: 177–8). After deliberating on the matter and recognising also that a Spanish currency depreciation move might help its industrial exporters, the government decided to follow the Franco-German line, against the advice of the Bank of Spain.

Interest rate policy is also revealing. As we have seen, economic policy after 1992 was 'locked into' the measures necessary to meet the EMU 'convergence criteria' to enable Spain to join the Single Currency in January 1999. This resulted in a number of contradictions and conflicts in economic policy matters (Kennedy 1996: 87–97). High interest rates were the price that was paid by Spain to keep the exchange rate in the ERM in the face of speculators attempts to drive the value of the peseta down in 1992 and 1993. The social costs of meeting the convergence criteria resulted in social unrest in the form of strikes and protests by the unemployed and trades unions. However, the policy direction, contradictions and all continued, and interest rates remained high. In September 1996, Aznar rejected a suggestion by Italy's prime minister Romano Prodi that the two countries join forces to delay the EMU project, or to seek a relaxation of the qualifying criteria (*The Economist* 14 December 1996: 2).

Subnational pressures can complicate the notion of what are portrayed as member-states' 'national interests' (see Chapter 2). The demand by CiU for the appointment of an observer from the autonomous communities in the Spanish permanent representation and other Spanish policy bodies concerned with EU decision-making continues to generate conflicts of interest with the PP government in the late 1990s (see Chapter 2).

Sometimes, the conflicting interests of member-states give rise to **clashes on third country matters** and, hence, finding a common external relations policy position has been difficult. For example, while EU member states were willing to condemn the Canadian government over the seizure by its navy of a Spanish trawler – the Estai – off the coast of Newfoundland in early 1995, there was a distinct reluctance, especially by the British (whose Cornish fishermen were jubilant at the attack on the tabloid-dubbed 'Spanish Armada'), but also by the Dutch and German governments, for reasons of their own commercial self-interest, to talk about trade sanctions and other reprisals against Canada. This coolness towards Spain's difficulties on the high seas was increased by Commission President Jacques Santer's ill-judged intervention to threaten just such sanctions, even before ambassadors of the EU member-states had convened a meeting to discuss the issue.

Conflicts over what one member-state considers to be **interference by other member-states in its internal affairs** can be of the most acrimonious sort. Such an encounter occurred between Spain and Belgium in February 1996 when the State Council (the senior judicial authority) of Belgium failed to extradite two suspected ETA terrorists to Spain. Subsequently it released them, on the grounds that they might not get a fair trial if they were extradited. Spain called an extraordinary meeting of the Schengen Convention to discuss the issue, regarding the Belgian action as a snub to the independence and fairness of its own judiciary.

The Commission sometimes acts to attempt to contain **member-state rivalry** and to prevent damage to EU policies and unity of purpose. The background to the setting up of the EBRD (European Bank for Reconstruction and Development) in 1990–91 brought the various member-states, including Spain, into such a dispute. The reasons for this were as follows. First, there was a basic rivalry between them which sprung from a desire to give their own industrial and business interests an advantage in the new markets of eastern and central Europe, which would be partly funded by the EBRD. Second, Spain raised objections arising from its fear of the shift north-eastwards of Community expenditure and investment. It feared particularly that German investment in its own economy would be lost to eastern and central Europe and that costs of EU policies would either rise dramatically or, worse, be spread more thinly. Spain resented, in particular, the speed at which these states were being embraced by the EU, compared to its own long wait on the EEC wings in the 1970s and early 1980s. Eventually, under pressure from the Commission, a unified front was maintained on the EBRD, despite these fragmenting forces, and the bank was established through an agreed formula.

Linkage politics serves as an important lever in EC/EU policy negotiations between member-states. During the Maastricht Summit in 1991, Spain won important concessions on its request for compensation to help implement environmental proposals. It did so by linking it to plans for greater social cohesion. By threatening to use its overall veto powers, Spain and its allies (Portugal, Greece and Ireland) won agreement on the Social Cohesion Fund which included financial provisions for environmental policy implementation. As we have already noted, concessions to the fishing industry in Spain have been linked to the negotiations to expand membership of the EU, to include the Nordic States.

Lobbying is central to the EC/EU policy-making. The degree of success and failure registered by those lobbying for Spanish interests is affected by numerous factors. Unhelpful in this respect is the paucity of neo-corporatism in the Spanish policy process (see Chapter 6). Spanish political and policy-making élites have been reluctant to encourage co-ordination between organised interests and the Spanish government on the forging of common EU policy strategies. Some sectors, such as the shipbuilding and mining industries, have had to fight directly at regional, national and EU levels to retain elements of the old subsidy regimes being outlawed by the EU, on grounds of unfair competition. Of course, Euro-federations of interest groups as well as national organisations, such as the CEOE and the regional governments, have also been employed as levers in the EU lobbying process by representatives of the private sector and its workforce (see Chapter 7).

Implementing European Union policies in Spain

The EU implementation process is characterised by a phenomenon known as **'variable geometry'**. This term describes the variations which occur when some member-states have committed themselves to a policy and others have declined or have failed to implement it. The Schengen agreement has brought about just such complications, not least for Spain, resulting in confrontations with Britain and France. For example, as Britain has not signed up to the Schengen agreement, British tourists have found themselves segregated and discriminated against at some Spanish airports (European Report 28 July 1995: 1). French reluctance to implement the agreement has also produced friction with Spanish migrants at their common borders.

The implementation of, and adherence to, EU policy is monitored by the European Commission, together with the EJC. However, it is assisted by the watchful eyes of other member-states who help to police the system and report suspected misdemeanours. Sometimes, this has worked against Spanish interests, but it has also worked in its favour. In 1991, the French government challenged the Spanish government over its subsidies to the steel industry and in 1993–94 the German government did likewise (Middlemas 1995: 521). But the Spanish government successfully challenged the British government in 1989 when the latter refused to allow Spanish fishing boats registered in the UK to fish for some of the British quota. Sometimes, conformity to EU directives can be extremely painful for member-states: the restructuring plan for the Spanish shipbuilding industry in 1995 involved the closure of two plants, the privatisation of three others and the shedding of 5,300 workers. In other cases, legislation has been passed to meet EU commitments, covering areas such as air and water quality, but without the resources necessary for proper implementation being made available.

There are a number of stages in the infringement proceedings taken by the Commission against errant member-states. **Formal enquiries** establish whether in fact the Commission believes that a misdemeanour has taken place. In June 1995, such an enquiry investigated whether Spanish state subsidies to Seat, the car manufacturer, amounted to a breach of EC/EU rules. **Letters of formal notice** raise with member-states the specific nature of the Commission complaints and give them time to respond and act to rectify matters. During the same year, such a letter was sent to the Spanish government concerning VAT refunds in the food sector. When it was dissatisfied with the answer it received from Spain, the Commission followed the next stage of the infringement procedure by sending the government its **reasoned opinion.** Failure to comply with such reasoned opinions can lead to further action being taken against a member state through **enforcement proceedings** which can ultimately lead to a fine imposed by the European Court of Justice (Nugent 1994: 114). Spain faced such actions by infringing a VAT directive on the issue of Spain's sporting associations exemption from VAT. Its overall record on implementing EC directives has been less blemished than other member states, especially Italy and Belgium. However, environmental protection directives have tended to be ignored most frequently in the past and industries, in breach of such directives, have sometimes preferred to pay fines imposed by the Commission rather than alter their ways (Molins and Morata 1994: 120).

Particular policy sectors have been more prone to the sometimes difficult relations which arise between Spain and the European Commission. Car manufacturing and air transport have been two major examples.

Seat

Difficulties encountered by the motor manufacturer Seat since Spain's entry to the EU generated a number of conflicts, which have not ebbed since its takeover by VW (Volkswagen). In 1995, the Spanish government announced a plan to invest 46 billion pesetas in a restructuring plan for Seat. The European Commission subsequently declared that it was reviewing this plan to ensure that it conformed to the overall strategy of VW in the European Union and was not going to amount just to the transfer of problems from one member state to another. To assist it in this matter, it asked member-states and other interested parties to comment on the proposals of the Spanish government (European Report 16 September 1995: 3.8). The reason for this, the Commission argued, was the necessity to ensure that whatever it recommended was going to stand up in the EJC, were it to be challenged by competitors or member-states. However, it was a measure of the poor relations which existed between Spain and the Commission on this issue that it was alone in its refusal among the 15 member-states to review during 1995 the state aid guidelines for the motor industry in the EU (the Commission has such guidelines which cover all sectors and are reviewed periodically). Spain had been at loggerheads with the Commission on the code since 1988 and had been granted numerous extensions to enable it to comply with the rules.

Towards the end of 1995, the Spanish authorities were authorised by the Competition Commissioner Van Miert to go ahead with proposals for grant-aid to Seat after reassurances that a 30 per cent reduction in capacity by Seat was built into the plan representing a 5–6 per cent reduction in overall VW production in Europe.

Iberia

A restructuring programme for the Spanish airline, Iberia, was proposed to the European Commission in January 1995 to make the company viable. It was built upon a cash injection of 130 billion pesetas by the Spanish government, as Iberia was owned by INI, and after that state-holding company was dismantled by its successors, Teneo and SEPI (see Chapter 5). Uproar followed as other European private sector airlines such as British Airways, Lufthansa, SAS and KLM all protested. They were particularly incensed because Iberia had received 120 billion pesetas in 1992, in what was regarded as a one-off concession. Publicly owned airlines, like Alitalia and Air France also closely watched developments. The Spanish government claimed that exceptional problems since then, such as recession, currency penalties (through the devaluation of the peseta in the ERM) and unforeseen events in its Latin American investments, especially difficulties in VIASA, the Venezuelan airline, necessitated a new programme. However, Iberia pilots began to hold strike action when threatened with pay cuts under the plan. The Industry Minister, Juan Manuel Eguiagaray travelled to Brussels in October 1995 during the strike (he travelled by government jet!) to discuss the investment programme with Neil Kinnock, the Transport Commission (Eguiagaray also met Van Miert, the Competition Commissioner, to discuss the Seat problem).

A proposal by the Spanish side to sell Aerolineas Argentinas, which the Commission had been pushing for as part of the restructuring plan, and also to undertake a programme of redundancies, received a positive response in Brussels. Eventually, the Commission agreed to clear an 87 billion pesetas rescue plan based on market principles (defined as one which a private investor would also have made). Iberia confirmed its intention to offload Aerolineas Argentinas in the deal (European Report 7 October 1995: 3.5).

From this case study we can observe how the EU (specifically the

Commission) has acted to assist the Spanish government to implement EU competition policy reducing state aid to industry. The action of the Commission also reinforced the Spanish governments attempts to reduce the level of its own subsidisation of Iberia.

In conclusion, it appears that in some policy areas at least the quality of policy implementation is being monitored and modified by the EU in response to weaknesses identified. Barke and Newton's study of the LEADER (*Liasons Entre Actions de Développement de l'Economie Rurale*/Integrated Rural Development Programme) initiative reveal, for example, communication difficulties between the different administrative levels of this 'rural' development policy. It points out that the EU Commission rethought its ideas on the initiative based on observations of its implementation (Barke and Newton 1997: 180).

Spain and the 1995 European Union presidency

Members-states' policy strategies are inevitably affected by **domestic political factors.** John Major and Tony Blair are not the only heads of state in the EU to discover this in the 1990s. The strength of the Spanish position in the EU was undermined by a series of domestic scandals and the absence of a majority government after 1993 (see Chapter 4). Despite pessimistic predictions though, the Spanish EU presidency of González in 1995 achieved some successes, against a background of domestic uncertainty and distraction.

The 1995 European Union presidency: a summary

The Spanish presidency of the EU was also marked by a number of wide circumstances and events which shaped its impact on EU policy agendas (Marks 1996: 9–14):

1 The fact that the Spanish presidency was preceded by France and followed by Italy meant that a common southern European thread ran throughout. The expansion of the EU at the beginning of 1995 to include Austria, Finland and Sweden, to some extent prompted a common agenda during these presidencies, directed at ensuring that southern Europe was not marginalised by northern European concerns. The Spanish presidency marked its commitment to southern Europe by hosting the EU Conference on the Mediterranean in Barcelona, in November 1995. It produced an aid package worth 4.7 billion ecus to finance assistance to 12 non-EU Mediterranean states between 1996 and 1999. In return for anticipated stability, security and economic return, the EU, led by Spain, guaranteed the gradual lifting of trade barriers on selected products to create a Mediterranean regional free trade area by the year 2010. However, the persistence of friction between Spain and Morocco over fisheries issues revealed the potential for conflicts of interest between the roles of EU President and head of state.

2 A peace deal in the Bosnia conflict, through the Dayton peace accord of November 1995, led to the commitment of NATO troops to the peace-keeping force in Bosnia. This brought home the full extent to which Spanish external relations policy had evolved since the early 1980s under González, as Spanish troops from the Euro corps were included in the NATO contingent which were committed to Bosnia.

3 The presidency of the EU assisted González in occasionally removing himself from domestic difficulties by enabling him to appear on some prestigious platforms: for example President Clinton's visit to Madrid in December 1995 and the signing of a new 'Transatlantic Accord' between the USA and the EU. Despite such respites, it was almost as calamitous a presidency as the Italian one which followed, in that, throughout, González clung very tenaciously to domestic power (see Chapter 3). It emphasised the constant air of domestic uncertainty and unpredictability that surrounds the EU presidencies.

4 The Spanish presidency revealed how summits of heads of states and government (in this case, the one at Madrid) can be used to achieve different ends. Despite the absence of much progress and the existence of a highly unfavourable background to the issue of EMU, the Madrid Summit did serve as force of cohesion to reaffirm the broad commitment of the member-states to the single currency and to finalise negotiations which were already well advanced. The Majorca Summit, in September, had a different purpose. It was informal and intended to articulate new ideas on EU integration, hosted as it was by one of the most pro-European member states (European Report, 23 September 1995: 1–3). In his invitation to European leaders, González said as much, but he also revealed the importance of public image in these matters when he pressed the leaders not to raise expectations about what the summit was going to achieve: it seemed as though the outcome of the event was being stage-managed before it even took place.

5 In the preparations for the 1996 Intergovernmental Conference, largely conducted through the work of the IGC Reflection Group (chaired by Carlos Westendorp, Spain's Secretary of State for EU Affairs), a parliamentary report was produced during the Spanish presidency which reflected many of the uncertainties surrounding EU development in the future. Although there had been some competition between the French and Spanish presidencies on the matter of who would have the honour of setting the IGC agenda, little was resolved during the Spanish presidency and the IGC agenda was defined only in quite broad terms, with potential for further movement on many issues (e.g. while Spain, Germany, Italy and Sweden favoured extending citizenship beyond member-state nationals to the permanent residents of the EU, the UK opposed this due to its fears of creeping EU federalism, and France objected on the grounds of racial tensions).

Since its election to office in May 1996 the PP government has shown itself also to be enthusiastically pro-European. For example the 1997 budget, which

included a pay freeze for public sector workers and a 20 per cent public investment cut, was designed to keep the budget deficit below the 3 per cent of GDP
threshold decided at Maastricht. On the matter of cuts to EU expenditure Aznar
has been less enthusiastic. In December 1998, on an official visit to the European
Commission, he rejected the proposal of the Austrian government to limit EU
spending for the period 2000–06 in contrast to the majority of member-states
who supported some cuts (European Report, 5 December 1998: 1.3).

Conclusion

Membership of the EC/EU provided a clear and early stimulus to the Spanish
economy, but it also had some negative effects. Community policies extended
across the economy, replacing the previous system of protectionism as a
shaping factor in various sectors. In agriculture, positive effects were felt in hor-
ticulture and production, while dairy farming and cereals experienced negative
effects. State monopolies were dismantled as a result of EC competition policy
and grants from the Structural and Cohesion Funds boosted investment in
infrastructures.

Increased integration was reflected in the rise in exports and imports
between Spain and the EC/EU (Salmon 1992: 53). Trade with the EC increased
from 31 per cent of imports and 52 per cent of exports in 1980, to 60 per cent
and 71 per cent respectively, in 1991. Accompanying this was a growing trade
deficit. After 1986, foreign investment moved upwards and in absolute terms:
Spain was the fourth largest recipient of foreign investment in 1989, after the
USA, the UK and France. This led to a substantial increase in the investment role
of multinationals in Spanish industry and throughout the economy.

Directing Spain's presence in the EU policy process have been its key political, bureaucratic and economic élites. In particular, the Foreign Ministry
through its Secretariat of State for the EC/EU lie at the heart of Spain's links
with the EU policy process. The international status of Felipe González, and the
high personal regard in which he is held in many European capitals, served
when he was prime minister as an important backdrop to Spain's speedy pro-
gression into the forefront of EU member states and integrationists. It remains
to be seen if José María Aznar can maintain that prominent position for Spain's
EU policy negotiators.

As in national politics, the policies and strategies of the PSOE and PP governments in the EU have had a marked regional and notably Catalan flavour to
them in the 1990s (see Chapter 2). Economic and political élites in Catalonia
have been amongst the strongest supporters of the EU project. Public support
for the EU generally in Spain has been broadly positive, though European elections have been mainly used by the public to air national grievances (a not
uncommon phenomenon in other member-states). European Union issues are
largely a concern of national and regional élites.

Wider Spanish priorities in the EU do stand out. Among these is the desire to be a central player in EU policy-making, balanced with an emphasis on southern European and Mediterranean needs in terms of trade, subsidies, strategic interests and policy generally (European Report, 28 November 1998: 5.2). Spain has also played a leading role in raising the profile of EU relations with Latin and Central America. Above all, it has been a strong advocate of further European integration through the various agreements and treaties to which it has been a signatory, including the SEA, Maastricht (with the Social Chapter), Schengen, the Single Currency and Amsterdam. European integration has attracted virtual cross-party unanimity, not only between PP and PSOE, but also the nationalist and regional parties who anticipate enhanced autonomy within a Europe of the Regions. With such wide unanimity in political, institutional and economic circles, it is little wonder that by 1997 Spain was one of the member-states considered by the IMF and OECD to be best prepared to join the first wave of single currency users.

References

Barke, M. and M.T. Newton (1997) 'The Practice of Local Rural Development in Spain', *Intellect: International Journal of Iberian Studies*, 10:3.

Breckinbridge, R.E. (1996) 'Lessons from the European Community and Spanish Democracy', *ECSA Newsletter*, European Community Studies Association.

The Economist (14 December 1996) 'Survey: Spain', p. 2.

European Report (28 July 1995) 1.

European Report (16 September 1995) 2069: 3.8.

European Report (23 September 1995) 2069: 1.3.

European Report (7 October 1995) 2073: 3.5.

European Report (28 November 1998) 2363: 5.2.

European Report (5 December 1998) 2365: 1.3.

Featherstone, K. (1988) *Socialist Parties and European Integration*, Manchester, Manchester University Press.

Gibbons, J. (1996) 'Spain', in J. Lodge, (ed.) *The 1994 Elections to the European Parliament*, London, Pinter.

Gillespie, R., F. Rodrigo and J. Story (eds) (1995) *Democratic Spain: Reshaping Relations in a Changing World*, London, Routledge.

Harrison, J. (1993) *The Spanish Economy: From the Civil War to the European Community*, London, Macmillan.

Kennedy, P. (1996) 'Europe or Bust? Integration and the Influence on the Economic Policy of the PSOE', *Intellect: International Journal of Iberian Studies*, 9:3.

MAPA (*Ministerio de Agricultura, Pesca y Alimentación*) (1992) *La Agricultura, La Pesca y La Alimentación*, Madrid.

Marks, M.P. (1996) 'The Spanish Presidency of the European Council: More Continuity than Change', *ECSA Newsletter*, European Community Studies Association.

Middlemas, K. (1995) *Orchestrating Europe*, London, Fontana Press.

Molins, M.M. and F. Morata (1994) 'Spain: Rapid Arrival of a Latecomer', in M.P.C.M

Van Schendelen (ed.) *National Public and Private EC Lobbying*, Aldershot, Dartmouth Press.

Nugent, N. (1994) *The Government and Politics of the European Union*, 3rd edn, London, Macmillan.

Rodrigo, F. (1995) 'Western Alignment: Spain's Security Policy', in R. Gillespie, R. Rodrigo, and J. Story (eds) *Democratic Spain: Reshaping External Relations in a Changing World*, London, Routledge.

Salmon, K. (1992) 'The Modern Spanish Economy: Integration into Europe', ACIS, *Journal of Contemporary Iberian Studies*, 5:1.

Salmon, K. (1995) *The Modern Spanish Economy: Transformation and Integration into Europe*, London, Pinter.

Sánchez de Dios, M. (1993) 'Executive Parliamentary Control', in A.A. Barbedo (ed.) *Spain and EC Membership Evaluated*, London, Pinter.

Scobie, H.M. (1998) *The Spanish Economy in the 1980s*, London, Routledge.

Index